Neoliberal lives

MANCHESTER
1824

Manchester University Press

Neoliberal lives

Work, politics, nature, and health in the contemporary United States

Robert Chernomas, Ian Hudson, and Mark Hudson

Manchester University Press

Published by Manchester University Press
Altrincham Street, Manchester M1 7JA, UK
www.manchesteruniversitypress.co.uk

British Library Cataloguing-in-Publication Data is available

ISBN 978 1 5261 1018 3 hardback
ISBN 978 1 5261 1019 0 paperback

First published 2019

The publisher has no responsibility for the persistence or accuracy of URLs for any external or third-party internet websites referred to in this book, and does not guarantee that any content on such websites is, or will remain, accurate or appropriate.

Typeset by
Toppan Best-set Premedia Limited

To the founders of the Crescentwood Saturday Soccer Club, a team that aims to be what neoliberalism is not, a place where players and their families from many corners of the world form a fellowship to work in support of one another and, to a lesser extent, play the beautiful game. As former Liverpool manager Bill Shankly said, it's about "everyone working for each other, everyone having a share of the rewards. It's the way I see football, the way I see life."

Contents

List of figures and tables

Figures

Tables

Acknowledgements

We would like to acknowledge the capable research assistance of Imalka Nilmogada, and the UM Undergraduate Research Fund for support. We also greatly appreciate the financial assistance of the Global Political Economy Research Fund from the Faculty of Arts at the University of Manitoba, which permitted us to hire Austin McWhirter, whose research assistance was absolutely top-drawer.

Thanks are due to many colleagues and associates in and outside the University of Manitoba, but our special gratitude goes out to: Mara Fridell, Dean Bavington, Clint Westman, Nick Garside, Reade Davis and the entire complement of faculty in the Economics and Society Program at the University of Manitoba (Fletcher Baragar, Jesse Hajer, Irwin Lipnowski, John Loxley, John Serieux, and Ardeshir Sepehri) for invaluable contributions and friendship, though they each might disagree with some of what is to follow.

1

A political economy for yacht owners

Just up the street from the Musée Picasso, in Antibes, France, a wandering tourist soaking in the Mediterranean atmosphere might stumble upon the Quai des Milliardaires, or at least the "Accès Interdite" sign at its gates. Beyond the sign, the wharves play host to a large proportion of the world's superyachts—generally understood to be pleasurecraft greater than 30 metres in length, but these days often exceeding 50 metres. The biggest sometimes won't fit, like the *Octopus*, which was owned by Microsoft co-founder, the late Paul Allen, who also owned the Seattle Seahawks of the National Football League, the National Basketball Association's Portland Trail Blazers team, and part of the Seattle Sounders Major League Soccer team. The *Octopus* is 126 metres, and requires a crew of 57 to keep its guests (it can fit 26 of them) comfortable, fed, and watered. Sadly for Mr. Allen, it is only the sixteenth largest superyacht in the world, though it does have a pool, a couple of helicopter pads, and a couple of submarines. Allen also owned a second superyacht (who doesn't need two superyachts?), *Tatoosh*, which is a more modest size, at a mere 92 metres, but seems more fun, with a movie theatre and a shaded, adjustable-depth swimming pool. For those aspirants who can't quite manage the build costs (estimated at $1 million per metre) and the annual operation (10 percent of the build cost annually), boats like *Octopus* and *Tatoosh* can be chartered. Apparently the second-largest superyacht in the world (*Eclipse*) goes for the bargain rate of $2 million per week, or almost $12,000 per hour. Food, fuel, water, and crew tips are additional, but for the celebrities, the hedge-fund managers, the global financiers, and the other 1 percent of the global population who hold half of its wealth, it's no problem.

Superyachts are operated and crewed in a largely regulation-free context. Crew—normally recently unemployed young adults, looking to pay off university or other debts, or maybe just looking for a taste of luxury-themed adventure and a glimpse of real wealth—are themselves reasonably well-paid, but work with no protections whatsoever. Twenty-hour days

1

are not uncommon in the rigidly gender-divided labor force required to keep the untreated teak decking in top condition, the guests instructed in jet-ski operation, the toilets sparkling, and the drinks filled. Utter discretion is mandatory, as is utter obedience. Unsurprisingly, some owners are reported to be quite friendly and generous. But others are tyrannical, and it's luck of the draw from gig to gig. Crew refer to the yacht owners, in an unfortunate but telling shorthand, as "my owner." Crew can be fired at a moment's notice without cause (unless "you just don't have the right look" can count as such) and serve utterly at the pleasure of either the owner or the renter. The yachts have also, until very recently, operated with little to no environmental regulation. The superyacht industry battled loudly against US-based regulations in 2016 that would require boats to be equipped with machinery to reduce their considerable nitrogen oxide emissions. With a few hundred thousand dollars' worth of fuel in the tank of a medium-sized superyacht, they are not very light on the carbon emissions, either. The US went through with the emissions regulations unilaterally, while the UN International Marine Organization abandoned its regulatory efforts.

The universe of the superyacht—with a tiny elite competing for status and prestige with one another, holding almost complete power over a dependent and subservient workforce, and operating in a regulatory void—is partially a result of many of the practices falling under the banner of "the neoliberal," while it simultaneously holds within it the image of a neoliberal utopia. The class divisions that make the superyacht possible, the making of a world in its image, and the consequences for human well-being, are the subjects of this book.

Neoliberalism is an often polarizing term that is as likely to raise hackles as it is to generate sympathy and understanding. Part of the reason that the term "neoliberalism" causes, in some, an instant shiver of discomfort is that it is currently almost exclusively used by its critics, and not always with much specificity. This has allowed some to claim that neoliberalism is nothing but a "knee-jerk slur," covering a host of different grievances (McWhorter, 2017). No one uses the term neoliberalism and then proceeds to wax poetic about the wonderful utopia created by its policies. It may be overused, and it may lack a single, agreed upon definition, but that does not mean that it is a useless term that means nothing and everything simultaneously. In fact, serious thinkers have given the definition of the term serious consideration.

Our aim is to define and illuminate neoliberalism within a coherent theoretical framework that allows for neoliberalism to be something, but not everything. In addition, we hope to reveal the pernicious effects of neoliberalization on some of the fundamental pillars of human development and flourishing. Through its effects on work, on human health, on our ignorance or enlightenment, on our capacities for politics, and our relations with non-human nature, we argue throughout this book that neoliberalism is stunting the vast majority of us.

Neoliberalism defined

The term has gained sufficient traction to enter the general lexicon. *Collins* dictionary, for example, defines neoliberalism as "a modern politico-economic theory favouring free trade, privatization, minimal government intervention in business, reduced public expenditure on social services, etc." This is a list of commonly understood neoliberal policies. However, as Notre Dame economist Philip Mirowski perceptively points out, neoliberalism should not be reduced to a fixed list of "ten commandments, or six tenets," but is an evolving ideology (Mirowski, 2009). The problem with the *Collins* definition is that it fails to provide a thread that runs through these policies, or a foundation upon which they are built. There is no obvious logic behind the list, and as such it leaves the term open to the charge of being a grab bag of policies that the Left doesn't like. In *A Brief History of Neoliberalism*, David Harvey provided a useful start: "Neoliberalism is in the first instance a theory of political economic practices that proposes that human well-being can best be advanced by liberating individual entrepreneurial freedoms and skills within an institutional framework characterized by strong private property rights, free markets, and free trade. The role of the state is to create and preserve an institutional framework appropriate to such practices" (Harvey, 2005, p. 2). Crucially, this definition highlights the emphasis on individuals' responsibility for their own economic fate, rather than having the state or any other collective (like a union) influence the distribution of goods and services in society. Neoliberalism is often associated with an expansion of the market both in terms of a retrenchment of the state and in terms of extending markets into places that they had not yet been (Heynen et al., 2007). According to Harvey, neoliberalism "holds that the social good will be maximized by maximizing the reach and frequency of market transactions, and it seeks to bring all human action into the domain of the market" (Harvey, 2005, p. 3).

Indeed, some of the political-philosophical roots of neoliberalism and some contemporary neoliberal rhetoric suggest that the state should simply withdraw from economic activity to be replaced by the market. Dardot and Laval document how, in fact, this conception of neoliberalism exists only due to the power and effectiveness of a strategic ideological push by early neoliberal theorists like Friedrich von Hayek, Ludwig von Mises, George Stigler, and Milton Friedman (Dardot & Laval, 2013, pp. 159–163). These intellectuals argued that "at bottom, the gulag and taxes were simply two elements on the same ideological continuum"

(Dardot & Laval, 2013, p. 162), and so freedom ultimately depended on the strict limitation of the size and scope of the state. Friedman drew the line at 10–15 percent of national product (Friedman, 2003). In fact, it took an extraordinary and coordinated political effort involving intellectual, ideological, and above all political work to transform the state along neoliberal lines.

Despite the anti-government, pro-market rhetoric, the actual role of the state in neoliberalism is surprisingly active. As Mirowski argues, it is misleading to describe the trend towards neoliberal policy as a removal of the intrusive impediments imposed by the state on the natural state of free-market affairs. Mirowski's contribution in revealing this was to trace the "intricately structured long term philosophical and political project" that very deliberately sought to transform "common sense" from the postwar Keynesian consensus to neoliberalism (Mirowski, 2009, p. 426). This involved coordinating theory, funding think tanks, lobbying governments and placing people in important government policy making positions (Mirowski, 2014). David Kotz focuses on the crucial role that the business community played in the transformation to neoliberalism. According to Kotz, although US business may never have been completely enamoured of three pillars of the postwar Keynesian accord—collective bargaining with unions, Keynesian full employment macroeconomic policy, and the welfare state—under considerable pressure from workers, big business, at least, came to accept these three components as inevitable features of the broader policy environment. For reasons we will discuss later in this chapter, the leading members of the business community became disenchanted with this state of economic affairs and very deliberately set out to get neoliberal policies enacted at the state and federal level. As was the case with the coordination of intellectuals detailed by Mirowski, this involved coordinating and disseminating opinions under organizations like the Business Roundtable, funding think tanks and other institutions that supported the preferred policies, like those populated by the academics studied by Mirowski, and influencing political outcomes through campaign donations and lobbying (Kotz, 2015). So, the neoliberal turn was not a result of the better ideas of the free market triumphing over the statist ideas of the postwar accord. Nor was it an inevitable return to the "natural" state of the market from the artificially imposed constraints of the government. Rather, it was a conscious effort by business, and the intellectuals that provided its ideological justification, to transform the role of the state. As Mirowski states about neoliberalism, "the conditions for its existence must be constructed" (Mirowski, 2009, p. 434). Neoliberal theorists have long understood the central role of the state in effecting that construction (see Bourdieu, 2003; Peck, 2010; Dardot & Laval, 2013; Cahill & Konings, 2017).

As Mirowski points out, an important part of neoliberalism is an acknowledgement that the policy environment must be actively created.

Yet, the fact that the business community and a group of intellectuals wanted to drive economic policy in a certain direction, and even the ample evidence that they organized to do so, does not inevitably lead to the conclusion that they succeeded in achieving these goals. If they did succeed, we still need to explain why. It is crucial, in this respect, that neoliberalism is understood in the broader context of the capitalist system and the particular historic moment in which it arose. As Cahill and Konings perceptively claim, only then can we understand why neoliberal ideas were embraced not only by business and their supporting intellectuals but much more broadly. The attempts to restructure capitalism after the late 1970s were conditioned and enabled by the economic malaise of the time and the fundamental dynamics of capitalism (Cahill & Konings, 2017).

If the claims about the small state are inaccurate, the emphasis on the market is also misleading. The state's role in neoliberalism is not so much to withdraw as it is to more blatantly side with business. It is true that in many areas neoliberal policy involves a reduction of the state and an increasing reliance on the market. As we shall see in Chapter 2, this is true of labor-market policy, in which context neoliberals argue that the redistributive role of the state, accomplished by regulating a minimum wage or providing income assistance, for example, must be minimized or eliminated. In this realm, the allegedly unstoppable forces of globalization and capital mobility are invoked to convince policy-makers that any active redistribution of income or wealth, or any regulation of wages, will result only in driving away jobs and investment, and hence do damage to those whom government wants to help. Colin Leys, for example, points to the difficulty governments have implementing labor market policies that favor unions, because firms would simply pull up their stakes and set up shop elsewhere. This does not render the state powerless, but it does restrict its use of power to fostering the process of commodification—the move from goods and services provided outside the market to being provided for by the market, with the purpose of making a profit. In other words, under neoliberalizing regimes, the state becomes an active participant in the incursion of markets into new social spaces, and of market-based competitive logics in governing formerly public, collective, or otherwise non-market aspects of life. Even services and institutions that remain public, such as education or healthcare, are reorganized to follow a competitive, market-mimicking logic. Thus, the state is restricted from action in one sphere (redistribution) while being enlisted for action in another (commodification). Leys, to put it mildly, is concerned about this transformation of the role of the state, arguing that it represents a shift in democratic accountability towards business and away from voters making it "incompatible with democracy" and "civilized life" (Leys, 2001, p. 5).

Geographer Jamie Peck's definition of neoliberalism better integrates the centrality of the state: "The defining characteristic of neoliberalism is its reliance on market-based arrangements and norms in the interest of monopoly capitalism through active use of state power" (Peck, 2010). The reference to "monopoly capitalism" indicates that, in addition to the state's role in commodification, it also works to protect large firms from competitive forces. This is what leads English sociologist Colin Crouch (2011) to argue that, although the language justifying neoliberal policy revolves around the socially resonant idea of free markets, a careful examination of actual neoliberal policy shows this to be a clever sleight of hand, hiding a program that is more pro-corporate than free market.

It is here that the difference between "classical" liberals and neoliberals becomes clear. Liberals are genuinely in favor of free, competitive markets, and approved of state policy that supported them, like anti-trust policy that prevents corporate concentration and maintains competition between firms (Mirowski, 2009). While liberalism has always drawn lines of various kinds (racial, geographic, gendered) around a community of the deserving and capable "free" who are the subjects of liberty, and that relies on the appropriate labor and subservience of a group of the constitutionally "unfree" (Losurdo, 2014), it also advanced a Smithian ideology of competition among enterprises, along with its half-hearted legal egalitarianism. Neoliberalism, on the other hand, nakedly advocates policies that buffer firms from market competition. Neoliberalism involves attempts to reduce competition within the business elite, whether that involves extending patent protection and intellectual property rules or weakening anti-trust law (Crouch, 2011). This even extends to using the state to protect failing business, as was the case with the bailouts of the financial sector. As Mirowski scathingly notes, neoliberal policy actually grants business "sweeping dispensations" from the discipline of the market (Mirowski, 2014, p. 98).[1]

If we combine these elements of neoliberalism, a useful definition of neoliberalism might be: a class-based project which emerged as a political practice in the late 1970s, aimed at redistributing wealth and power towards the capitalist class (Duménil & Lévy, 2011). It makes ample use of the state in doing so through the uneven refashioning of institutions and relations in the image of the market (Leys, 2001; Mirowski, 2009; Kotz, 2015). Competition is maximally constrained for owners while workers are increasingly exposed to it (Crouch, 2011; Mirowski, 2014).

Neoliberalism in context: theories and acronyms

We view neoliberalism not as an inevitable or natural stage of capitalism but as a result of a specific class-based response to a set of historical conditions that arose in the 1970s. Despite its historical specificity, neoliberalism should also be placed in the overarching context of the general dynamics of the capitalist economic system. This book is broadly in the tradition of historical materialism that places the production and reproduction of the necessities of life at the center of the analysis. Political and cultural life are understood to be related to the way in which we organize the production and distribution of social wealth as part of an overall social regime. Within a capitalist system, that means that class conflict and the need to generate profit are positioned as central driving forces of social change. On one hand, a part of the fundamental logic of capitalism is that business constantly seeks to transform the natural and social world in a manner that will facilitate capital accumulation. Similarly, when limits to accumulation (whether political, ecological, cultural, or otherwise) appear, the nature of capitalism demands that they be "overcome." In this quest to alter the conditions under which business operates, capitalists are aided by the centrality of profits to the health of the economy. In the capitalist system, declining profitability is problematic for the economy because firms will reduce their investment, economic growth will fall, unemployment will increase, and income growth will slow. This is particularly true for the citizens of the US relative to other nations because of its extraordinary reliance on the private sector for investment. When profits fall, firms' efforts to alter the broader policy framework in a manner more conducive to profits will generate considerable sympathy among the general population suffering through an economic downturn. However, the centrality of profits does not mean that the capitalist system is a blank check for business. Often policies that increase the profitability of firms have detrimental impacts on the rest of the society and so various opposing groups in society will resist, or even reverse, the expansion of profit-enhancing rules if they perceive that particular aspects of life should remain buffered from this influence.

Neoliberalism represents a particular response to a historically specific set of circumstances. There is nothing inevitable about the extent to which neoliberal policies have been adopted. While other nations have faced the same global economic context, they have not adopted the neoliberal package with the same fervor as the US. More socially democratic countries provide a great deal more economic production and income distribution through the public sector by levying higher rates of taxation. Interestingly, the countries that have taken a more skeptical approach to neoliberal economic policy have performed better than the US in many ways.

The idea that the broad policy environment at any time, in any particular place, is the result of social struggles by different groups with different and often opposing interests has a great deal in common with Karl Polanyi's thinking in *The Great Transformation* (Polanyi, 1944 [1957]) despite the fact that he was not, strictly speaking, in the historical materialist tradition. Polanyi coined the term the "double movement" to describe two contrasting trends in capitalism. The first is to strip away the social relationships that protected what he termed fictitious commodities to make them subordinate to the laws of self-regulating markets. For example, labor is a fictitious commodity because, unlike other commodities, it is not produced for profitable sale in the market. Labor is really nothing more than the activity of people. Historically, the value of labor was "embedded" in political, religious, and social relationships rather than being determined solely by the market. For example, career choices were determined by tradition. At an even more basic level, income was protected by custom and policy. However, these protections created problems for business because the social floor under income made workers less desperate to subject themselves to the wage slavery of factory discipline. By making income solely determined by the market, and, therefore, workers dependent on the labor market for their livelihood, the market for labor would function in a manner favorable to business. This move to make society subject to the discipline of the market involved a deliberate and disciplined political project to strip away the social protections that surrounded people's livelihood. According to Polanyi, exposing the fictitious commodities to the logic of the market would cause the destruction of both society and nature. Again, taking labor as the example, "For the alleged commodity 'labor power' cannot be shoved about, used indiscriminately, or even left unused, without affecting also the human individual who happens to be the bearer of this peculiar commodity" (Polanyi, 1944 [1957], p. 76). According to Polanyi, as a result of the starvation wages, crushing workday and hazardous job environment that accompanied the imposition of market forces on labor, society acted to protect itself by, to a certain extent, removing elements of labor from the realm of the market. In Polanyi's view, the devastation pursuant to the creation of free-standing and self-regulating markets creates the second half of the double movement as society, reluctant to see its own annihilation or that of the environment around it, seeks to re-embed the fictitious commodities under social protection. The state was pressured to provide a basic income for the poor, safety and health laws were instated, the working day regulated. This book accords with Polanyi in two important respects. It shares with Polanyi, first, the belief that organizing society along market principles must involve a deliberate political project to strip away social protections, and, second, that the outcomes of this project are often problematic, at least for what Polanyi called labor and land, but what can be more broadly thought about as the intertwined relations of human and non-human nature.

This work also positions itself in the literature that expressly ties long swings in the capitalist economy to the particular institutional structure that emerges from the conflict between classes. It has long been recognized that capitalist economies go through long waves of boom and bust cycles.

The Regulation Approach (RA) links the cyclical dynamics of capitalist economies with institutional structures. RA scholars argue that institutions emerge to govern and stabilize the conflicts and crises that inevitably emerge in a capitalist economy. A coherent institutional structure will emerge and persist when it can, at least temporarily, create stability and legitimacy in the process of generating profits. It is the crucial role of "regularizing" or normalizing the process of making profits that gives the regulation school its name, not merely the study of regulation, narrowly defined (Jessop & Sum, 2006, p. 4). While RA is far from a homogeneous single entity, and has been adopted for a wide variety of political stripes from the more radical historical materialist to more reformist theories, RA does focus on a set of social institutions that come together to facilitate a specific kind of context in which firms generate profits (Jessop & Sum, 2006, p. 8). To take just one concrete example, Fordism is often taken to be a particular institutional structure, which consisted of mass-produced durable goods, high productivity, and a proportionate division of value added between firms and their employees (Aglietta, 1979; Jessop, 1997).

An offshoot of RA, Social Structure of Accumulation (SSA) theory explains long waves through the ability of the broad economic policy environment to facilitate or hinder firms' pursuit of profits. The SSA is defined as the set of formal and informal rules and institutions that influence firms' profits but are outside of the direct decision making discretion of the individual firm. This theory claims that the SSA forms a coherent policy environment and will be backed by an accompanying ideology. In the boom period, in the first part of the cycle, the SSA will abet profits. However, inevitably the cycle will tip into crisis during the bust period, often because the same institutional rules that aided profits in the boom period hinder them because of either changed conditions or the internal contradictions in the rules of the SSA. In an economic system that relies on private investment, low profits are problematic not just for firms and their owners but for all of society, so the bust period will instigate a quest for a new SSA that will restore profits. The specific form that the new SSA takes will depend on the relative strength of different classes or groups in society. Once a set of rules is found that restore profits, these create the conditions for the long-term boom that marks the beginning of the next SSA (Bowles et al., 1986). Most authors in the SSA tradition argue that there have been three long waves in the US, each of which ended in a major economic crisis (in the 1890s, 1930s and 1970s). The extent to which the crash of 2008 marks the end of what many of them call the neoliberal SSA is the subject of much more controversy (McDonough, Reich, & Kotz, 2010; Lippit, 2014; Kotz, 2015).

In SSA theory, there is predictability to both the general institutional structure and its inevitable crisis. SSAs generally come in two types depending on the balance of class forces. In the first, capital is strong.

In this type of SSA, firms' greater relative political clout results in an institutional structure that benefits firms at the expense of their workers and other citizens. In this type of SSA, workers' wages will tend to stagnate. Government will be unwilling or unable to impose regulations that increase costs on firms, like environmental or safety regulation. While this will generate a profit-enhancing environment in the boom part of the long swing, it creates the seeds of its own destruction because firms needing to sell their products will run up against the barrier of an income-constrained population. Both the Great Depression and the 2008 crisis are seen in this light. The crisis of a strong capital SSA is the result not of declining profits or profit squeeze but of their inability to realize profit through the sale of their commodities (Duménil & Lévy, 2011). The second type of SSA features relatively weak capital. Although profits must always be ensured in any SSA, in this type, citizens or workers have relatively greater power in influencing the institutions of the SSA. In this SSA wages tend to grow more rapidly and the profit-seeking behavior of firms is moderated by government constraints. The crisis of a weak capital SSA is caused by profits being squeezed by increased costs, as was the case, according to many SSA analysts, in the 1970s (Kotz, 2015).

This book positions neoliberalism as a class-driven response to previously encountered barriers to capitalist expansion and argues that, in important ways, the US is the most advanced case of this transformation. In the language of the SSA, the neoliberal set of institutions reflects a specific period in US capitalism where business is particularly strong. Talking about business "strength" may seem a bit vague, since strength and power in a class-based system require economic, political, and cultural bases that can be hard to discern. We can make this more concrete by looking at the rise of neoliberalism in the US.

Business support for neoliberalism in the United States

The Great Depression caused a profound reconsideration of the rules of the economic game in the US. Faced with the apparent success of wartime Keynesian deficit spending in jump starting the economy and an increasingly militant working class angered by the injustices of the Depression, business in the US conceded to an institutional environment in which the working class shared more broadly in productivity gains, workers' rights and protections were advanced within the workplace, and some aspects of life were removed from dependence on the market and provided for publicly (for example, education, social security, Medicaid). This institutional structure has gone under a wide variety of names (the post-war accord, regulated capitalism) and there is still some controversy around the extent to which these institutions were fully adopted, but the broad basic structure should be fairly familiar to anybody over the age of 50. First, Keynesian fiscal and monetary policies were used to achieve full employment. This represented a new acknowledgement that unemployment was not necessarily the result of the shortcomings of the out-of-work, but a result of the functioning of the broader economic system that could be alleviated by government intervention. Second, the welfare state was dramatically expanded. This had the dual role of protecting the income of the unemployed by decommodifying (or in Polanyi's terms, re-embedding) at least a basic, minimal standard of living and maintaining the consumption, and therefore the demand for products, of those without employment income. Third, unions became an established part of the industrial relations landscape. This was formalized in legislation like the Wagner Act, which made it easier to form unions and forced firms to undertake collective bargaining on a limited array of workplace issues when workers formed into unions (Kotz, 2015). In addition, government regulation of firms' behavior became more widely accepted during this period. In the early stages of the post-war period, regulation was fairly limited, often to sectors with strategic importance, as was the case with the Glass Steagall Act, which restricted the activities of the banking industry to avoid a repeat of the 1929 crash. As the postwar period progressed, regulation became an increasingly salient feature of the economy. During the early 1970s, for example, both the Occupational Safety and Health Administration (OSHA) and the Environmental Protection Agency (EPA) were created.

In the decades after World War II, tight labor markets (and other pro-worker changes to labor markets) did cause a rise in wages. It is no coincidence that this was a period in which labor, organized into politically powerful industrial unions, enjoyed much more clout. During this period wages grew more rapidly, and more broadly, than in any other historical period, the US experienced the emergence of a blue-collar middle class, and inequality declined as incomes at the bottom and middle of the spectrum increased more rapidly than those at the top (Piketty & Saez, 2003; Galbraith, 2012; Piketty, 2013). A couple of factors specific to this period enabled increases in both wages and profits. The first was that productivity was increasing rapidly because of technological innovation in production, meaning that each worker could produce more in each hour of work. This reduced cost per unit and created the opportunity for wage increases without cutting into profits. It also created the need for a mass market for US products. The second factor was a lack of international competitors for the US after the European and Japanese economies were destroyed during the world war, so increased demand by the US workforce was likely to be provided for by US-based companies. Thus, the broad-based income gains that were, in part, due to high employment, played an important role in maintaining profits as well. The demand for the products

Figure 1.1 US profit rate (percent)

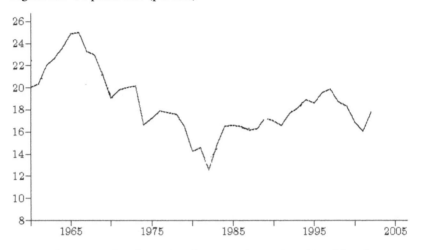

Source: G. Duménil and D. Lévy, "Costs and Benefits of Neoliberalism:
A Class AnalysisI In G. Epstein (ed.), *Financialization and the World
Economy* (Aldershot: Edward Elgar, 2005)

of American firms was also bolstered by both the direct spending of the
government on things like the interstate highway system and its transfers
to households through social benefits such as unemployment insurance.

Inevitably, the post-war boom collapsed. Starting around 1965, corporate
profits fell precipitously for almost twenty years (Duménil & Lévy, 2004,
pp. 24–28; Kotz, 2015, p. 63). It was this fall in profits that created the
economic turmoil in the US. High rates of unemployment, low investment
and sluggish economic growth were the inevitable result. Figure 1.1 shows
clearly that the profit rate declined through the 1970s and then began
to recover after the early 1980s. This was, of course, part of the promise
of neoliberal economic ideas. Their policies were aimed at restoring profits,
although they were often not particularly explicit about this goal.

The causes of the fall in profits are the subject of much debate in
heterodox economic circles (Pollin, 2003; Brenner, 2006; Duménil &
Lévy, 2011; Shaikh, 2011; Kotz, 2015) but what is much more clear is that,
starting around 1980, business and government took active measures
to restore profits, embarking on a practical application of neoliberal
principles which had been percolating intellectually for several decades
(Duménil & Lévy, 2012; Kotz, 2015). Broadly speaking, neoliberalism
marked a profound shift in the economic underpinnings of countries,
which shifted power to business in several ways. First, by abandoning
traditional Keynesian demand-side stabilization in favor of monetarist
policy aimed at controlling inflation by manipulating interest rates, high

levels of employment were abandoned as a policy goal, putting downward pressure on workers' wage demands. Second, a supply-side program of flattening progressive tax rates to create incentives for investment, savings, and work redistributed after tax income to the rich. Third, to further reduce costs to firms, the regulatory role of the government was greatly pared back, and, where it still existed, traditional bureaucratic regulation was replaced with cost-benefit analysis and market solutions. Finally, the welfare system and labor market were reformed by, among other things, policies reducing the power of unions and making government benefits to the unemployed more miserly. This was euphemistically known as "flexibility," but the distributional effects against labor and for business should be obvious (Jenkins & Eckert, 2000, p. 313). To this list of national policies we could add the international trend to eliminate barriers to trade and financial flows, forcing workers in the US to compete with lower wage labor in the developing world while capital was free to find the location in which it could earn the highest return (Duménil & Lévy, 2012).

In keeping with the theoretical claims of Polanyi, RA, and SSA, the neoliberal turn was not a natural or inevitable transition from policies that were failing to those that would succeed. Rather, it was a result of a very deliberate series of policy interventions meant to restructure the economic rules along the lines desired by a relatively powerful business community.

Essayist Lewis Lapham marks the beginning of the concerted effort to organize and fund the transformation to neoliberal economic policy in the US in 1971, with a call to arms called "Attack on the Free Enterprise System," written by Lewis Powell, solicited by, and for confidential circulation to, the Chamber of Commerce. In it, Powell warned that "survival of what we call the free enterprise system lies in organization, in careful long-range planning and implementation, in consistency of action over an indefinite period of years, in the scale of financing available only through joint effort, and in the political power available only through united action and national organizations" (quoted in Lapham, 2004). Several now well-known businessmen took up the call including: newspaper magnate Richard Mellon Scaife, weapons and chemical manufacturer John Olin, Vicks Chemical's Smith Richardson, beer baron Joseph Coors, and the Koch brothers (one of whom, David, ran as the Vice Presidential candidate for the Libertarian Party in 1980) who made their money in oil. Coors and Scaife combined to provide the start-up cash for The Heritage Foundation in 1973 and the Koch family financed The Cato Institute in 1977 (Lapham, 2004) along with a variety of other libertarian, pro-market think tanks and centers including the Reason Foundation, the Institute for Humane Studies, the Centre for the Study of Public Choice, and the James Buchanan Centre (MacLean, 2017). These new organizations joined with previously established institutions like the

American Enterprise Institute (AEI) in an effort to turn the tide of ideas towards what they would call free market. The fact that they received generous financial support and institutional direction from business should also provide some indication of just who would benefit from their economic ideas.

Two sociologists, J. Craig Jenkins and Craig Eckert, who have studied what they call "the new conservative economics," discovered that different institutions specialized in different policy areas. The AEI, for example, was the driving force behind promoting monetarism to combat inflation, fiscal conservatism, and the Government Regulation Program that promoted deregulation. The Heritage Foundation backed the supply-side economic policies of corporate tax reduction and deregulation. The Hoover Institution concentrated on criticizing social welfare programs like social security and income maintenance (Jenkins & Eckert, 2000). This is not to say that all of these organizations were always pulling in the same direction. There are, theoretically, potential conflicts between the balanced budgets advocated by a fiscal conservative and the sharp tax reductions of supply siders. However, despite these divisions, a quick comparison of the policies implemented in the neoliberal era and those promoted by these institutions should suffice to demonstrate their remarkable success.

On the off chance that there remains any doubt about who was directing these institutions or who benefited from their research and advocacy, a glance at their boards of directors should put this to rest. Important business groups like the Business Roundtable, the Chamber of Commerce, and the National Association of Manufacturers cooperated with these institutes and there was considerable cross pollination of boards. In fact, of the 287 policy directorships in these organizations, 82.5 percent were held by 221 corporate officers and private entrepreneurs (Jenkins & Eckert, 2000, p. 325).

Funding also flowed from the business community to these organizations. The Scaife Foundation donated around $20 million to Heritage in the 17-year period between 1985 and 2002. Total donations from business foundations to Heritage totalled $45 million during this period (Backhouse, 2005, p. 380). Of course, individual corporations also contributed, with donations from companies like AIG, Philip Morris, Lockheed Martin, and Exxon Mobil. The big contributor to the AEI's budget (which had grown to $50 million by 2009) was the Bradley Foundation, with lesser contributions from Olin, Scaife and Exxon. The Koch families' money went largely to the Cato Institute, to which Scaife and Olin also contributed (Media Matters, n.d.). Even though millions of dollars have been lavished on these organizations to influence the direction of economic policy, in the grand scheme of research foundations, institutions like the AEI are not among the biggest players. The assets of the Ford Foundation were over $9 billion in 2002 compared to the Bradley Foundation's more modest

$500 million. (The big recent mover in the conservative foundation world has been the Walton Foundation, which is focussed largely on educational donations, with assets of over $1 billion in 2009 (Media Matters, n.d.).) Rather, the success of these organizations was their single-minded use of the funds that they did attract.

In order to have a significant effect, of course, the ideas fermenting in the think tanks and business forums must be translated into policy. The growing impact of the conservative think tanks during this period is difficult to empirically capture but some scholars have attempted to quantify their influence. Perhaps the best study on this front was conducted by Andrew Rich. He used three measures to assess think tank influence during the 1990s: a survey of congressional staff and journalists, the number of times they testified before Congress and the number of times they were cited in a newspaper. According to the Rich survey, in 1993 the top five think tanks with the "greatest influence on the formulation of public policy in Washington" were: Brookings, Heritage, AEI, Progressive Policy Institute and Cato. By 1997 those same institutes occupied the top five positions, but the pecking order had changed in favor of the more conservative organizations. Heritage had moved up to the top spot, with Cato third and AEI fourth (Rich, 2004, p. 81). Sixty-eight percent of the survey respondents claimed that conservative think tanks had a greater influence than liberal think tanks, while only 5 percent argued that liberal think tanks wielded greater influence (Rich, 1997). Rich also found that, between 1991 and 1999, conservative think tanks testified before the House or Senate almost one and a half times more often than liberal or centrist organizations (Rich, 2004, p. 94). Conservative think tanks were also "substantively" mentioned in newspapers almost four times more frequently than their non-conservative counterparts during these years (Rich, 2004, pp. 93, 95).

While influencing what constitutes economic common sense can shape the political landscape through changing the ideas of the voting public and policy-making elite, more direct political influence was also helpful for business after 1980. Conservative think tanks have been successful in placing people in a position to advise Presidents, particularly those from the Republican Party, increasing the likelihood that economic ideas will be converted into economic policy. Reagan's Presidential campaign relied heavily on conservative think tanks to provide intellectual approval for his policies. This was coordinated by Martin Anderson, a senior fellow at the Hoover Institution and key Reagan policy advisor, who believed that gathering a team of intellectuals to support the ideas of the candidate would dramatically increase his credibility (Abelson, 2009, p. 136). Once in power, the Reagan administration drew heavily from the think tanks that helped formulate his campaign platform. Between 1981 and 1988, almost two hundred members of conservative think tanks went to work for the Reagan government. Hoover (55), Heritage (36), and AEI (34) were particularly large sources of personnel for the Reagan team (Abelson, 2009, p. 138).

It was during the Reagan years that the Heritage Institute came to prominence as a policy force in Washington. After Reagan was elected in 1980, Heritage presented its report, *Mandate for Leadership*, containing policy proposals cobbled together from its own research and that of other like-minded think tanks, to presidential advisor Edwin Meese III, who commented that the government would "rely heavily on it." By 1982, Edwin Feulner, the head of Heritage, claimed that more that 60 percent of the proposals in the report had been, or would be, adopted. Although it is likely that Feulner was overstating the impact of the document, it did become known as the "bible" of the Reagan administration (Abelson, 2009, p. 139).

Business groups also responded to Powell's 1971 call by organizing themselves more coherently to clearly express their policy preferences and to coordinate lobbying activity. For example, the Business Roundtable was founded in 1972. Its founding document identified rising wages as a source of declining profits in the early 1970s. Its membership grew through the 1970s so that by 1979 it included nearly seventy of the top one hundred financial and non-financial corporations in the United States. It advocated for reductions in corporate taxes, raising the retirement age, and cutbacks in environmental legislation. It opposed consumer protection advocated by Ralph Nader and legislation to improve the bargaining power of unions, especially the Labor Law Reform Act of 1978. In March 1981, the Business Roundtable publicly endorsed Ronald Reagan's entire economic program, including high-interest monetary policy and cuts to taxes, social spending, and regulations (Kotz, 2015, p. 72).

A particularly transparent example of the influence of business lobbying on politicians is the American Legislative Exchange Program (ALEC) founded in 1973. ALEC is not really a research and policy organization like those mentioned previously, although it does produce research reports and policy studies. Rather, its main role is to craft "model" bills and resolutions that can be easily turned into law by sympathetic politicians, mostly at the state level. ALEC's funding comes from the, by now, usual suspects in the business foundation world including Scaife, Coors and Koch, but also draws considerable funding from individual firms. Its list of corporate donors is a virtual who's who of corporate America from General Motors to Bank of America to Microsoft to McDonald's. Donor firms get veto power over the wording in the legislation cooked up by ALEC (Nichols, 2011). ALEC claims to have introduced a remarkable 3100 individual pieces of legislation in one year (1999–2000). Its recent activities include: the Automatic Income Tax Reduction Act, which would provide an automatic biennial tax rate decrease; the Public-Private Fair Competition Act, which would establish whether state agencies compete "unfairly" with the private sector; and the anti-union Right to Work Act, which removes an employee's obligation to pay union dues (Rogers & Dresser, 2011). ALEC's bill pipeline was not confined to these areas, but extended to writing legislation on the environment, public schools, and healthcare. ALEC bills have been successfully adopted, sometimes word for word at the state level. One might claim that this was politics "by business, for business," rather than any romantic, inclusive notions of "the people."

Generally speaking, these efforts bore fruit. While no doubt many neoliberal supporters still consider their work at best a partial triumph, the remaining chapters in this book will demonstrate that, by almost any measure, they have been remarkably successful in implementing the neoliberal policy package. As Figure 1.1 shows, these policies did have a restorative effect on the profit rate. However, this restoration has caused devastating effects on the potential for human development. Looking at how humans create themselves and their worlds on material foundations of health and the natural environment, through work and politics, the book chronicles how neoliberalism has foreshortened human potential. At a time when neoliberalism's effects are stirring various forms of popular resistance and opposition, this book will be a catalogue of sorts for the range of processes that need to be confronted if the realization of human potential is to be freed from the increasingly cramped and exclusive quarters to which neoliberalism seeks to confine it.

The rest of the book

Neoliberal capitalism is a class-based political project undertaken to more favorably position business in its struggle to enhance the conditions for profitability—a project that reaches deeply into the weave of social and ecological life. It involves both the increasing role of money and markets in the determination of life chances and the systematic push of corporations—as bearers of neoliberal reason and as beneficiaries of neoliberal transformations—into previously protected spheres of life. Each of the chapters will analyse a crucial sphere that capital has successfully increased control over, privatized, or commodified. We emphasize these particular spheres on the basis of their fundamental role in answering Martha Nussbaum's (2011, p. 32) question "What does a life worthy of human dignity require?" We suggest that each of the areas has an indispensable role in supporting human dignity. Capital's deepening intrusion into these spheres has not only exposed them to the logic of accumulation (and worked to turn them into sites of accumulation) but also reduced the possibilities of oppositional politics, as the market logic and dynamics come to be seen as applicable to everything.

One of the key activities through which humans develop themselves, and in capitalism through which their conditions of life (and that of their children) are largely determined, is work. Since the 1980s, workers (and the so-called middle class) in the US have experienced stagnant wages, the longest workweek in the industrialized world and unprecedented household debt. In the words of Federal Reserve Chair, Alan Greenspan, labor has been "traumatized." Even after the 2008 crisis, the inequality of wealth and income in the US continued unabated. In Chapter 2, the results and mechanisms responsible for this inequality will be explored along with its complement, macroeconomic instability. There has been considerable attention paid to the increase in inequality during this period, mostly focusing on changes to government redistribution as taxes and the welfare state have declined in tandem. The pre-redistributive arena of economic life in the US economy has received much less attention. We will argue that the labor market in the US has turned against workers because many of the social protections that had previously been fought for, and won, by US workers have been clawed back as a result of business dominance in the policy arena during the neoliberal era. It is within the sphere of work that neoliberalism as a class-based project is perhaps most visibly apparent. Neoliberal labor-market policies represent a transformation in the labor market from an institutional regime that both removed some elements of provisioning from the realm of the market and included structures that increased workers' bargaining power to one in which labor-market institutions and policy are increasingly designed to remove the protection for workers in an overall context of increasing competition between workers nationally and globally.

Chapter 3 will examine how neoliberal capitalism is reshaping relations between humans and nature—a second sphere crucial to the prospects for human development. As the scale and depth of industrial production's negative environmental effects became clearer in the 1970s, Americans made the legitimacy of the state contingent on mitigating the damage. A raft of far-reaching environmental legislation and regulation (under a Republican administration) resulted. In the neoliberal era, the response to environmental transformation has taken a markedly different approach. Deregulation is perhaps the most obvious neoliberal threat to the maintenance of a habitable planet, as state-imposed limits to capital's access to resources and sinks are removed, but deeper transformations are involved as well. Rather than being understood as a set of limits to the never-ending accumulation of capital, socio-natural systems and their components have been recast as capital itself, or as new frontiers of profitability. As all of nature is targeted for privatization, commodification, and reconfiguration as an assemblage of value-creating "ecosystem services" (carbon sequestration, nitrogen fixation, water filtration, species habitat, etc.), new regimes of property, and new relations between people and their environments, are emerging with considerable effects on the distribution of assets and life chances, as well as on the way we conceive of nature and our place within it. This chapter will address the means through which, rather than adapting our economic priorities and relations to the socio-natural limits of the planet, neoliberal capitalism is attempting to transcend those limits by re-conceptualizing and reorganizing life, landscapes, and ecosystems in its own image.

Our third foundation for human development, health, is the subject of Chapter 4. It will explain why Americans pay so much more for healthcare and do so poorly on measures of health outcomes compared to other rich countries. Part of the reason for this particularly inefficient state of affairs in the US is that the conditions in which people exist create worse health outcomes than in other nations. Worse, neoliberal policy has caused these economic determinants of health to deteriorate relative to the conditions that existed in recent US history. As a result, people in the US live shorter, less healthy lives than people in comparably wealthy nations, or for that matter, even compared to nations with considerably lower incomes.

The healthcare system that attempts to deal with the relatively unhealthy US populace is singularly poorly equipped to do so. The US relies more on for-profit private healthcare insurance and delivery than any other country in the industrialized world. Indeed, during the neoliberal period, healthcare delivery has increasingly been transferred to business. The medical industry over-prescribes care for some and denies access to others depending on the profit imperative. Healthcare in the US will be analyzed as the result of two opposing interests. On one hand, the trend towards neoliberal policy in healthcare, which means increased commodification and reliance for profit corporations, is reinforced by the medical industry that benefits from this state of affairs. On the other, average Americans express tremendous dissatisfaction with this system. We will interpret the Affordable Care Act (Obamacare) as a neoliberal cooptation of this dissatisfaction.

Chapters 5 and 6 focus on neoliberalism's implications for political agency. Chapter 5 examines how the one of the most important institutions for the development of capable democratic participants—education—has been intensely subjected to the logic of for-profit commodification as a result of neoliberalism. Laws have been passed, deregulation applied, mergers taken place, and austerity budgets imposed so that corporations can profit from public resources while increasing their control over the education system responsible for fostering a population capable of thoughtful and informed democratic participation.

Government funding of American public universities has plummeted as a result of fiscal constraints created by neoliberal policy in the areas of taxation and deficits. Unable to live on increasingly meagre government funds, public universities in the US have come to rely increasingly on corporate donations and rising tuition rates. This has created problematic results in three important areas. First, although the university as a truly independent and unbiased bastion of research was more the ideal than reality, in the neoliberal period corporate financing has undermined both the independence and the objectivity of university research. The subjects of inquiry have become increasingly shaped by the demands of funding and even the results of those investigations have been biased towards the interests of research funders. Second, the content and structure of what is taught at the university have been altered by the demands of both corporate funding and the requirement that post-secondary education train workers rather than create citizens. Finally, in the postwar period, tuition at public universities was subsidized to make university access less dependent on the income of students or their families. As universities have increased tuition fees to make up for declining government funding, post-secondary education is increasingly the realm of the affluent, compromising its role facilitating social mobility between generations.

As with many of the other neoliberal timelines in this book, the transformation of K-12 education (from kindergarten to grade 12) started under the Reagan administration in the early 1980s. As a result of the application of neoliberal principles, students who start off at a disadvantage because of their socio-economic position will find themselves further impeded because of the schools they are more likely to attend, while the already existing advantages of the socio-economically privileged are reinforced. Further, neoliberal values have been applied to running K-12 education, from how students are tested to increasing school choice, with largely detrimental impacts. The overarching impact of these changes has been to produce a citizenry deprived of equality of opportunity in life chances but also constrained in its ability to fully and equally participate in public life.

The transformation of the political system has been both a cause and an effect of neoliberalism. Chapter 6 looks at how the primary means of democratic expression and political agency for the large majority of the population in the US have been (further) limited under neoliberalism. The chapter first looks at the various ways that democracy has been thinned under neoliberalism, highlighting a profound shift in political power towards the wealthy, and a corresponding decimation of working-class power. Beyond this, however, neoliberal policies could not have been implemented in even a nominal democracy without at least a modicum of support from its victims. This chapter will thus also explore why many Americans voted and acted against their material interests during this period. Remarkably, large sections of the American electorate vote for and support policies that favor the very business class that has profited from their economic decline. Standard explanations for this "false consciousness" range from a compliant media, unlimited corporate campaign funding, and an electorate susceptible to the subsequent information bias. The results of this political transformation have become increasingly pervasive in the everyday life of ordinary Americans, re-shaping their relations with elites, with one another, and with nature.

The final chapter will examine the policies of President Donald Trump. The election of President Trump has been characterized by some analysts as a death blow for neoliberalism. We will examine President Trump's policies to determine the extent to which they are a rejection or continuation of neoliberal policy.

Note

1 These are hardly the only works that have used the term neoliberalism. Others that attempt to define the term or apply it to different arenas include: Birch & Mykhnenko, 2010; Plant, 2010; Braedley & Luxton, 2010: and Brown, 2015.

References

Abelson, D. (2009). *Do Think Tanks Matter?* 2nd edn. Montreal: McGill-Queens University Press.

Aglietta, M. (1979). *A Theory of Capitalist Regulation: The US Experience.* London: Verso.

Backhouse, R. (2005). The Rise of Free Market Economics: Economists and the Role of the State since 1970. *History of Political Economy*, 37(1), 355–392.

Birch, K., & Mykhnenko, V. (2010). *The Rise and Fall of Neoliberalism.* London: Zed Books.

Bourdieu, P. (2003). *Firing Back: Against the Tyranny of the Market 2.* New York: Verso.

Bowles, S., Gordon, D., & Weisskopf, T. (1986). Power and Profits: The Social Structure of Accumulation and the Profitability of the Postwar U.S. Economy. *Review of Radical Political Economics*, 18 (1–2), 132–167.

Braedley, S., & Luxton, M. (2010). *Neoliberalism and Everyday Life.* Montreal: McGill-Queen's University Press.

Brenner, R. (2006). *The Economics of Global Turbulence: The Advanced Capitalist Economies from Long Boom to Long Downturn 1945–2005.* New York: Verso.

Brown, W. (2015). *Undoing the Demos: Neoliberalism's Stealth Revolution.* New York: Verso.

Cahill, D., & Konings, M. (2017). *Neoliberalism.* Cambridge: Polity.

Crouch, C. (2011). *The Strange No-Death of Neoliberalism.* Cambridge: Polity.

Dardot, P., & Laval, C. (2013). *The New Way of the World: On Neoliberal Society.* Trans. G. Elliot. London: Verso.

Duménil, G., & Lévy, D. (2004). *Capital Resurgent.* Cambridge, MA: Harvard University Press.

Duménil, G., & Lévy, D. (2011). *The Crisis of Neoliberalism*. Cambridge, MA: Harvard University Press.

Duménil, G., & Lévy, D. (2012). The Crisis of the Early 21st Century. In R. Bellofiore & G. Vertova (eds), *The Great Recession and the Contradictions of Contemporary Capitalism*. Aldershot: Edward Elgar.

Friedman, M. (2003). Le Triomphe de Liberalisme. (H. Lepage, Interviewer) Politique Internationale (No. 100). Retrieved August 2, 2017, from www.politiqueinternationale.com/revue/read2.php?id_revue=15&id=163&content=texte&search=.

Galbraith, J. (2012). *Inequality and Instability*. Oxford: Oxford University Press.

Harvey, D. (2005). *A Brief History of Neoliberalism*. Oxford: Oxford University Press.

Heynen, N., McCarthy, J., Prudham, S., & Robbins, P. (2007). *Neoliberal Environments: False Promises and Unnatural Consequences*. New York: Routledge.

Jenkins, J., & Eckert, C. (2000). The Right Turn in Economic Policy: Business Elites and the New Conservative Economics. *Sociological Forum*, 15(2), 307–338.

Jessop, B. (1997). Survey Article: The Regulation Approach. *The Journal of Political Philosophy*, 5(3), 287–326.

Jessop, B., & Sum, N. (2006). *Beyond the Regulation Approach: Putting Capitalist Economies in Their Place*. Cheltenham: Edward Elgar.

Kotz, D. (2015). *The Rise and Fall of Neoliberal Capitalism*. Cambridge, MA: Harvard University Press.

Lapham, L. (2004). Tentacles of Rage: The Republican Propaganda Mill, A Brief History. *Harpers Magazine*, September.

Leys, C. (2001). *Market-Driven Politics: Neoliberal Democracy and the Public Interest*. London: Verso.

Lippit, V. (2014). The Neoliberal Era and the Financial Crisis in the Light of SSA Theory. *Review of Radical Political Economics*, 46(2), 141–161.

Losurdo, D. (2014). *Liberalism: A Counter-History*. New York: Verso.

MacLean, N. (2017). *Democracy in Chains: The Deep History of the Radical Right's Stealth Plan for America*. New York: Viking.

McDonough, T., Reich, M., & Kotz, D. (2010). *Contemporary Capitalism and Its Crises: Social Structure of Accumulation Theory for the 21st Century*. Cambridge: Cambridge University Press.

McWhorter, J. (2017). When People Were Proud to Call Themselves "Neoliberal". *The Atlantic*, May 30. Retrieved July 20, 2017, from www.theatlantic.com/business/archive/2017/05/history-of-neoliberal-meaning/528276/.

Media Matters. (n.d.). http://mediamattersaction.org/transparency/.

Mirowski, P. (2009). Post Face: Defining Neoliberalism. In P. Mirowski & D. Plehwe (eds), *The Road from Mont Pelerin (pp. 417–456)*. Cambridge, MA: Harvard University Press.

Mirowski, P. (2014). *Never Let a Serious Crisis Go to Waste*. London: Verso.

Nichols, J. (2011). ALEC Exposed, August 1–8. *The Nation*.

Nussbaum, M. (2011). *Creating Capabilities: The Human Development Approach*. Cambridge, MA: The Belknap Press of Harvard University Press.

Peck, J. (2010). *Constructions of Neoliberal Reason*. Oxford: Oxford University Press.

Piketty, T. (2013). *Capital in the 21st Century.* Cambridge, MA: Harvard University Press.

Piketty, T., & Saez, E. (2003). Income Inequality in the United States, 1913–1998. *The Quarterly Journal of Economics,* 118(1), 1–41.

Plant, R. (2010). *The Neo-Liberal State.* Oxford: Oxford University Press.

Polanyi, K. (1944 [1957]). *The Great Transformation.* Boston, MA: Beacon Press.

Pollin, R. (2003). *Contours of Descent: US Economic Fractures and the Landscape of Global Austerity.* London: Verso.

Rich, A. (1997). *Perceptions of Think Tanks in American Politics: A Survey of Congressional Staff and Journalists.* Washington, DC: Burson-Marstellar Worldwide Report.

Rich, A. (2004). *Think Tanks, Public Policy, and the Politics of Expertise.* New York: Cambridge University Press.

Rogers, J., & Dresser, L. (2011). ALEC Exposed: Business Domination Inc, August 1–8. *The Nation.*

Shaikh, A. (2011). The First Great Depression of the 21st Century. In L. Panitch, G. Albo, & V. Chibber, *Socialist Register, Vol. 47, The Crisis This Time.* New York: Monthly Review Press.

2

Work and incomes: nice for some

"You work three jobs? ... Uniquely American, isn't it? I mean, that is fantastic that you're doing that." President George W. Bush to a divorced mother of three in Omaha, Nebraska, in 2005. (Bush, 2005, p. 152)

Fran Marion, an African American woman with two children, works at a Popeyes fast food franchise in Kansas City, Missouri (Rushe, 2017). Her tale makes for sobering reading, and is all-too common an experience for the workers in the United States. Ms. Marion worked two jobs—for a combined shift of 9:00 AM to 1:30 AM—and with the resulting income was, for a while, just able to put a substandard roof over her family's heads. At her Popeyes shift, she processes an order every two minutes or so, grossing the company an estimated $950. Ms. Marion takes home $76. The stark reality for low-wage workers in the US is that wages simply aren't sufficient to pay for the bare necessities. Wages are, to put it differently, not high enough to materially reproduce the labor power for which they are exchanged. Just over half of the spending at both state and federal levels on public assistance programs goes to working families, meaning that the US public foots about $152.8 billion per year to help low-wage workers access basics like healthcare, housing, and food (Jacobs, Perry, & MacGilvary, 2015). Often even this isn't sufficient. After the city condemned the house she was renting due to the landlord's perpetual neglect, Ms. Marion became homeless. Her two teenage children lived an hour away with friends. She couch-surfed with a fellow fast-food worker and her family. Meanwhile, the seven publicly traded fast-food corporations on the top-ten list pulled in $7.44 billion in retained profit in 2012, while disbursing $7.7 billion in dividends and share buybacks. The top-ten's low wages and lack of benefits for front-line workers cost an estimated $3.8 billion in socialized costs (Allegretto et al., 2013).

Workers have recently undertaken an effective campaign to address this problem, under the banner of the Fight for $15 movement. Ms.

Marion is an active and vocal leader in the Kansas City chapter. Targeting cities, Fight for $15 has successfully pushed councils to adopt by-laws that raise the minimum wage to be paid by businesses. Starting with SeaTac, Washington, and spreading to dozens of cities across the US, labor activists have succeeded at the municipal level where Congress has refused to budge at the federal level. In Kansas City, for example, the council voted in July, 2015 to increase the minimum wage to $13 by 2020, and local activists had secured enough signatures to put a $15 minimum wage on the ballot in November of that year.

Conservative lawmakers at the state level, however, had different ideas. At the behest of business and trade associations, the Missouri state legislature passed—against the veto of its Governor—what is called a "pre-emption bill." These bills, increasingly popular within Conservative and corporate-dominated state legislatures, forbid municipalities from passing by-laws on a variety of issues—but most crucially wages. The Missouri pre-emption bill which ensured that the $15 minimum wage proposition never appeared on the ballot actually began as a pre-emption of by-laws that would ban plastic grocery bags. Amendments on the question of wages and on mandated leave benefits were tacked on later (Hancock, 2015). Missouri is not alone in passing or threatening pre-emption bills on the minimum wage. Alabama, Arizona, Texas, and Oklahoma are all working to strip cities of their authority to mandate wage increases. They are supported by the efforts of the American Legislative Exchange Council (ALEC), discussed in the first chapter, which provides model legislation for just such purposes, conveniently available online to neoliberally inclined, business-friendly state lawmakers.

This is the model towards which neoliberalism strives. Drawing on a labor force of highly exploited workers, leveraging whatever forms of marginalization or oppression are culturally available, and appropriating for free or at below-cost the necessities of commodity production, a small minority strives to enrich itself and entrench its power at the expense of the rest. Working with all of the tools provided through ownership and wealth, they have embarked on a successful project to beat back profit-dampening regulation and legislation, prevent organization by workers, and transfer jaw-dropping proportions of wealth and income towards themselves. With her grounded experience on the short-end of neoliberalism, Ms. Marion's analysis is pointed:

"We are the foot soldiers for these billion-dollar companies. We are the ones doing the work and bringing the money," she says. "At the top of America, when it comes to Trump and them, their goal is to keep us down," she says. "Between these billion-dollar companies and Trump, it's a power trip." … "We are still coming. No war has been won over night and we are not giving up." (Rushe, 2017)

Work is something of a double-edged sword. On one hand, work is the source of tremendous pride, self-worth and identity. At the very least, the income derived from labor feeds the family and hopefully allows a bit more besides. Being the bread winner is a source of justifiable pride. Further, most people identify themselves by the job they do. When people are asked what they do, the answer is rarely "I'm a gamer" or "I play center field on the local slow pitch team." It is almost always "I'm an accountant" or "I'm a steelworker." A job is often associated with a person's contribution to society. It is the arena in which most of our successes will be achieved. This was famously recognized by Marx's claim that work is an expression of human creativity in a double sense; that, through labor, we not only transform the world around us but also transform ourselves. The pleasure associated with labor is the ability of people to consciously re-shape the world around them to suit their wants and desires, as well as developing themselves physically and intellectually in the process. Crucial to this process is the ability of people to come together and cooperate in order to meet societally shared goals and objectives.

On the other hand, work—particularly under social relations characterized by a hierarchy of classes—is the source of many of life's great frustrations and disappointments. For most people, what they do, how they do it and what they create is beyond their control at work. Further, what they earn, and, even worse, whether they will even continue to hold down employment, is determined by some powerful, suit-wearing figure in the executive suite. It is no wonder that the principal dream peddled by the lottery merchants is freedom from work: freedom from wondering whether the next pay check will stretch to cover your family's expenses, freedom from the badgering and belittling demands from supervisors, freedom from work's daily grind. This second, alienating and exploitative, side of work is a prominent feature of selling labor in a wage-driven capitalist economy. The creative nature of work is subverted when workers agree to submit to the dictates of their employer in exchange for their pay. The employee no longer controls how they will produce, what will be produced or how they will interact with other workers. Rather, these things are determined for them, to a large extent, by a labor process dictated to them by the employer. Part of that control is the extent to which their work is compensated with income capable of enabling them to participate meaningfully in society. The working poor are not only alienated in the sense that they have a lack of control over what they do on the job, but they also experience a lack of control over their spending off the job. Being forced to go without what many others in society take for granted is a great source of powerlessness and frustration for low-income workers. Even worse, the threat of unemployment can make wage labor a precarious proposition. This too was recognized by Marx, who argued that firms must exploit their labor to the fullest extent possible in order to increase profits. Further, the ability of firms to make their employees work hard and accept lower wages rests on the threat of unemployment. If there were no unemployment, the threat of firing would lose its sting and workers would be in a much stronger bargaining position in the labor market.

It is the degree to which employees feel that they control their labor and the extent to which they feel they are fairly paid that determines, in large part, the fulfillment they get out of their work lives. In the first chapter, we posed the question "what does a life worthy of human dignity require?" In the world of work, it would require a great deal more of the first of work's double edge than the second. Work should be meaningful, fulfilling, creative, secure, and fairly compensated. The question is whether neoliberal labor market policies facilitate or hinder these worthwhile goals.

The context for transformation

The "Golden Age" of US capitalism, between the late 1940s and the late 1960s, was characterized by high rates of profit, high levels of investment, rapid productivity growth, low inflation, low unemployment, and rising real wages. It was also characterized by historically powerful checks on business's power in the labor market. The failures of the free market during the Great Depression and the economic success of government military spending during World War II created a political climate where growth and full employment became the responsibility of the state. The US government sought to reduce severe economic instability using monetary and fiscal policy, including progressive taxes and unemployment insurance, to avoid severe downturns. This period marked the dramatic expansion of the welfare state to mitigate the inequities and hardship resulting from the market distribution of income, but these programs had the additional effect of strengthening the bargaining position of labor because a guaranteed income, even a meager one, in the absence of a job diminished the threat of unemployment.

The period immediately after World War II was also one of intense labor–management strife. As an indication of the degree of labor unrest, in 1947 there were 207 strikes involving more than one thousand workers resulting in 26 million workdays lost. In 1950 these numbers had increased to 424 strikes and 30 million days idle (Bureau of Labor Statistics, 2017). In an effort to achieve some degree of labor peace, corporations accepted an accord with the historically militant US labor movement. Labor accepted constraints on its most disruptive methods of industrial action, such as wildcat strikes when workers would simply "down tools" and walk off the job, as well as corporate control over production, technology, plant location, marketing, and the labor process. In return, business provided job security, rising wages, and union recognition. Unions delivered an orderly and disciplined labor force and corporations rewarded workers with a share of the income gains made possible from productivity growth. Low unemployment, a relatively generous social safety net, and strong unions created an economic context in which workers had a degree of power in the labor market (for a more complete discussion see Bowles et al., 1986; and Pollin, 2003). While the corporate control over the labor process meant that alienation was a very real fact for postwar workers, exemplified by the routine regimented boredom of the assembly line, unions permitted much greater control over their work lives than was previously the case. Further, the stability and predictability of income growth created a broad, middle class of laborers, allowing workers to participate in the growing culture of mass consumption.

The "Golden Age" did not last. The 1970s were characterized by a falling rate of profit, a productivity slowdown, accelerating inflation, rising unemployment, stagnating investment and an end to growth in real wages. In the US, business and government responded to this economic malaise by turning to policy prescriptions designed to cut costs to firms in an effort to restore profits.[1]

Neoliberal labor market: policies

Neoliberal policies removed the social protections that had been part of the "Golden Age" accord, dismantling government supports that ensured that workers' incomes were not solely determined by the market for labor. As a result, after 1980 a sweeping series of changes to the policies surrounding the US labor market resulted in income being determined increasingly by the market alone.

Business in the US became more overtly hostile to what it considered to be its overly protected employees. Firms that had previously made at least moderate commitments to long-term employment and collective bargaining with their employees aggressively shifted to an insistence on more flexible labor arrangements. They increased the number of outside contractors and part-time employees. Production was shifted or contracted out to lower-wage nations. Unions were fought, resisted and discouraged with increasing intensity (Ehrenreich, 2016). In realizing these goals, the business community sought a wide-ranging change to the policy environment in which they operated. While a complete list of all the changes during this period is beyond the scope of this chapter, we will try to demonstrate that a remarkably wide array of policy changes was used to achieve this goal. Indeed, many of the policies are well outside labor market policy narrowly defined.

Labor market policy: tipping the scales of class power

We will begin with what most would define as narrow labor market policy. The post-1980 period was characterized by declining government support for the unemployed. One excellent example of this was the change from the Assistance for Families with Dependent Children (AFDC) to Temporary Aid for Needy Families (TANF) during the Clinton administration. TANF is federal funding that is channeled through the states for social assistance. While permitting considerable latitude for states to determine their own eligibility requirements, the federal government insisted on some common, and quite punitive, rules for states to receive funding. Recipients were eligible only for a maximum of five years. Recipients must work to be eligible for benefits, and it ended automatic Medicaid coverage. Only households that are in severe financial distress are eligible for TANF, although the precise criteria vary by state. In 2012, a single mother with two children must earn less than $800 per month and have assets of less than $2000 to be eligible in the majority of states (Falk, 2014). The increased eligibility requirements have meant that fewer people in poverty are claiming TANF benefits. In 1996, 68 percent of families in poverty received TANF but, by 2013, only 26 percent did so (Center on Budget and Policy Priorities, 2015, p. 6). Rates vary considerably by state. While, in California, a single parent with two children would get $704 in 2016, TANF benefits were $170 in Mississippi and $215 in Alabama for a family of three (Center on Buget and Policy Priorities, 2016, p. 12). In 32 states TANF rates provide an income that is less than 30 percent of the poverty threshold (Edin & Shaefer, 2015, p. 172). Of all the states, only Maryland and Wyoming have increased their TANF benefits since 1996 when adjusted for inflation. In all other states benefit rates are lower, some considerably so. In 23 states, TANF benefits were more than 30 percent lower in 2016 than they were in 1996 in real terms (Center on Buget and Policy Priorities, 2016, p. 12). The decline in support for the poor has two crucial impacts beyond the obvious effects on the ability of those on social assistance to meet their basic needs. First, it makes out-of-work laborers increasingly desperate to take employment. Second, it increases the threat of being out of work for those employed. Both of these impacts create more power for firms in their dealings with their labor force.

Another important manner in which workers' income is separated from the pure logic of the market is through the minimum wage. The federal minimum wage was introduced in 1938, at an inflation-adjusted hourly rate of $3.51 (in 2016 dollars). It increased roughly in line with productivity growth through the "Golden Age" to $8.68 in 1968 (Schmitt, 2012). It remained relatively constant at around $8.00 for the 1970s and then fell consistently through the 1980s to $6.00, hovering between $6.00 and $7.00 until the 2007 increases under Obama (Desilver, 2017). Labor productivity continued to grow throughout this period, such that, had the federal minimum wage continued to track productivity, it would have hit $21.72 per hour by 2012. Even getting half of the productivity gains would have put the minimum just over the hard-fought-for level of $15.00 by that same year (Schmitt, 2012). States and municipalities, of course, are free to set their minimums higher than the federal level, and some do. Thirty-one states, as of January 2018, have minimum wages higher than the federal floor. However, many of these are only slightly higher, and even in those states and municipalities in which minimums are significantly higher than the federal, only very recently have they regained their inflation-adjusted levels prior to their significant decline through the 1970s and 1980s. Let's take the minimum-wage champion city of Seattle, Washington, as an example. Seattle has in the 2010s produced considerable anxiety from within neoliberal circles for scheduling some significant increases to their minimum wage. Employers, depending on their number of workers and whether those workers get tips or benefits, must pay $15.00 per hour as the minimum wage starting sometime between 2017 and 2021 (Torres, 2016). This was a hard-won struggle by Seattle workers. However, putting it in historical context shows that, by 2015, Seattle was only just getting back to where the inflation-adjusted minimum wage was back in 1968 (Perry, 2016). In other words, between 1968 and 2015, minimum wage workers got exactly none of the productivity gains. Things are far worse in pretty much every other jurisdiction. As was the case with social assistance programs like TANF, the reduction in minimum wage weakened a crucial state support that increased worker bargaining power.

The rules surrounding unionization were also weakened after 1980. While unions were an accepted, if not exactly welcomed, feature of the industrial relations landscape prior to the 1980s, firms became increasingly hostile to the increased bargaining power for workers and intrusion on corporate flexibility that they created. The Director of Labor Education Research at Cornell, Kate Bronfenbrenner, found that, between 1999 and 2003 in 57 percent of union elections, firms threatened to close down workplaces. Employees were threatened with lay-offs in 47 percent. In two-thirds of the elections, workers were required to attend weekly one on one anti-union meetings with their supervisor. In 34 percent of the elections, workers engaging in pro-union activity were fired. She also noted that this represented a marked increase in these kinds of anti-union activities compared to previous periods (Bronfenbrenner, 2009).

These anti-union tactics were facilitated by changes to the rules surrounding unionization that made it more difficult for unions to obtain and maintain certification. To take just one example, states have increasingly passed "right to work" legislation that prohibits workers from paying mandatory union dues when they are employed in a unionized workforce. While this legislation is couched in the language of freedom of choice, it considerably weakens unions because it permits workers to opt out of paying dues but still benefit from the gains that unions win from employers. Unsurprisingly, studies have found that union organizing is lower in right-to-work states (Ellwood & Fine, 1987; Davis & Huston, 1995; Hogler et al., 2004).

There are a number of ways to measure the impact of neoliberal policies on the power of workers in the labor market. Union membership has fallen from 20 percent of wage and salary workers in 1983 to 11 percent in 2015 (Dunn & Walker, 2016). Another, related, measure is the willingness and ability of workers to go on strike to back their demands for higher wages and better working conditions. Between 1966 and 1974, there was an average of 352 work stoppages involving at least 1000 workers per year. After 1981, workers became much less militant. In the decade of the 2000s, the most strike-filled year was 2000 in which there were only 39 large walkouts. In 2009 there were five (Perelman, 2011, p. 49).

Like Robin Hood in reverse, neoliberal labor market policy strove to decrease government payouts to the poor while simultaneously reducing the amount that it took from the rich. Two different waves of tax reduction, the first under Reagan in the 1980s and the second under Bush Jr. in the 2000s, cut a variety of different taxes on upper income earners. As a result the tax system in the US was far less progressive by the mid-2000s than it was in the 1960s. In the 1960s the top marginal tax rate on earned income was 91 percent, by 2003 it had fallen to 35 percent. Corporate and estate taxes, which fall more heavily on high income earners, have also been reduced during this period. The result has been that the average tax rate on all income for the very rich top 0.1 percent of income earners in the US decreased from over 60 percent in 1970 to about 40 percent by the mid-2000s (Piketty & Saez, 2007, p. 15). The reduction of tax progressivity is in keeping with the neoliberal desire to make outcomes increasingly determined by the market. At the same time it had the important consequence of increasing after-tax income inequality, as we shall see later in the chapter. It also freed up income for the very rich to spend on influencing the political system even further in their favor, a topic that we will explore in Chapter 6. Finally, it reduced the amount

of money that was available for government spending, creating a justification for reducing the size of the state.

Macro policy: shifting the terrain of struggle

In addition to the more narrow labor market policies listed above, broader
macroeconomic policies transferred power from workers to firms. During
the "Golden Age" unemployment in the US stayed, for the most part,
between 4 percent and 6 percent. Part of the reason for this was the
commitment to use fiscal (deficit spending during recessions) and monetary
(influence over the interest rate) policy to maintain full employment.
Full employment as a policy goal was abandoned after the 1980s. In
terms of fiscal policy, the federal government did consistently run deficits,
which does increase employment, but it was done in a manner that did
not particularly enhance the consumption or incomes of the working
class. While the political rhetoric of the neoliberal era was about "fiscal
balance" and "financial responsibility," only Clinton acted on that rhetoric
by balancing the federal budget. Reagan, both Bush presidencies, and
Obama all continued to run deficits—and larger ones than all the pre-1980
non-World War II years (even as a percent of GDP). For the Reagan and
George W. Bush administrations, these were a product of increased
military spending and tax reductions that primarily benefited the rich
(a point to which we will return). For Obama, they were the product of
Keynesian counter cyclical spending following the 2008 crisis. Although
the language of financial responsibility has been used to cut spending,
balancing the budget has never been the actual concern of governments
during the neoliberal period. The overriding concern has been to reorient
state spending, abandoning its use to support employment and working-
class purchasing power during downturns, and eliminating non-market
forms of income and public provisioning.

The goal of monetary policy also moved from providing full employment
to combating inflation. With inflation rates climbing towards 10 percent
in the late 1970s, the Federal Reserve (Fed) Chair, Paul Volcker, and his
successor from 1987 to 2006, Alan Greenspan, raised interest rates
dramatically in an effort to clamp down on demand and control inflation.
While reducing demand to control inflation has a sanitized, painless
ring to it, what it really means is causing unemployment. Between the
late 1970s and around 1997 monetary policy was consistently contractionary. Faced with the choice of creating employment or fighting the specter
of inflation, Volcker and Greenspan chose to throw people out of work
(Greider, 2001).

Greenspan followed a more expansionary, lower interest rate policy
only after 1997. It was not a sudden change in Greenspan's monetary
philosophy that caused the alteration, but the unexpected discovery that

even when unemployment fell to 4 percent, while wages increased, it did not lead to "wage inflation" (Greider, 2001). Usually lower unemployment causes wages to rise, but in the late 1990s Greenspan came to the conclusion that, in the US, this connection had largely been severed because workers had become, in his words, "traumatized" (cited in Perelman, 2011, p. 48).

> Increases in hourly compensation ... have continued to fall far short of what they would have been had historical relationships between compensation gains and the degree of labor market tightness held ... As I see it, heightened job insecurity explains a significant part of the restraint on compensation and the consequent muted price inflation ... The continued reluctance of workers to leave their jobs to seek other employment as the labor market has tightened provides further evidence of such concern, as does the tendency toward longer labor union contracts. The low level of work stoppages of recent years also attests to concern about job security ... The continued decline in the state of the private workforce in labor unions has likely made wages more responsive to market forces ... Owing in part to the subdued behavior of wages, profits and rates of return on capital has risen to high levels. (Greenspan, 1997)

Between 1979 and 1983 the unemployment rate rose from 6 percent to over 10 percent. It was not until the late 1990s that the unemployment rate dropped below 6 percent for any length of time. The rhetoric surrounding the use of monetary policy to control inflation is misleading in two ways. First, it masks the unemployment-creating mechanism through which inflation is controlled. So, the burden of controlling inflation falls squarely on the working population who are either out of work or have their wages constrained. Second, it masks what the contractionary policy is really designed to combat. While the stated target is inflation, the real goal of monetary policy is to ensure that wages do not cut into profits. In the words of Greenspan historian and *The Nation* columnist, William Greider, "If working-class wages rose smartly, that was a sign of inflation threatening prosperity. If stock prices rose explosively, that was evidence of good times ahead" (Greider, 2005).

Some of the architects of these policies were quite frank about their goals. In the UK, which followed similar fiscal and monetary policies, Alan Budd, professor of economics at the London Business School and economic advisor to Margaret Thatcher, described, in astonishingly candid terms, what occurred during the 1980s. Contractionary monetary policy and neoliberal fiscal policy were seen by the Thatcher government as "a very good way to raise unemployment. And raising unemployment was an extremely desirable way of reducing the strength of the working classes ... What was engineered—in Marxist terms—was a crisis of capitalism which re-created the reserve army of labor, and has allowed the capitalist to make high profits ever since" (Cohen, 2003).

In addition to the changes to national fiscal and monetary policy, international trade policy underwent a transformation after 1980. Between 1960 and 1970, the US exported more to the rest of the world than it imported, resulting in a positive trade balance. In the 1970s this was reversed, causing considerable concern about the inability of US companies to compete with imports at home and export abroad. One popular explanation for the trade deficit was that other nations were not allowing US goods and services into their markets. The solution was to pursue free trade deals with other nations that would guarantee access. After 1980, the US signed a raft of free trade deals, the most globe-spanning of which was the World Trade Organization (WTO) following the Uruguay Round of negotiations in 1995. The US also signed numerous bilateral and regional trade agreements like the 1994 North American Free Trade Agreement now renegotiates on the United States – Mexico – Canada Agreement.

The logic behind free trade is that it benefits consumers through greater competition, and US firms by expanding export markets. However, it also tilted power in the labor market away from workers and towards firms. As *New York Times* columnist and Nobel Prize winner Paul Krugman explained, "When we import labor-intensive manufactured goods from the third world instead of making them here, the result is reduced demand for less-educated American workers, which leads in turn to lower wages for these workers." "Fears that low-wage competition is driving down US wages have a real basis in both theory and fact" (Krugman, 2007). Another Nobel economist, Joseph Stiglitz, argued that free trade, as it is currently implemented, means that "American workers understand that they have to compete with those abroad, and their bargaining power is weakened" (Stiglitz, 2014).

Neoliberal policy surrounding the labor market was couched in the pro-market language of incentives. Those on the lower end of the labor market had their supports curtailed, making them "responsible" for their own success. High earners were relieved of their tax responsibilities, ending the "penalties" for success. Both changes moved the US towards aligning overall income with what could be generated in the market. However, these changes had the effect of reducing workers' power in the labor market.

Neoliberal labor market: impact

These neoliberal economic policies were very good for profits and helped business in the US bounce back from the doldrums of the 1970s. A quick glance back at Figure 1.1 shows clearly that the profit rate declined through the 1970s and then recovered after the early 1980s. This was, of course, part of the promise of neoliberal economic ideas. Their policies were aimed at restoring profits, although they were often not particularly explicit about this goal. An important part of the restoration of profits was the basket of neoliberal labor-market policies listed above. While the proponents of neoliberal labor-market policy promised not only a restoration of profits but also increases in production and incomes for the majority of the population, it was far more successful at delivering the former than the latter.

The partial restoration of profitability did not quite bring the US back to the halcyon days of economic growth that existed prior to 1970. During the boom period of the post-war "Golden Age" from 1950 to 1973 real economic growth averaged 4.2 percent per year. During the neoliberal boom from 1980 to 2007 this dropped to 3 percent (Bureau of Economic Analysis, 2012). So, even by this broad measure of economic success the post-1980 US economy was relatively unsuccessful.

The economy looks even worse when we examine where the gains from that more limited growth went. Income made from production is divided up between different groups in society. One of the most obvious divisions is between profits and what is paid to workers. During the "Golden Age" prior to 1980, in part because the economic structure created some balance between the power of employers and employees in the labor market, when improvements in production resulted in greater worker productivity, the gains were shared between profits and wages. Figure 2.1 shows that, as we discussed with reference to the minimum wage, as productivity increased, wages increased at roughly the same rate up until the late 1970s. When neoliberal labor market policies started to be introduced after 1980, the gains from production started to go far more to profits than to wages and benefits for workers (see also Fleck et al., 2011). As a result, the share of national income in the non-farm sector taken home by workers in wages and other compensation declined from around 64 percent in 1980 to 60 percent in 2007 and 56 percent by 2013 (Bureau of Labor Statistics, 2017; see also Aron-Dine & Shapiro, 2007, pp. 1–2; Elsby et al., 2013; Lawrence, 2015). It is important to point out here that income gains at the top came at the expense of most of the rest. In their investigation into the rising income of the top 1 percent of income earners, sociologists Thomas Volscho and Nathan Kelly found that declining union rates, lower taxes on the rich, free trade and increasing asset values provide the bulk of the explanation (Volscho & Kelly, 2012). According to economist David Kotz, the decline in workers' wage share accounted for 84 percent of the increase in after tax profits for non-financial firms in the US (Kotz, 2015).

By removing the minimal protections that provided workers with a modicum of power in the labor market before 1980, neoliberal labor-market

Figure 2.1 Labor productivity and real hourly compensation, US nonfarm business, 1950–2014

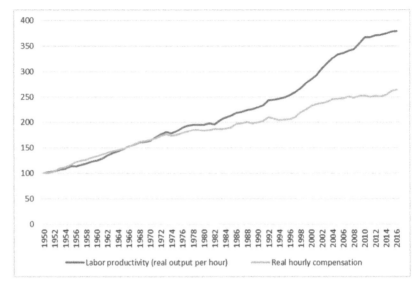

Source: Bureau of Labor Statistics: *Labor Productivity and Costs*, https://data.bls.gov/cgi-bin/dsrv?pr. Labor productivity measures are calculated as growth in real output relative to growth in hours worked

policy has restored profits, but it has created income stagnation for US wage earners. According to economist Lester Thurow (1996, p. 2), US real per capita GDP rose 36 percent from 1973 to 1995, yet the real hourly wages of non-supervisory workers declined by 14 percent. In 2006, Joel Rogers, director of the Center on Wisconsin Strategy, calculated that, if wages had tracked productivity since 1980 as they had after World War II, "median family income in the U.S. would be about $20,000 higher" by the early 2000s than it was (Tasini, 2006). Inequality experts Thomas Piketty and Emmanuel Saez also show that between 1973 and 2000 the average income of the bottom 90 percent of US taxpayers fell by 7 percent. Incomes of the top 1 percent rose by 148 percent, the top 0.1 percent by 343 percent, and incomes of the extremely well-off in the top 0.01 percent rose by an amazing 599 percent (Piketty & Saez, 2003). Even during the economic boom period from 2001 to 2006, workers did not gain nearly as handsomely as business. Wages and salaries grew at a modest 1.9 percent per year after adjusting for inflation during this period while corporate profits after inflation increased by 12.8 percent annually. The economic collapse wiped out many of these modest gains. Between 2007 and 2009 the real income of the bottom 99 percent of the population fell by 11.6 percent, while the income of the top one percent increased by 49 percent. The gains during the post-2009 recovery have been similarly skewed towards the top income earners. Between 2009 and 2012, the top 1 percent enjoyed real income gains of 31.4 percent (95 percent of the total), but the bottom 99 percent managed only real income growth of 0.4 percent (Saez, 2013). These sobering income numbers for most of the population are the reason that the post-1980 period has been described as the "Great Stagnation" (Cowan, 2010).

There is some evidence that the number of people living in extreme poverty has increased during this period. Between 1996, the year that TANF was introduced, and 2011 the number of people in the US living on $2 a day, the World Bank definition of deep poverty that is usually applied to the developing world, more than doubled, to 1.5 million households containing around 3 million children (Edin & Shaefer, 2015). According to the 2011–15 American Community Survey by the US Census, over 500,000 homes in the US "lack complete plumbing facilities," meaning they are without at least one of: running water, a tub or shower or a functioning flush toilet (US Census Bureau, 2015). While poverty is often associated with unemployment, it is also an issue for the employed. According to a report by the National Employment Law Project, 26 percent of private sector workers in the US earn less than $10 an hour. If these workers were to put in a 37-hour week for 50 weeks, their earnings would be $18,500 a year (National Employment Law Project, 2012).

The lack of income gains for many Americans comes despite an increase in the time spent in paid employment. A growing number of people took on two or three jobs. All told, by the 2000s, the typical American worker worked more than 2200 hours a year—350 hours more than the average European, more hours even than the typically industrious Japanese put in. It was many more hours than the typical American middle-class family worked in 1979 – 500 hours longer, a full 12 weeks more. Americans now sleep between one and two hours less than they did in the 1960s (Reich, 2010, p. 86). Contrary to any stereotypes of the lazy poor, those at the lower ends of the income spectrum have increased their work hours more than those at the top. The annual hours worked of the bottom 20 percent of income earners increased by 22 percent between 1979 and 2007. The richest 5 percent increased their hours worked by a more tolerable 7.6 percent during the same period (Mishel, 2013). According to the Brookings Institution, what increase in incomes there were for the median American family were the result of increased hours worked, which went up by 26 percent between 1975 and 2009, mostly as a result of women doubling their hours of paid employment (Greenstone & Looney, 2011). The trend towards working long hours for pay impacts men and women differently. While it is men who more often work long hours in waged or salaried jobs, the pressure for long hours has forced many women out of the labor market. One study found that 86 percent of women who quit professional or managerial jobs did so because of the requirement to work long, inflexible hours (Stone & Lovejoy, 2004). Another attributed 28 percent of the decline in female labor participation in the US relative to other OECD countries to the lack of policies to facilitate a work–life balance (Blau & Kahn, 2013). The increase in work time has created considerable stress within the family. Longer hours are associated with relationship problems with spouses and children (Buck & Neff, 2012; Roberts & Levenson, 2001). Workers who put in more hours report that they lack the time and energy to help with domestic chores or child-rearing responsibilities (Shields, 1999).

Yet, even increased hours at work have not alleviated the income stagnation for the American family. Higher expenses have more than eroded the increase in incomes that longer workdays made possible. Elizabeth Warren argues that the cost of two cars, health insurance, mortgage payments, day care, and other necessities meant that a two-income family in 2006 had $1500 less discretionary income than their single-income counterparts of the previous generation (Warren, 2006). It is true that some of them bought houses beyond their means, manipulated by Wall Street's snake-oil sales pitch, but by Warren's account they were not suckered into luxury consumption, but desperate to maintain their historical standard of living.

With workers facing stagnant or falling real wages, longer hours and increasing economic fragility, borrowing became an increasingly attractive option. Companies found that extending credit was a lucrative addition to their usual business of actually producing goods and services. Households found themselves trapped in a vicious cycle of growing debt of two very different types. Mortgage debt was induced by the dream of home ownership coupled with historically very low interest rates and a deregulated lending market, meaning that high debt could be justified by lower debt payments. The second type of debt, like that on credit cards or payday loans, carried punitive interest rates, resulting in much higher payments per dollar of debt. Overall debt levels began to rise rapidly around the mid-1980s, when it stood at about 60 percent of income. By 2007, the ratio of total household debt to personal disposable income topped out at 138 percent before falling slightly to 128 percent in 2009 (Allegretto, 2011, p. 21). While the US population, in general, was falling further in debt, this was disproportionately true for workers. In 2007, 86 percent of families in which the head of the household was working for someone else carried debt in the US, compared to 77 percent of all families. A larger percentage of working-class families (54 percent) also carried some credit card debt relative to the general population (46 percent) (Baragar & Chernomas, 2012). Debt to finance consumption was a widespread feature of the economic reality for twenty-first-century US workers. In return, a larger portion of the money wage was handed over to the financial sector through the increasingly habitual interest (including mortgage) payments of households.

Well over a century ago, renowned, conservative economist John Bates Clark claimed that workers should be paid the value of what they produce: "If they create a small amount of wealth and get the whole of it, they may not seek to revolutionize society; but if it were to appear that they produce an ample amount and get only a part of it, many of them would become revolutionists, and all would have the right to do so" (Clark, 1899). By standards of justice held by turn-of-the-twentieth-century conservatives, then, US workers would now be well within bounds were they to be signing up for barricade duty. Neoliberal labor market policy has shifted the balance of power away from compensation to workers and to the profits of firms. Compared to the pre-1980 period, workers are keeping a smaller proportion of what they produce. This shift has been so profound that the wages of most workers in the US have stagnated for this entire period. Most US households have not enjoyed the same kind of income growth or income security after 1980 as they did in the decades before, while enduring greater debt loads and working longer hours.

The growth of corporate profits relative to worker compensation is also reflected in a growing inequality between the very rich and the rest of society. Between 1967 and 2009, the share of total income that was earned by the richest 20 percent of the population has increased from 44 percent to 50 percent. Figure 2.2 shows that the other 80 percent of the population has actually taken home a lower share of income. The real gains have come at the very top of the income spectrum. In fact, the higher up the income spectrum, the larger the gains during this period. The top 5 percent of earners saw their share of income increase from 17 to 22 percent. The post-2008 recession has actually made inequality worse. Between 2007 and 2014 the Gini coefficient (a measure of inequality, in which 0 indicates perfect equality and 1 represents the most unequal case of one person having everything) rose from 0.37 to 0.39 (OECD, 2016). Rising CEO compensation has contributed to this trend. In 1965, the average pay of the CEOs at the top 350 US firms (ranked by sales) stood at about twenty times the average compensation of their workers. Figure 2.3 shows that this ratio increased steadily, but fairly slowly until about 1990 when it exploded to around 400 to 1 in the late 1990s. Despite some moderation since those heady days for business bigwigs, CEOs take home over two hundred times the compensation of their average worker (Mishel, 2012).

A comparative look at other OECD nations suggests that the rapid rate of increase in inequality in the US, as well as its extent, is not the sole product of some non-political, globalized process. The US is one of the most unequal of the wealthy nations. Of the 35 countries of the

Figure 2.2 US share of income by quintile

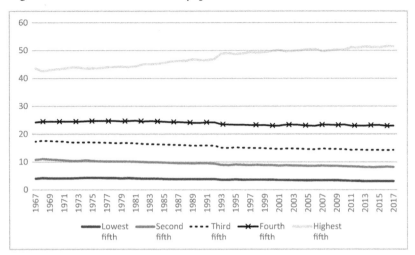

Source: US Census Bureau, *Current Population Survey, Annual Social and Economic Supplements*

Figure 2.3 US ratio of CEO to worker compensation, 1965–2010

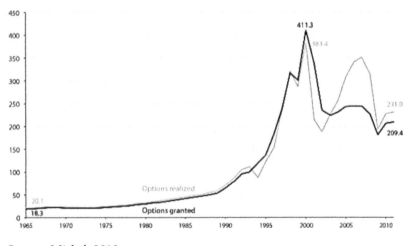

Source: Mishel, 2012

OECD listed in Figure 2.4, the US ranks as the 3rd least equal, surpassed by only Mexico and Chile in 2014 (OECD, 2016).

The distribution of wealth in the US has been even more unequal than the distribution of income. In 2009, the wealthiest 10 percent of the population owned 76 percent of total US net worth (all assets minus

Figure 2.4 Income inequality in OECD nations: Gini coefficients

Source: OECD Income Distribution Database

Figure 2.5 Share of wealth, top 10 percent, selected OECD nations, 2010–12

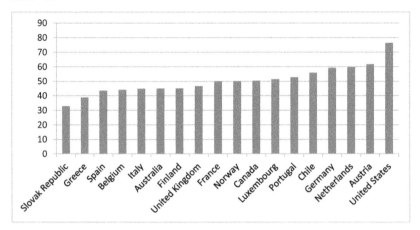

Source: OECD.Stat, Wealth Distribution

all liabilities). Like income inequality, this has become more severe during the neoliberal period. In 1983 the wealthiest 10 percent owned 68 percent (Wolff, 2010; see also Congressional Budget Office, 2016). It is also an outlier internationally. Figure 2.5 shows that the US has the most concentrated wealth of any country tracked by the OECD. Somewhat surprisingly, this inequality in wealth has worsened after the 2008 economic crisis. While discussions about a declining stock market and a poorly performing business sector might have provided the impression that the rich were a bit hard done by after 2008, the decline in the value of the housing market was much more severe, which has a larger impact on families with less wealth since their major asset is usually a home. As a result, between 2007 and 2009 the wealthiest 20 percent of households saw their wealth decline by 16 percent, on average, per year. The bottom four-fifths (the rest of the population) had reductions in wealth of 25 percent annually in this period (Allegretto, 2011, p. 3). The average wealth of the top 1 percent of the population stood at 225 times the median in 2009, up from 125 in 1962, and the highest ratio in history (Allegretto, 2011, p. 7).

The extent to which inequality is a genuine societal problem is the subject of some debate. In the early 2000s, Republican politicians like Mitt Romney were describing discussions about the degree of inequality in the US as "class warfare." In an infamous research report, Citigroup analysts noted that the US (along with Canada and the UK) was becoming a "Plutonomy," in which the rich absorbed a disproportionate share of the income. Rather than a call to arms against rising inequality, the report urged investors to profit from this trend by abandoning companies servicing the "average" consumer and focusing on luxury brands, like Bulgari and Kuoni, in the Plutonomy Stock Basket that had outperformed competing indexes "by 6.8% per year since 1985" (Kapur et al., 2005). Free-market economists, like Milton Friedman, have argued that income inequality can be justified on moral and efficiency grounds. In terms of efficiency, inequality is needed to create effort and innovation as it is only the financial rewards that come with market success that lead people to work hard and take the risks of investment. Morally, unequal incomes are the result of individuals' differing contributions to society, according to Friedman.

However, there is reason to be skeptical on both these fronts. In terms of efficiency, recent research suggests that there is no positive statistical connection between inequality and economic growth. Quite the opposite is true. According to a 2014 OECD working paper, "income inequality has a negative and statistically significant impact" on economic growth. What is particularly problematic for economic growth is "the gap between low income households and the rest of the population," while having those with higher incomes moving away from the rest of society is less of a problem (Cingano, 2014; see also Arjona, Ladaique, & Pearson, 2002). In more moral terms, Piketty noted that many at the high end of the income distribution do little to earn their lavish rewards. According to Piketty, between 1990 and 2010 the fortune of Lilianne Bettencourt, the heiress of L'Oréal, "who never worked a day in her life" (Piketty, 2013, p. 440), grew from $2 billion to $25 billion. Even those who have put in some time at the office, like the iconic entrepreneur Bill Gates, whose wealth increased from $4 billion to $50 billion over the same period, do not merit their affluence. Gates's wealth was created in large part by monopoly rents and the work of thousands of engineers and scientists rather than any individual genius on his part. Further, his wealth grew at the same rate after he stopped working (Piketty, 2013).

While the economic benefits of inequality are increasingly being called into question, it is clear that inequality creates a wide variety of social and economic problems, most of which are felt most keenly by those at the lower end of the income spectrum. In their book *The Spirit Level*, British epidemiologists Kate Pickett and Richard Wilkinson found that countries with higher levels of inequality scored worse on measures of violence, education, health, and social mobility (Wilkinson & Pickett, 2010). While the precise reason that this connection exists is still being debated, the authors argue that it stems from the lack of a sense of belonging that exists in unequal societies.

Stagnant wages, the longest workweek in the industrialized world and growing debt were not only problems for the increasingly stressed and overworked individuals who suffered under the post-1980 economic structure. Those same conditions also sowed the seeds for the economic collapse of 2008 in the wake of the mortgage market meltdown. For many analysts, the crisis was caused by the collapse of the housing market but this is an incomplete explanation for two reasons. First, the collapse of the housing market was, in part, driven by the low household incomes. US workers facing stagnant real wages and the longest workweek in the industrialized world resorted to borrowing to maintain their consumption, including their homes. Business found it profitable to extend extraordinary levels of credit as a complement to increasing profitability in the sphere of production. The result was a dramatic increase in worker indebtedness and the instability that would inevitably follow when those bills came due (Palley, 2011). The first sign of the impending crisis was triggered by highly indebted households contracting their spending. The resulting reduction in sales created excess fixed-capital capacity for business, which responded with a rapid decline in investment. The financial crisis that erupted in September of 2008 contributed to the decline in investment as expectations for future profitability collapsed and credit contracted.[2] Second, the housing market and subsequent financial collapse were the result of the deregulatory policies that were a crucial part of the post-1980s policy environment.[3] This was not some external "shock" to the economic system, but a result of the profit-seeking behavior of firms in a deregulated industry in the context of stagnant household incomes. The entire tragic episode can essentially be summarized in three sentences. Loans were being made to increasingly risky customers, on increasingly speculative terms. Worse, the banks that made the loans earned income through commissions, as opposed to the more traditional method of having the loan repaid, because they sold the mortgages on to others in bundled securities. As families started to default on what they thought was going to be their dream home, the banks and investment firms that had purchased mortgage-backed securities found themselves holding badly overvalued assets (Hudson, 2009).

Alternatives: the Nords

The World Economic Forum (WEF) is a Geneva-based foundation whose annual meeting of chief executives and political leaders, held in Davos, Switzerland, is a gathering of the truly rich and powerful. The WEF is funded by a thousand corporations, each of which has annual revenues of more than $1 billion. Every year the WEF produces its Global Competitiveness Report, which ranks the competitiveness of the world's economies. The top ten countries of World Economic Forum Growth Competitiveness Index Rankings for 2011 in rank order were; Switzerland, Sweden, Singapore, the US, Germany, Japan, Finland, Netherlands, Denmark, and Canada (Schwab, 2010, p. 15). What was most interesting about this list was how many of these countries have strong rules that explicitly go against the neoliberal economic policy agenda by using government intervention to regulate industry, strengthen the power of workers in the labor market, and redistribute incomes. This is not a one-year anomaly. European countries that have been more cautious about neoliberal policy than the US (especially the Nordic nations) have fared well in the WEF competitiveness rankings year after year. In 2005, the report lauded these nations for the quality of their public institutions, budget surpluses, low levels of corruption and high degree of technological innovation. Although these states had high taxes and a strict regulatory framework, they were characterized as having "excellent macroeconomic management overall," according to Augusto Lopez-Claros, chief economist at the WEF.

> Integrity and efficiency in the use of public resources means there is money for investing in education, in public health, in state-of-the-art infrastructure, all of which contributes to boost productivity. Highly trained labor forces, in turn, adopt new technologies with enthusiasm or, as happens often in the Nordics, are themselves in the forefront of technological innovations. In many ways the Nordics have entered virtuous circles where various factors reinforce each other to make them among the most competitive economies in the world, with world class institutions and some of the highest levels of per capita income in the world. (Lopez-Carlos, 2005)

The US cannot claim a great advantage over other nations when it comes to economic growth (Table 2.1), but the score is more unambiguous on more social measures. Unfortunately for the US it is unambiguously inferior. In a nation that celebrates the "rags to riches" story of social mobility, where anyone can be president, the difference between a son's income and his father's in the US was the third lowest of 12 OECD nations, behind only Italy and the UK (another neoliberal paragon) in 2010. Three of the top four socially mobile nations, as measured by the intergenerational difference in income between a father and his son, were Denmark, Norway, and Finland (OECD, 2010, p. 185). According to the

Table 2.1 Economic growth: percent change in real GDP per capita, PPP

	1980–2008	1990–2008	2000–2008
Denmark	64.21	34.14	7.80
Germany	62.18	30.58	11.61
Sweden	68.44	39.61	17.68
United States	68.80	35.00	8.75

Source: Calculated from OECD StatExtracts – GDP per head, US$, constant prices, constant PPPs

Table 2.2 Poverty rates before and after taxes and transfers: total population, mid 2000s (%)

	Before	After
Sweden	27	5
United States	26	17

Note: The poverty rate is defined as 50 percent of the current median income.
Source: OECD.statextracts Income distribution – Poverty

report, "redistributive and income support policies are associated with greater intergenerational social mobility" (OECD, 2010, p. 184). Tables 2.1 and 2.2 show that in more social democratic economies, like Sweden, which have followed a very different macroeconomic model, there is less poverty while they still maintain a competitive and vibrant economy.

The US also scores very poorly in terms of social justice. In 2011, the OECD report on social justice ranked the US twenty-seventh out of 31 countries, ahead of only Greece, Chile, Mexico and Turkey (OECD, 2011, p. 8). The score was compiled by looking at how well countries fared on six measures: poverty prevention, access to education, labor market inclusion, social cohesion and non-discrimination, health, and intergenerational justice. The US didn't rate very highly on any of these measures. Its best ranking was a modest sixteenth in both labor market inclusion and social cohesion. It was a particular laggard (twenty-ninth) in the area of poverty, which the OECD described as "alarming" (OECD, 2011, p. 7). The top five places in the social justice ranking went to Iceland, Norway, Denmark, Sweden and Finland. Further, the World Health Organization Commission on Social Determinants of Health argued that "Nordic countries, for example, have followed policies that encouraged equality of benefits and services, full employment, gender equity and low levels of social exclusion". This, said the Commission, "is an outstanding example of what needs to be done everywhere." According to Sir Michael Marmot, the Commission Chair, health policy needs to focus on "creating the conditions for people to be empowered, to have freedom to lead flourishing lives" (World Health Organization, 2008). You might call it the triumph of the Nords.

Conclusion

In the three decades after World War II, the US (although admittedly to a lesser extent than many of the other advanced, wealthy nations), implemented labor-market policies that increased workers' bargaining power and protected them from relying exclusively on what their labor could command in the market for their income. Government followed full-employment monetary and fiscal policy. Social assistance, although never particularly generous, was increased. Minimum wages were instituted and rose steadily until the late 1960s. Unions were recognized as legitimate bargaining agents. In response to declining profits for US firms, after 1980, the US labor market was deliberately restructured by a series of political decisions that steadily eroded these protections.

Work could be one of the primary sources of people's fulfillment and satisfaction. In some important ways, people feel that paid work is their contribution to society and is the location from which they draw their sense of self-worth. Yet is also a crucial arena of stress and dissatisfaction, where people feel thwarted and constrained. People want some degree of control over their working lives. They want meaningful employment that pays them an income that, as John Bates Clark acknowledged, pays them a fair wage for what they produce. The labor market after 1980s represented a move away from fulfillment and towards frustration for most US workers. Unemployment was higher, hours were longer, wage gains were minimal or non-existent. Further, these supposed good times were bought to an end by the failure of the housing market and the broader economy, which could be directly traced to the labor market and deregulatory policies that were a fundamental component of the overall policy package put in place to restore profits after 1980.

Notes

1 The precise cause of the fall in profits is still a matter of considerable controversy. See, for example, Brenner, 2006.
2 For a more complete discussion of how the structure of the U.S. economy created the 2008 crisis see: Kotz, 2009; McDonough et al., 2010; McNally, 2010; Duménil and Lévy, 2011; and Varoufakis, 2011. For a more general explanation on the role of money and monetary policy on economic stability see Lavoie et al., 2010.
3 For more on the role of finance in the economic crisis, especially the role of the rise of new financial instruments and speculative investments, see Minsky, 1986; Spotton Visano, 2006; Crotty, 2009; Martin, 2011.

Bibliography

ALEC. (n.d.). *Living Wage Mandate Preemption Act.* Retrieved June 14, 2018 from ALEC: www.alec.org/model-policy/living-wage-mandate-preemption-act/.

Allegretto, S. (2011). *The State of Working America's Wealth 2011.* Washington, DC: EPI Briefing Paper #292.

Allegretto, S., Doussard, M., Graham-Squire, D., Jacobs, K., Thompson, D., & Thompson, J. (2013). *Fast-Food, Poverty Wages: The Public Cost of Low-Wage Jobs in the Fast-Food Industry.* Berkeley, CA: UC Berkeley Center for Labor Research and Education.

Arjona, R., Ladaique, M., & Pearson, M. (2002). *Social Protection and Growth,* OECD Economic Studies, No. 35. Paris: OECD.

Aron-Dine, A., & Shapiro, I. (2007). *Share of National Income Going to Wages and Salaries at Record Low in 2006.* Washington, DC: Center on Budget and Policy Priorities.

Baragar, F., & Chernomas, R. (2012). Profits from Production and Profits from Exchange: Financialization, Household Debt and Profiability in 21st Century Capitalism. *Science & Society,* 76, 319–339.

Blau, F., & Kahn, L. (2013). *Female LaborSupply: Why Is the U.S. Falling Behind.* Cambridge, MA: NBER Working Paper Paper No. 18702.

Bowles, S., Gordon, D., & Weisskopf, T. (1986). Power and Profits: The Social Structure of Accumulation and the Profitability of the Postwar U.S. Economy. *Review of Radical Political Economics,* 18 (1–2), 132–167.

Brenner, R. (2006). *The Economics of Global Turbulence: The Advanced Capitalist Economies from Long Boom to Long Downturn 1945–2005.* New York: Verso.

Bronfenbrenner, K. (2009). *No Holds Barred—The Intensification of Employer Opposition to Organizing.* Washington, DC: Economic Policy Institute.

Buck, A., & Neff, L. (2012). Stress Spillover in Early Marriage: The Role of Self-Regulatory Depletion. *Journal of Family Psychology,* 26(5), 698–708.

Bureau of Economic Analysis. (2012). *National Income and Product Accounts Tables: Percent Change from Preceding Period in Real Gross Domestic Product,* June 28. Retrieved July 11, 2012, from Bureau of Economic Analysis: www.bea.gov/national/index.htm.

Bureau of Labor Statistics. (2017). *Estimating the U.S. Labor Share,* February. Retrieved June 27, 2017, from Monthly Labor Review: www.bls.gov/opub/mlr/2017/article/estimating-the-us-labor-share.htm.

Bureau of Labor Statistics. (2017). *Work Stoppages Involving 1,000 or More Workers, 1947–2016.* Retrieved June 20, 2017, from www.bls.gov/news.release/wkstp.t01.htm.

Bush, G. (2005). *Public Papers of the Presidents of the United States: George W. Bush Book 1.* Washington, DC.: US Government Printing Office.

Center on Budget and Policy Priorities. (2015). *An Introduction to TANF.* Washington, DC: Center on Budget and Policy Priorities.

Center on Buget and Policy Priorities. (2016). *TANF Cash Benefits Have Fallen by More Than 20 Percent in Most States and Continue to Erode.* Washington, DC: Center on Buget and Policy Priorities.

Cingano, F. (2014). *Trends in Income Inequality and Its Impact on Economic Growth,* OECD Social, Employment and Migration Working Papers. Paris: OECD.

Clark, J. (1899). *The Distribution of Wealth: A Theory of Wages, Interests and Profits.* New York: Macmillan and Co.

Cohen, N. (2003). *Gambling with Our Future,* January 13. Retrieved March 15, 2007, from New Statesman: www.newstatesman.com/200301130012.

Congressional Budget Office. (2016). *Trends in Family Wealth, 1989 to 2013*. Washington, DC: Congressional Budget Office. Retrieved November 28, 2018, from www.cbo.gov/publication/51846.

Cowan, T. (2010). *The Great Stagnation*. New York: Penguin Group Inc.

Crotty, J. (2009). Structural Causes of the Global Financial Crisis: A Critical Assessment of the "New Financial Architecture". *Cambridge Journal of Economics*, 33(4), 563–580.

Davis, J., & Huston, J. (1995). Right-to-Work Laws and Union Density: New Evidence from Micro Data. *Journal of Labor Research*, 16(2), 223–229.

Desilver, D. (2017). *Five Facts about the Minimum Wage*, January 4. Retrieved June 20, 2017, from Pew Research Center: www.pewresearch.org/fact-tank/2017/01/04/5-facts-about-the-minimum-wage/.

Duménil, G., and Lévy, D. (2011). *The Crisis of Neoliberalism*. Cambridge MA: Harvard University Press.

Dunn, M., & Walker, J. (2016). *Union Membership in the United States*. Washington, DC: US Bureau of Labor Statistics.

Edin, K., & Shaefer, H. (2015). *$2.00 a Day: Living on Almost Nothing in America*. New York: Houghton Mifflin.

Ehrenreich, J. (2016). *Third Wave Capitalism: How Money, Power, and the Pursuit of Self-Interest Have Imperiled the American Dream*. Ithaca, NY: Cornell University ILR School.

Ellwood, D., & Fine, G. (1987). The Impact of Right-to-Work Laws on Union Organizing. *Journal of Political Economy*, 95(2), 250–273.

Elsby, M., Hobijn, B., & Sahin, A. (2013). The Decline of the U.S. Labor Share. *Brookings Papers on Economic Activity*, 1–52.

Falk, G. (2014). *Temporary Assistance for Needy Families (TANF): Eligibliity and Benefit Amounts in State TANF Cash Assistance Programs*. Washington, DC: Congressional Research Service.

Fleck, S., Glaser, J., & Sprague, S. (2011). The Compensation-Productivity Gap: A Visual Essay. *Monthly Labor Review*, January, 57–69.

Frank, R. (1996). *The Winner-Take-All Society: Why the Few at the Top Get So Much More Than the Rest of Us*. New York: Penguin Books.

Frank, R. (1999). *Choosing the Right Pond: Human Behavior and the Quest for Status*. Oxford: Oxford University Press.

Getter, D., Jickling, M., Labonte, M., & Murphy, E. (2007). *Financial Crisis? The Liquidity Crunch of August 2007*. Washington DC: Congressional Research Service.

Greenspan, A. (1997). *Testimony Before the Committee on the Budget, United States Senate*, January 21. Retrieved March 12, 2007, from Federal Reserve Board: www.federalreserve.gov/BOARDDOCS/Testimony/1997/19970121.htm.

Greenstone, M., & Looney, A. (2011). The Great Recession May Be Over, But American Families Are Working Harding Than Ever, July 8. *Brookings Up Front*.

Greider, W. (2001). Father Greenspan Loves Us All, January 1. *The Nation*. Retrieved November 28, 2018, from www.thenation.com/article/father-greenspan-loves-us-all/

Greider, W. (2005). The One-Eyed Chairman, September 1. *The Nation*.

Hancock, J. (2015). Missouri Legislators Vote to Block Kansas City from Raising Minimum Wage, September 16. *The Kansas City Star*. Retrieved August 30,

2017, from www.kansascity.com/news/local/news-columns-blogs/the-buzz/article35423013.html.

Hogler, R., Shulman, S., & Weiler, S. (2004). Right to Work Legislation, Social Capital, and Variations in State Union Density. *The Review of Regional Studies*, 34(1), 95–111.

Hudson, I. (2009). From Deregulation to Crisis (Winnipeg, MB: Fernwood, 2009). In W. Anthony & J. Guard (eds), *Bankruptcies and Bailouts*. Winnipeg, MB: Fernwood.

Jacobs, K., Perry, I., & MacGilvary, J. (2015). *The High Public Cost of Low Wages*. Berkeley, CA: UC Berkeley Center for Labor Research and Education.

Kapur, A., Macleod, N., & Singh, N. (2005). *Plutonomy: Buying Luxury, Explaining Global Imbalances*. Citigroup. Retrieved November 28, 2018, from https://delong.typepad.com/plutonomy-1.pdf.

Kotz, D. (2009). The Financial and Economic Crisis of 2008. *Review of Radical Political Economics*, 41(3), 305–317.

Kotz, D. (2015). *The Rise and Fall of Neoliberal Capitalism*. Cambridge, MA: Harvard University Press.

Krugman, P. (2007). Divided over Trade, May 14. *New York Times*. Retrieved June 17, 2018, from www.nytimes.com/2007/05/14/opinion/14krugman.html.

Lavoie, M., Rochon, L.P., & Seccareccia, M. (2010). *Money and Macroeconomic Issues: Alfred Eichner and Post-Keynesian Economics*. Armonk, NJ: M.E. Sharpe.

Lawrence, R. (2015). *Recent Declines in Labor's Share in US Income: A Preliminary Neoclassical Account*. Cambridge, MA: Harvard University Press.

Lichtenstein, N., & Shermer, E. (2012). *The Right and Labor in America*. Philadelphia: University of Pennsylvania Press.

Lopez-Carlos, A. (2005). *Video Interviews*. Retrieved August 12, 2006, from The Global Competitiveness Report 2005–2006: www.weforum.org/site/homepublic.nsf/Content/Global+Competitiveness+Report+2005–2006:+Interview.

Martin, R. (2011). *Fixing the Game: Bubbles, Crashes, and What Capitalism Can Learn from the NFL*. Cambridge, MA: Harvard Business Review Press.

Marx, K. (1847). *Wage Labour and Capital, translated in 1891 by Frederick Engels, chapter on "Relation of Wage Labour to Capital"*. Retrieved November 28, 2018, from www.marxists.org/archive/marx/works/1847/wage.

Marx, K. (1889). *Capital Volume 1*. New York: Appleton & Co.

McDonough, T., Reich, M., & Kotz, D. (2010). *Contemporary Capitalism and Its Crises: Social Structure of Accumulation theory for the 21st Century*. Cambridge: Cambridge University Press.

McNally, D. (2010). *Global Slump: The Economics and Politics of Crisis and Resistance*. Winnipeg: Fernwood.

Minsky, H. (1986). *Stabilizing an Unstable Economy*. New Haven, CT: McGraw-Hill.

Mishel, L. (2012). *CEO Pay 231 Times Greater Than the Average Worker*, May 3. Retrieved June 25, 2012, from Economic Policy Institute: www.epi.org/publication/ceo-pay-231-times-greater-average-worker/.

Mishel, L. (2013). *Vast Majority of Wage Earners Are Working Harder, and for Not Much More: Trends In U.S. Work Hours and Wages over 1979–2007*, January 30. Retrieved June 29, 2017, from Economic Policy Institute: www.epi.org/publication/ib348-trends-us-work-hours-wages-1979–2007/.

Mortgage Bankers Association. (2007). *National Delinquency Survey, 4th quarter, 2007*. Washington, DC: Mortgage Bankers Association.

National Employment Law Project. (2012). *Big Business, Corporate Profits, and the Minimum Wage.* New York: National Employment Law Project.

OECD. (2010). *Economic Policy Reforms: Going for Growth.* Paris: Organization for Economic Cooperation and Development.

OECD. (2011). *Social Justice in the OECD: How Do the Member States Compare?* Paris: Organization for Economic Cooperation and Development.

OECD. (2016). *OECD Income Distribution Database.* Retrieved June 30, 2017, from OECD: http://stats.oecd.org/.

Palley, T. (2011). America's Flawed Paradigm: Macroeconomic Causes of the Financial Crisis and Great Recession. *Empirica,* 38(1), 3–17.

Perelman, M. (2011). *The Invisible Handcuffs of Capitalism: How Market Tyranny Stifles the Economy by Stunting Workers.* New York: Monthly Review Press.

Perry, M. (2016). Some Early Results From Seattle's Radical Experiment with a $15 an Hour Minimum Wage: Fewer Jobs, Fewer Hours. American Enterprise Institute. Retrieved November 26, 2018, from www.aei.org/publication/some-early-results-from-seattles-radical-experiment-with-a-15-an-hour-minimum-wage-fewer-jobs-fewer-hours/.

Piketty, T. (2013). *Capital in the 21st Century.* Cambridge, MA: Harvard University Press.

Piketty, T., & Saez, E. (2003). Income iInequality in the United States, 1913–1998. *Quarterly Journal of Economics,* 118(1), 1–39.

Piketty, T., & Saez, E. (2007). How Progressive Is the U.S. Federal Tax System? A Historic and International Perspective. *Journal of Economic Perspectives,* 21(1), 3–24.

Polanyi, K. (1944 [1957]). *The Great Transformation.* Boston, MA: Beacon Hill Press.

Pollin, R. (2003). *Contours of Descent: US Economics Fractures and the Landscape of Global Austerity.* London: Versoa

Reich, R. (2010). *Aftershock: The Next Economy and America's Future.* New York: Knopf.

Roberts, N., & Levenson, R. (2001). The Remains of the Workday: Impact of Job Stress and Exhaustion on Marital Interaction in Police Couples. *Journal of Marriage and Family,* 63(4), 1052–1067.

Rushe, D. (2017). Fran Works Six Days a Week in Fast-Food, and Yet She's Homeless. "It's economic slavery.", August 21. *The Guardian.* Retrieved from www.theguardian.com/us-news/2017/aug/21/missouri-fast-food-workers-better-pay-popeyes-economics.

Saez, E. (2013). *Striking it Richer: The Evolution of Top Incomes in the United States (Updated with 2012 Preliminary Estimates).* Berkeley, CA: University of California Berkeley.

Schmitt, J. (2012). *The Minimum Wage Is Too Damn Low.* Washington, DC: Center for Economic and Policy Research.

Schor, J. (1996). *The Overspent American: Why We Want What We Don't Need.* New York: Basic Books.

Schwab, K. (2010). *The Global Competitiveness Report 2010–2011.* Geneva: World Economic Forum.

Shields, M. (1999). Working Long Hours and Health. *Health Reports,* 22(2), 37–55.

Skidelsky, R. (2009). *Keynes: The Return of the Master.* New York: PublicAffairs.

Smith, A. (1981). *An Inquiry into the Nature and Causes of the Wealth of Nations.* Indianapolis: Liberty Fund.

Spotton Visano, B. (2006). *Financial Crises Socio-Economic Causes and Institutional Context.* New York: Routledge.

Stein, B. (2006). In Class Warfare, Guess Which Class Is Winning, November 26. *New York Times.*

Stiglitz, J. (2014). On the Wrong Side of Globalization, March 16. *New York Times.*

Stone, P., & Lovejoy, M. (2004). Fast-Track Women and the "Choice" to Stay Home. *The Annals of the American Academy of Political and Social Science,* 596(1), 62–83.

Tasini, J. (2006). The DLC Won't Talk About Corporate Power, July 25. *Huffington Post.*

Thurow, L. (1996). *The Future of Capitalism.* New York: Penguin Books.

Torres, B. (2016). A Year In, 'The Sky Is Not Falling' From Seattle's Minimum-Wage Hike, March 31. *The Seattle Times.* Retrieved November 26, 2018, from www.seattletimes.com/business/economy/a-year-in-the-sky-is-not-falling-from-seattles-minimum-wage-hike/.

US Census Bureau. (2015). *Selected Housing Statistics.* Retrieved June 28, 2017, from 2011–2015 American Community Survey: https://factfinder.census.gov/faces/tableservices/jsf/pages/productview.xhtml?pid=ACS_15_5YR_DP04&src=pt.

Varoufakis, Y. (2011). *The Global Minotaur: America, the True Origins of the Financial Crisis and the Future of the World Economy.* London: Zed Books.

Volscho, T., & Kelly, N. (2012). The Rise of the Super-Rich Power Resources, Taxes, Financial Markets, and the Dynamics of the Top 1 Percent, 1949 to 2008. *American Sociological Review,* 77(5), 679–699.

Warren, E. (2006). The Middle Class on the Precipice: Rising Financial Risks for American Families. *Havard Magazine January–February.*

Wilkinson, R., & Pickett, K. (2010). *The Spirit Level: Why More Equal Societies Almost Always Do Better.* New York: Bloomsbury Press.

Wolff, E. (2010). *Recent Trends in Household Wealth in the United States: Rising Debt and the Middle-Class Squeeze—An Update to 2007.* Levy Economics Institute Working Paper No. 589. Annandale-on-Hudson, NY: Levy Economics Institute.

World Health Organization. (2008). *Inequities Are Killing People on Grand Scale, Press Release,* August 28. Retrieved August 3, 2011, from World Health Organization: www.who.int/mediacentre/news/releases/2008/pr29/en/index.html.

3

Every last molecule on earth: neoliberalism's "nature"

On the investment bank Credit-Suisse's website, an article appears that encapsulates much of what we hope to convey with this chapter. The article deals with the aftermath of Hurricane Andrew, which made landfall at the town of Homestead, Florida, on August 24, 1992. Packing winds of about 225 km per hour, it levelled Homestead, and proceeded across southern Florida, killing 65 people and destroying some $25 billion worth of property (in 1992 dollars). Somewhere in the neighbourhood of 63,000 homes in Dade County were completely destroyed, with another 100,000 suffering significant damage. It still stands as the one of the most expensive weather events in US history, after Katrina and Sandy (though as we write, the bills for the 2017 hurricane season are still being tallied). However, the catastrophe was "far from catastrophic for investors" (Klement, 2016), according to Credit-Suisse, since the event spurred a financial innovation that has since been a boon to those wealthy enough to afford a high buy-in, and some risk.

Realizing just how inconveniently expensive hurricanes and other troublesome phenomena understood to be the fault of "nature" were becoming, the insurance and reinsurance industries concluded that they might be in trouble as climate change produced more droughts, floods, and storms. They needed to spread the risk of expensive, weather-related disasters out beyond the traditional insurance markets, over a much, much larger pool of financial capital. The global pool of capital operative in insurance and reinsurance is about $350–$400 billion. For most of us, this sounds like quite a sum, but one Katrina costs insurers about $75 billion and can put serious strain on, or even break, the market's capacity to adequately spread risk. The US bond market alone, however, comprises about $29 trillion. If some of that capital could be attracted into sharing some of the risk that insurers and reinsurers were bearing, insurance companies' fear of being financially wiped out by a series of geographically proximate disasters would be greatly reduced. Enter the "catastrophe bond," or cat bond, for short. This is the key financial innovation developed in response to fears of increasingly frequent and intense disasters, and it is an instructive lens on how neoliberalism responds to environmental problems.

Here's how it works. Say you have $200 million lying around looking for a decent return. One of the options available is to make a bet on whether a particular event will occur in a particular area. The event might be an earthquake in Japan, or a hurricane in the southeastern US, or a tropical cyclone in Australia. You agree to park your money in a fund (which is in turn invested for the agreed-upon period). If the trigger event doesn't happen, you get a pretty good return—historically around 6–8 percent above what you could get with a US government bond with roughly the same maturity. If it does happen, then you lose a portion or the entire amount invested and it goes to cover the disaster-based losses of whoever issued the bond, usually an insurance company in partnership with an investment bank.[1] To take an example, you might bet that a named storm on the eastern seaboard of the US is not going to surpass a certain storm surge high-water mark. If it goes above a specified height, then you might lose some or all of your principal (depending on how high above the mark the surge actually goes), which would then cover the losses of insurers who are faced with big payouts to policy holders whose homes and businesses are under water.[2]

So, while, for most of humanity, climate change poses a serious threat to life, livelihood, lifestyle, and community, it has not taken long for it to be transformed into a means of further accumulation for the wealthy. The costs are to be borne socially, and disproportionately by the poor, while the powerful are positioning themselves to profit, as poorer countries must pay to insure themselves against disasters whose likelihood and severity are increased by past and continuing fossil-fuel burning mostly by the rich. Furthermore, if markets are to be the central tool with which societies deal with the consequences of our having surpassed the planet's capacity to absorb carbon dioxide—which is the neoliberal solution—then they need to be able to see the situation in monetary terms. So a hurricane is transformed into a trigger event probability and an associated value of lost (and insured!) life and property. They also need to offer the prospect of profit for investors, of course, in order to lure capital.

In order to make these things happen, along with other neoliberal environmental policies and practices, we are asked to fundamentally change the ways that human and extra-human nature are entangled with one another. Although this word "entangled" is a bit jargony, it is not a simple task to find language that adequately describes our "relationship" to nature. Even the idea of a "relationship" implies two distinct things interacting. But that's not quite right when we consider the social and the natural. They aren't completely distinct. Nature is not actually something which is totally independent of society—though it has its own history that precedes us – nor can we conceptualize something called "society" without already presuming a particular "nature" within it. Both are now internal to the other (Moore, 2015). However, we do experience something we commonly think of as "nature" in particular ways. We do so through recreation and leisure, through labor (both alienated and otherwise) that transforms and reorganizes ecosystems and their elements, and through our metabolic processes (breathing, eating, drinking, etc. ...). We understand that there are qualities to different "natures," some pleasant, some dangerous, some disgusting. We understand that some parts of what we think of as "nature," like fresh water or soil, are indispensable to life. Neoliberalism, however, intends to transform this understanding and experience of nature. Neoliberalism, as a suite of practices and ways of understanding that are designed to facilitate the transfer of wealth and power to the already-wealthy and powerful, asks us to see, comprehend, and treat nature as a matrix of commodified or commodifiable values, each infinitely divisible and exchangeable for every other.

Neoliberalism's transformation of the ways society and nature organize and constitute one another can be seen most clearly through changing patterns of property relations and rights, including new forms of state-mediated access to nature's "sources" and "sinks," the emergence of new, environmentally related commodities and markets, and the increasing treatment of non-human life as a frontier of accumulation. This chapter looks through these examples at the ways in which neoliberalism attempts to force a particular reorganization of the "web of life" (Moore, 2015) in the service of capital, and examines how this reorganization impoverishes us and the planet.

Historical materialism and nature

Marx recognized that our relationship with non-human nature, as it unfolded through the process of labor, was the necessary foundation of our development as humans. He recognized that in working with "nature" to transform it through work, in order to reproduce ourselves physically and socially, we entered into an unavoidable tangle with it. Through this tangle, we transform both nature and ourselves ("we" being nothing more than an aspect of nature). Marx understood very clearly that "one can look at history from two sides and divide it into the history of nature and the history of men. The two sides are, however, inseparable; the history of nature and the history of men are dependent on each other so long as men exist" (Marx, 1845). This is actually a key, and poorly understood, aspect of Marx's historical materialism, illuminated best by John Bellamy Foster's work *Marx's Ecology* (2000).

Under capitalist relations, though, and in particular through the wage–labor relation, this process of development is subverted. We become alienated from both our own natures and non-human nature—we experience the world increasingly through commodity exchange, rather than through a collective, conscious effort to understand and transform the world. Marx, and many who have followed in his tradition, point out other problematic aspects of the way capitalism transforms and reconfigures socio-natural relations. Early on, Marx pointed out that the geography of production, which concentrates and isolates material and energy flows, results in a "rift" in our metabolic relationship with nature (Marx, 1981b, p. 949). While initially providing a critique of capitalist agriculture, which simultaneously "robbed the soil of its fertility" in the countryside while producing concentrated waste in the cities, the idea of the metabolic rift has been applied to a plethora of environmental problems, from climate change to fisheries (Foster, 1999; Clausen & Clark, 2005; Clark & York, 2005).

Drawing on Marxist crisis theory, a second stream of historical materialist critique points out the connections between the basic dynamics of accumulation and environmental degradation. The logic of competition to which firms are variously exposed under capitalism creates an incentive to lower costs through whatever means possible. As we discussed in the previous chapter, labor costs are one such possibility. Another avenue which has been open to and commonly used by businesses in this pursuit has been the externalization of costs of production onto nature—dumping pollutants, or freely appropriating what firms see as "natural resources" without allowing them time or conditions to replenish. James O'Connor (1991) has famously referred to this as the "second contradiction of capitalism," through which supply-side crises are generated by drawing down the Earth's capacity to provide low-cost inputs, and sinks for unwanted output. As resources become scarcer, including the atmospheric, aquatic, or terrestrial space for dumping pollution, production costs rise, creating a profit-squeeze.

Others have taken this notion further, positing that capitalism, rather than being something that simply *acts upon* nature, is a mode of "organizing nature" (Moore, 2015). This view, which attempts to transcend the old division between the "social" and the "natural," suggests that we must understand capitalism and nature as mutually co-constitutive—each is internal to the other. As Moore puts it, "society is not only a producer of changes in the web of life, but also a *product* of it" (2015, p. 78). Under capitalism, this co-constitution of society and nature is driven by the logic of accumulation, and the world is partitioned (not only spatially) into zones of exploitation, in which labor generates surplus value through the production of commodities, and zones of appropriation, in which capital draws on the unpaid work of human and extra-human nature.

This latter point is crucial in understanding the ecological contradictions of capitalism, and the limits that accumulation encounters. According to Moore, capitalism relies perpetually on the appropriation of free work provided by nature (and by unpaid human work, particularly but not exclusively that performed by women) in order to stave off crisis. It is only through massive appropriations of free (or as close to free as possible) work in order to enhance labor productivity that capitalism has been able to overcome earlier crises. He focuses particularly on four central inputs to the production process that have been central in this dynamic: labor, energy, food, and raw materials. As capital's ability to appropriate free work wanes as it annexes various geographical and commodity frontiers into the circuit of capital, and we near what Moore predicts to be the end of these "Four Cheaps," capitalism's profitability comes under intense pressure, and new means of transcending ecological limits to accumulation are sought—some of which, at least, further intensify the destruction of human and non-human nature.

With this understanding of how historical materialists have attempted to grapple with the relations between capitalism and nature, we can now turn to examine how neoliberalism, as a class-led attempt to restore its wealth, power, and privilege in the wake of the profit downturn beginning in the mid-1960s, is restructuring these relations, wreaking ecological havoc, and remaking our collective experience and understanding of nature.

Perhaps the most obvious way that neoliberal politics work their way into air, water, soil, and "nature" more broadly is through changing the terms on which states allow capital access to these life-supports. While this is sometimes seen through the concept of "deregulation," it is really much broader than that. States aren't simply "pulling back" from defending the environment, becoming more passive and letting markets somehow take over. They are actively changing the rules of the game to enable capitalists to more aggressively draw on nature's sources and sinks as conditions of production (O'Connor, 1998). We can start with more obvious examples of this, and work our way up through the more complex and insidious.

Owning it all

One aspect of the neoliberal dream, as it relates to environmental questions, is to expand the logic of the market by assigning private property rights to everything. Such extension of private property rights over former commons, public land, or shared resources is not completely novel, though the fact that carving up nature and putting it up for sale is so routinely discussed shows how far we have already traveled down this road. Writing in 1944, Karl Polanyi was at pains to highlight the strangeness of making markets for nature. "What we call land is an element of nature inextricably interwoven with man's institutions," he wrote. "To isolate it and form a market out of it was perhaps the weirdest of all undertakings of our ancestors" (Polanyi, 1944 [1957], p. 187). Resistance to the incursion of private property and the enclosure of land (and resources) is also not new. Marx, in his initial foray into political economy in the pages of the *Rheinische Zeitung* in 1842, took up the cause of Prussian peasants who were being subject to the expansion of private property at the expense of customary practice and common property. The poor, in this case, were being denied the right to gather dead wood in forests belonging to large landholders. It had been made a penal offense, and peasants were being criminalized for exercising a right (access to an aspect of nature) they had customarily enjoyed. The wood—dead as well as alive—was newly considered the private property of the landowner, and the peasants gathering it newly considered thieves. When they were caught, they were turned over to the landowner to perform forced labor (Foster, 2000, pp. 66–67). A couple of decades later, in *Capital*, Marx discusses at length the violence of the English enclosures of the fifteenth to eighteenth centuries, through which common agricultural land was transformed into privately owned pasture for the benefit of the landowning elite (simultaneously creating a body of "free" laborers for the factories). So, the partitioning of the world and the attempt to have it all owned has been a longstanding project, as has resisting it.

The neoliberal trajectory, however, is to push this longstanding process of the extension of private property as far as possible, ensuring that the web of life is structured maximally by contractual relations of exchange founded on enforceable private property rights. Writing on the issue of water (a non-negotiable condition of life on this planet), fellows of the Austrian economic school's Mises Institute make the case, for example, for the "privatization of all bodies of water, without exception," claiming that only through such privatization will we be able to deal with over-fishing, piracy, shark attacks, unsafe boating, oil spills, and other sub-optimal outcomes which the authors allege stem from the "tragedy of the commons" (Block & Nelson, 2016). Actually, when Garret Hardin originally developed his argument about the "tragedy of the commons," he was arguing in part for an authoritarian government that could wrest control over decisions about reproduction from families, thus controlling the growth of human population—not exactly a libertarian dream. Nonetheless, privatizers have used Hardin's analysis of open-access resources (which should not be confused with commons, which are often heavily regulated, tightly managed, and exclusive to a particular group (Ostrom, 2002)) for decades now to argue that resource depletion and pollution are the result of inadequately assigned property rights and markets. While this hypothesis was formalized in the work of Ronald

Coase (2013 [1960]), it has been seized upon by neoliberal forces[3] in an attempt to frame a lack of private property, rather than its gross over-extension, as the fundamental source of environmental problems. The common-sense appeal is that, like partying renters who leave the place in ruins when the lease is up, humans who don't own a thing have no reason to care for it. Only with exclusive rights over the benefits deriving from a chunk of land, a fishery, a river, a genetic code, a stretch of beach, or a rainforest do we become disinclined towards its immediate, longterm, planned, or negligent destruction. Fisheries are often cited as the most clear-cut case of this, since everything outside of the 200-mile limit exclusive economic zones established under the UN Law of the Sea is considered fair game for all (see, e.g., Easterbrook, 2009). As such, there is an incentive to grab what you can, lest your rivals gain the upper hand, with the end result being an empty ocean.

The think tanks, policy advocates, and intellectuals that mobilize this articulation of property rights and environmental protection thus turn Polanyi around, suggesting that the new, strange, and problematic practice is the attempt, through government, to limit or otherwise infringe upon previously existing private property, the origins of which, steeped in the bloody dispossession and decimation of previous communities inhabiting that property, remains obscured. Seen in terms of the double-movement, the illegitimate move in the eyes of neoliberals is not the subdivision of the web of life into fictitiously independent parcels of land (or fish populations, or atmospheric carbon-sequestration capacity ...) but the effort to constrain what people can do with and on it. Groups like the Heritage Foundation and the Cato Institute begin from the premise that the fundamental value in need of protection is individual liberty, which springs exclusively from enjoyment of private property. They thus work to protect the property rights established during the "first leg" of the double-movement—the creation of markets in land—against the incursion of limits pursued during the "second leg." Any government-imposed limits on property (with the exception of a very restrictive set of uses which would be injurious to neighbours) are understood in this framework to be "regulatory takings," tantamount to the actual seizing of land (Spencer et al., 2014; Pilon, 1995). Environmental regulation, then, as a form of regulatory taking which reduces the value of property, should be kept to an absolute minimum, and, when absolutely unavoidable, must be compensated (as specified, in their view, by the "Takings Clause" of the Fifth Amendment).

Instead of regulation, they argue, the environment would best be protected by the incentive structure created by a system of universal and enforceable private property rights. The vision is one in which commons or other forms of public "natures" are relegated to the trash heap, and the world and everything it in ("every molecule on earth," as one commentator for the conservative Canadian think tank The Fraser Institute, put it) has become an exclusive, alienable commodity. In such a context, argue the neoliberal advocates (again, drawing selectively on Coase), owners would rationally steward the source of value that is their property (like a fishery, or a woodlot), and social actors could negotiate compensation among themselves when any conflict arose (downstream pollution of a river, for example). So, the neoliberal ideal, when it comes to structuring socio-natural relations, is to do so through contract and unrestricted property rights.

That, at least, is the theory. In line with the dual-track nature of practical and theoretical neoliberalism, the project to redistribute wealth, resources, and power to capital involves a much messier mixture of grabbing what can be had for free, and capitalizing that which cannot. Primarily, the goal here is to allow capital unimpeded (or facilitated) access to those elements of nature which enable accumulation. Where that purpose can be fulfilled, as it has been historically, through unpaid appropriation, that is the preference. Where it must rely on commodification and capitalization, however, as the case must be when a market is to be created, that is the next best thing.

The privatization of nature, as suggested above, has a long history tied up with various property rights battles. Under neoliberalism, it has accelerated, taking on appearances that range from the farcical to the terrifying to the tragic. As problematic as early environmental politics were in North America, environmentalists have a long history of tying human development to some kind of connection with "wilderness." Early conservationists and preservationists tied this to all kinds of racist, sexist, nationalist, and classist politics (Taylor, 1997; Nash, 2014 [1967]) but the idea that people develop themselves and flourish in part through interaction with a non-human world endures. Sometimes this is expressed through work. In other cases, particularly in heavily industrialized societies, people seek it out increasingly through recreation. The United States has 640 million acres of public land, mostly in the West, to which urbanites and sportspeople flock in order to get some kind of connection to the non-human. In addition to being recreation sites and (grossly insufficient) protections for biodiversity, this land is, of course, also the site of a great deal of extraction and industry, such as logging, mining, and grazing. The state and federal agencies charged with the management of this land have been historically bound to relationships with extractive capital, and have, with varying degrees of enthusiasm, accommodated capital's need to access nature in the form of standing timber, underground resources, and forage (Hudson 2011; Hirt, 1996; Robbins W., 1982). However, public lands have been the target of resource developers since their establishment, and those with an eye to pulling oil, gas, logs, minerals, or forage from those lands have battled ceaselessly either to have them privatized, turned over to the states (and then privatized) or opened up even more widely to extraction. Though widely criticized for facilitating extraction, the public land managers—particularly the National Parks Service and the US Forest Service—began to pay more and more attention to "recreational use values," "ecosystem values," and "wilderness values" in the 1990s and early 2000s. Middle-class Americans have for generations trekked to national parks, national forests, Bureau of Land Management (BLM) lands, state forests, wilderness refuges, and monuments to recreate. People looking to encounter the non-human world, to experience an interaction with other life, have for the most part done so on public lands, and they've been able to do so without exorbitant costs. $10.00 will get you a night's stay on many USFS or BLM campgrounds, and a few are even still free.

The existence of such vast acreage under something approaching a commons—belonging to the entire US citizenry even if managed unevenly for their benefit—does not sit well with a neoliberal approach, and in 2012 Western states kicked off a renewed effort[4] to wrest it from the control of the federal government. Utah got the ball rolling with the Transfer of Public Lands Act (TPLA), which demanded that the federal government hand every acre managed by the USFS or the BLM lying within Utah (60 percent of its land) back to the state. In the following year, bills or resolutions following in the TPLA's footsteps were passed in Idaho, Montana, Nevada, New Mexico, and Wyoming (Ketcham, 2014). Observers note that states do not have anything like the resources necessary to manage that much land, and expect that some would be opened to development and the rest sold off (Streep, 2017; Robbins, 2017).

The TPLA set an initial deadline of 2015 for the extinguishment of federal title, and the transfer of public lands into state control. Like the Sagebrush Rebellion, the TPLA and its imitators claimed to be spawned by a popular frustration with local affairs being controlled by an Eastern establishment. In reality, as Bruce Babbitt, then Governor of Arizona, suggested, "behind the mask the Sagebrush crowd is really nothing but a special-interest group whose real goal is to get public lands into private ownership" (Ketcham, 2014). The same is true for the public land transfer "movement" today, and in fact surveys suggest that Westerners don't support land transfer (Colorado College State of the Rockies Project, 2016) and believe that public lands belong to all Americans (Public Opinion Strategies/FM3, 2014).

Public opinion is not the driver of neoliberal politics, however (e.g. see MacLean, 2017). In 2012, a piece of model legislation appeared on the website of the American Legislative Exchange Council (ALEC), entitled the Disposal and Taxation of Public Lands Act (ALEC, 2012) which is eerily similar to the TPLA. It's no coincidence. The TPLA is a collaborative product of Utah state representative Ken Ivory and industry representatives in ALEC's Energy, Environment, and Agriculture Task Force, through which the bill was vetted before being brought to the Utah statehouse (Ketcham, 2014).

The federal government has, for all intents and purposes up until now, ignored the Act and its copycats across the West. Litigation would be the only possible way forward for the Western states to win their battle, and the legal case is highly dubious (Williamson, 2012; Ruple, 2016). That does not, however, mean that the pursuit of privatization is being abandoned. The national Republican Party's official 2016 platform was unequivocal: "It is absurd to think that all that acreage must remain under the absentee ownership or management of official Washington. Congress shall immediately pass universal legislation providing for a timely and orderly mechanism requiring the federal government to convey certain federally controlled public lands to states" (Republican National Committee, 2016). An ominous early signal that there might be a concerted push on this front came on the very first day of the new congress, when the House of Representatives passed a resolution (championed by yet another Utah rep, Rob Bishop) by which transfers of land from the federal government to lower levels of government would no longer require a financial offset to balance out any increase to the deficit that would occur as part of the transfer (Streep, 2017). In other words, there would be no value attributed to any land passed from federal control to state or local control.

In April, 2017, a further ripple of concern went through the ranks of public land defenders (some of whom are politically liberal environmentalists, but many of whom are Republican members of the hook and bullet crowd) when President Trump signed Executive Order 13792. This Order mandated a review and recommendations by the Secretary of the Interior concerning the fate of 27 parcels of land or sea designated as National Monuments. The review was to consider whether the designations were appropriate, whether they restricted land use in or around the Monuments, what their implications were for the economic development and fiscal health of states, tribes, and localities, and whether they were restricted to the "smallest area compatible with the proper care and management of the objects to be protected" (Zinke, 2016).

Of course, as the neoliberal urge to privatize would open up protected lands to extraction, it would simultaneously result in millions of acres of currently public land being fenced off. What are now substantial wilderness and recreational spaces accessible to all would become the property of the very few with the wealth to purchase them. Neoliberalism's answer to this is that people's desire to experience wilderness, to share space or even interact with non-human life, must be supported through their willingness and ability to pay. Such is the logic—to which we will return—of neoliberal valuation: *the continued existence of all things is contingent on their positive contribution to exchange value.* Indeed, such privatized spaces in which the relationship between human and non-human life is mediated through the cash nexus are springing up. Hunting—a long-established practical relation between human and non-human life—provides one example.

In the mid-1970s, Texas was home to 316 privately owned game ranches that collectively held about 57,000 exotic deer and sheep (Butts, 1979). By 2007, there were more than five thousand such private game ranches, with most of the expansion coming in the 1980s and early 1990s (Middleton, 2007). By 2010, Wildlife Partners LLC—a San Antonio-based exotics breeder, buyer, and management consulting firm—estimates that there were 400,000 exotics (now re-branded as "Texotics," in order to give them a little local flavour) living behind high fences, with 50,000–60,000 "free ranging" (those having escaped enclosure and their offspring) (Wildlife Partners, n.d.). Most of these exotics are hunted, along with a selection of local species, for a fee, and often as part of hunting packages. Hunters in the US are a small and diminishing percentage of the population, but they have higher-than-median incomes, and those who do hunt spend heavily—particularly the trophy-hunters. Hunters spent $14 billion in pursuit of birds and animals in 1991, and two decades later they were spending over $33 billion (US Department of the Interior, US Fish and Wildlife Service, and US Department of Commerce, US Census Bureau, 2011).

For the high-end and corporate clients seeking an experience in the "great outdoors," there are establishments like Greystone Castle Sporting Club, a "6,000 acre ranch and castle facility [which] allows ... an unmatched range of sporting and hunting activities combined with luxurious accommodations and gourmet dining." At Greystone, one might opt to hunt a variety of birds, local whitetail, or any of an impressive array of exotics. While on the low-end, a hog trophy fee is just $300, taking home a kudu trophy will cost a more substantial $15,000. Alternatively, there is the Ted Nugent-approved Ox Ranch, which covers 18,000 acres, enables clients to hunt anything from addax to zebu, with trophy fees ranging from $750 for a culled whitetail to $35,000 for a top-quality European red stag. When you aren't roaming the land with your pistol, rifle or bow, you can hand-feed the giraffes, shoot machine guns, drive a World War II Sherman tank, or do yoga.

If your preference for a wildlife encounter is one that ends with the wildlife's survival, there is a neoliberal encounter for you, too. Resorts in popular US tourist destinations like Florida, Hawaii, or Cancun, for example, offer an opportunity to "swim with dolphins," an experience that is becoming increasingly popular in part due to its integration with the cruise ship industry. For about $100, cruise passengers or other customers can enjoy an hour of pool time with a couple of dolphins, getting towed around on their dorsal fins, pushed along by their noses, and posing for hug-and-kiss photographs. For a small additional fee, Dolphin Discovery (with locations throughout Mexico and the Caribbean) allows customers to enjoy

> privacy, comfort and personalized service at our new Dolphin VIP Lounge area. If you're the kind of person willing to experience the best, our VIP Lounge offers you the best option to relax with the one of a kind view of the Caribbean Sea while you immerse in our infinity pool or have a premium drink from a selected liquor collection. Delight yourself with the international exquisite buffet that includes seafood, pasta, salads and more in an air-conditioned room full of windows so you can keep enjoying the perfect Caribbean view.

There's probably at least a little dolphin mixed in with that seafood buffet, given that, despite enormous successes in reducing bycatch, the tuna fishery kills about a thousand dolphins per year (NOAA, 2016). Opponents of these kind of captive-dolphin experiences suggest that there are a host of problems with keeping cetaceans in captivity, from increased mortality to stress-induced psychosis.

There are, it (should not, but) does need to be said, some problematic ethical considerations in both of these examples. In the case of what critics call "canned hunting," for example, animals are sometimes shot at feeding stations or in fenced enclosures at private game ranches, strictly for the trophy. But even bracketing the moral consideration we might extend to the non-human life in both of these situations, the rise of private hunting facilities and dolphinariums represent neoliberal logic taken to its conclusion. Life is annexed and made subservient to a precise market logic in which exchange value rules. Individual beings are read in this register purely as cash value, and even species' survival is dependent on the economic value they render. The landscape of the Texas hill country—the species composition of its flora and fauna, and its ecology—has been transformed according to the market for privatized recreational hunting. Humans' desire for a "connection" of some kind with wildlife is channeled into an effortless and highly profitable managed experience. Dolphins are either supplied through captive breeding programs or captured wild and transported to the concrete pools in which they will spend their lives endlessly replicating marketable behaviors for life-jacket-sporting tourists. Within these spaces, a fully commodified and privatized encounter (whatever one might think of its quality) with the non-human is given full expression.

Lest these examples be considered too "niche," consider their amplification and application to whole human societies under neoliberal logic and practice. When Lawrence Summers—a significant card in the neoliberalizing deck—was Chief Economist at the World Bank, he wrote the following in a memo to staff:

> The measurement of the costs of health-impairing pollution depends on the foregone earnings from increased morbidity and mortality. From this point of view a given amount of health-impairing pollution should be done in the country with the lowest cost, which will be the country with the lowest wages. I think the economic logic behind dumping a load of toxic waste in the lowest-wage country is impeccable and we should face up to that. ("Furor on memo," 1992)

This is not a case of a bad apple. It is a frank expression of the logic through which environments, and the human societies that co-constitute them, are remade under neoliberal dominance. As we will elaborate further later in the chapter, health, illness, degradation, flourishing, life, and death are meted out according to calculations of net present value.

Open season

Full privatization, and the assignment of property rights to everything existing remains a work-in-progress. Land, waterways, air, and even some non-human animals have yet to be fully transmuted into private property. Yet much of this remains important for the production of surplus, and profits decline along with the complexity, time, and money involved in accessing non-human nature. As such, neoliberal forces would prefer that it be accessible to capital with the minimum of regulatory fuss. The battle to declare open season on resource development, and to otherwise make nature cheaply or freely available to capital has not been won, but it has had significant victories in rolling back the limits that were placed on market-driven and market-determined resource exploitation in the 1960s and 1970s.

Capital needs access to what James O'Connor called "conditions of production" (1998). These are fictitious commodities (things that we attempt to treat as commodities, but which aren't, in fact, created as commodities) like labor, nature, and public infrastructure that, arranged appropriately, form necessary foundations for production, but which individual capitalists aren't required to restore or replace as they get used. When it comes to the "nature" category, we can, following O'Connor, think of the conditions of production as being simultaneously our conditions of life: clean air, a stable climate, potable water, clean and fertile soil. Because these are conditions of life, movements arose to protect them by regulating capital's access to them.

Spurred in part by the publication of *Silent Spring* in 1962 (Carson, 1962), demands for environmental protection became more urgent, and civil society organizations, during a remarkable decade and a half from the mid-1960s until the early 1980s, pushed Republican and Democratic federal governments into passing a flurry of environmental laws. Beginning with the Wilderness Act in 1964, through the National Wild and Scenic Rivers Act of 1968, the National Environmental Policy Act of 1969, the reorganization of federal executive environmental responsibilities under the Environmental Protection Agency in 1970, the Coastal Zone Management Act of 1972, the Clean Air and Clean Water Acts[5] of early 1972 and 1973, the Endangered Species Act of 1973, the Federal Land Policy and Management Act of 1974, the Surface Mining Control and Reclamation Act of 1977, and a supporting cast of several other statutes began to set national, legal limits on resource extraction and development in order to shield our "conditions of life" from untrammelled exploitation as "conditions of production" (Coggins & Nagel, 1989). These laws represent a bright example of Polanyi's double-movement. Americans newly sensitized to the environmental effects of untrammeled development and resource exploitation threatened a massive withdrawal of consent from a government whose legitimacy came into question over the issue of its capacity and willingness to protect the environment. Beginning with the tenure of Secretary Stewart Udall and through the administrations of Walter Hickel (under President Nixon) and Cecil Andrus (under President Carter), even the notoriously extraction-friendly Department of the Interior began to consider environmental protection as an important part of its mandate (Coggins & Nagel, 1989).

Capital chafed under even the moderate new limits imposed by expanded protected areas and the weight of new regulations that recognized water, air, and soil as conditions of life. Under President Ronald Reagan, the momentum swung rapidly back towards deregulation, despite public concerns arising from toxic scandals in the late 1970s and early 1980s, such as Love Canal, Times Beach, and Warren County. Reagan's own environmental stance was made clear when he weighed in on the hotly contested proposal for the establishment of Redwood National Park. In front of a room full of timber owners, while still a candidate for Governor of California, Reagan assured his audience that "we've got to recognize that where the preservation of a natural resource like the redwoods is concerned, that there is a common sense limit. I mean, if you've looked at a hundred thousand acres or so of trees—you know, a tree is a tree, how many more do you need to look at?" (Cannon, 2003, p. 302).

Capital's battle to turn US public lands over to private resource developers, and to confound the regulatory mandate of the EPA found its most committed vehicle in Reagan's appointments of James Watt as

Interior Secretary and Anne Gorsuch (later to become Anne Gorsuch Burford) as Director of the EPA. Both were short-lived, very likely due to their over-zealous efforts to press a pure neoliberal logic onto the nation's public lands and its entire "web of life."

James Gaius Watt was brought into the administration from the Mountain States Legal Foundation (MSLF), a conservative public-interest law firm founded with an initial gift from the ultra-conservative Joseph Coors in 1977. The MSLF self-describes as a "legal foundation dedicated to individual liberty, the right to own and use property, limited and ethical government, and the free enterprise system, that defends constitutional liberties and the rule of law" (Guidestar, 2017). He carried the MSLF's aggressive neoliberal agenda into a department with a long history of enabling resource extraction, but one that was also viewed as insufficiently committed by resource developers. The key principles of his administration were summed up by one commentator as follows:

> (1) federal ownership of land, if not unconstitutional or unconscionable, is at least A Bad Idea; (2) to the extent that land remains in federal ownership, valuable land should be reclassified or transferred to make them more easily accessible to resource developers; and (3) the resources of the federal lands should be made available to private developers to the maximum possible extent, at minimum cost, and with the fewest possible regulatory restrictions. (Coggins & Nagel, 1989)

While Watt was unable to push through the more radical aspects of his agenda (in particular the wholesale transfer of public lands from the federal government), he carried the fondest wishes of extractive industry further than they had dared hope possible prior to 1981. Watt resigned under pressure from Senate and the White House in October of 1983—the trigger event being his comment, when describing the alleged diversity of his coal advisory commission, that "We have every kind of mixture you can have. I have a black, I have a woman, two Jews and a cripple. And we have talent" (Weisman, 1983). However, as short as his tenure was, his legacy of opening up US public resources as a site of accumulation has been lasting and disastrous. His treatment of offshore oil and gas leasing is illustrative.

Under Secretary Watt, the price of offshore oil and gas leases plummeted, and the number of acres leased shot up precipitously. Watt accomplished this by shifting the way that the federal government offered offshore leases, from leasing smaller individual blocks within an area (like the Central Gulf of Mexico, for example) to leasing entire areas under a single bid. Prior to these changes, the largest offering ever was the 1975 leasing of 2,870,344 acres in the Gulf. The first area-wide lease following Watt's changes was just shy of 38 million acres. Few companies had the wherewithal to bid for and develop such large areas, leaving the bids open only to fewer, larger corporations (about half of all federal offshore leases are held by just 20 companies), and resulting in fewer, smaller bids on a per-acre basis. This has had a lasting and large effect on fossil fuel corporations' capacity to access offshore oil and gas, and on the return to its public owners—the American people. Gramling and Freudenberg's (2010) analysis of the impact of the shift to area-wide leasing shows that under the older model, in place from 1954 until 1982, the American public earned an average of $2224.71 per acre on offshore lease sales. Following Watt, that per acre amount sunk to just $263.33. In addition, the US federal government has a laughably low royalty rate on offshore production, lower than most US states, yielding the American public "one of the lowest takes in the world" from oil and gas, according to the US Government Accountability Office (2007). Not satisfied with this, Watt dropped the rate on many leases from 16.6 percent to 12.5 percent. In 1995, the US Congress doubled down on its offshore giveaway, passing the Outer Continental Shelf Deep Water Royalty Relief Act, which enabled oil companies to exploit "millions of barrels of oil and billions of cubic feet of gas without paying a nickel's worth of royalties" (Gramling & Freudenberg, 2010). As Gulf oil in particular was made cheaply available, the number of leases shot upward, from 3,520 leases prior to 1983, to 21,179 between 1983 and 2008—a sixfold increase even as the revenue earned by the federal government fell (Gramling & Freudenberg, 2010). In short, the legacy of Watt was to open up the publicly owned resources of the Outer Continental Shelf to cheap exploitation by some of the world's largest corporations. In tandem with longstanding US energy policy that resulted in what Gramling and Freudenberg describe as a "cycle of dependency, profit, and risk taking" (Gramling & Freudenberg, 2012), this handover proved disastrous not just in terms of opening up public resources at cut-rate prices, and enabling further contributions to the US's already grossly disproportionate historical contributions to greenhouse gases but in terms of a catastrophic short-term event.

Despite assurances that new technologies and fail-safes made uncontrolled deep-water oil spills very improbable, with this scale of development, the improbable becomes likely. The 2010 tragedy of the *Deepwater Horizon*, which was engaged in drilling 2.5 miles into rock under 5000 feet of water, tapping oil that was under 6000 pounds of pressure per square inch through BP's Macondo well, was the realization of that "improbability." Eleven rig workers were killed, seventeen were injured, and some 4.9 million barrels of oil blew into the Gulf of Mexico's waters over five months. The environmental consequences were, and continue to be, vast. While much of the impact won't be understood for years, or perhaps decades, preliminary assessments suggest that the combination of unrecovered oil and chemical dispersant has resulted in the deaths of an estimated five thousand marine mammals and a million offshore and coastal seabirds. Turtles, a thousand of which were found dead immediately following the spill, have been stranding at much higher than normal rates, along with dolphins and whales. Coral communities, bottom-dwelling organisms, seaweed diversity, and oyster populations have all been heavily impacted by the spill. Clean-up workers and coastal residents have been and will continue to suffer illness as a result of exposure to oil and chemical dispersant. Part of the "clean-up" (and we shouldn't even for a moment imagine that the oil has been "cleaned up" since anywhere from a quarter to a half of the oil remains unaccounted for) involved the unprecedented use of huge volumes of two variants of the dispersant Corexit (just over 4 million litres was applied at the surface, and just under 3 million litres were injected directly to the wellhead). Drawing on data from 28,000 participants, the National Institute of Environmental Health's GuLF Study is attempting to track the immediate and long-term health impacts of the spill and the response. One result from this is the finding that exposure to Corexit is associated with a wide variety of human health problems, over and above exposure to the oil itself (McGowan et al., 2017). While debate will continue for some time over the wisdom and effectiveness of using chemical dispersants, the bottom line is that once a spill happens, even if the much-advertised "world class response" *is* present, that response is less about cleaning up, and more about making decisions as to who and what will bear the brunt of the damage. Is it better to keep the oil suspended in the water column, dispersed into micro-droplets, or allow it to rise to the surface as a slick? Should we let the damage fall in the deep sea, or the marshes and beaches? Is it better for response workers to breathe in toluene and benzene fumes from surface oil, or be exposed to dispersant? These represent the decision-making framework for oil spills. While we watch in horror as events like the Deepwater Horizon unfold, and continue to describe them as "accidents," they are in fact inevitable results of a world wedded to oil, and governed by the risk-management framework of neoliberalism.

Most explanations of the *Deepwater Horizon* disaster tend to focus on the proximate causes of technological failure (a concrete core installed by Halliburton ruptured under the pressure of a natural gas surge, which then climbed the rig's riser and ignited on the platform). However, Gramling and Freudenberg provide a much more convincing historical and structural analysis, indicating that the policies put in place by Watt, and followed up by the 1995 Royalty Relief Act, actively and deliberately encouraged the kind of risky deep-water plays represented by Macondo— plays that took us to the edge of our technological capacity and then tipped us over it. The Reagan administration had set out to facilitate cheap and lightly-regulated access not only to the nation's resources but to the ecosystems through which they are accessed, and the conditions of life to which they are attached—in this case, the oceans.

All the while, the body charged with regulating capital's access to Americans' oil was utterly compromised by its contradictory roles of revenue collection and regulation—a condition robustly illustrated two years prior to the Macondo Blowout when an investigation revealed that staff in the Department of the Interior's Minerals Management Service (MMS), charged with the collection of royalties revenue, "accepted gifts, steered contracts to favored clients and engaged in drug use and illicit sex with employees of the energy firms" they were also responsible for regulating. It was the same MMS that approved BP's Oil Spill Response Plan, which has been shown to be inaccurate and false on a number of issues ranging from the company's skimming capacity (claimed to be an astounding 491,000 barrels per day, when in fact they managed to skim about 3 percent of the total spill), the likelihood and timing of a spill reaching the coast (reported to be 21 percent probable within one month, when in actuality the spill reached the coast in 9 days), the likely impacts on wildlife ("no adverse impact" on sea turtles and endangered marine mammals—true only if we believe they go to a better place when they die), and the contact name for an expert on spills and wildlife (a professor who was reported to be at the University of Miami, but who had in fact left twenty years prior, and who had also been deceased for four years) (Gramling & Freudenberg, 2012, pp. 64–66).

The lack of protective oversight combines with the relentless pressure to cut costs and save time (the same thing, really) that drives capitalist decision making, to inevitably produce catastrophe. The *Deepwater Horizon* was being leased for $500,000 a day, and its operational service requirements cost another $500,000. Additionally, it was needed by BP elsewhere, to begin drilling at another site. The corner-cutting that combined to produce the disaster was all designed to save time. It was a product of the need for capital to reduce the span between investment and the realization of profit, enabled by a willing state committed to ensuring that private capital would not be constrained by oversight or regulation. In the neoliberal calculus, this case suggests, enhancing access to the conditions of production outweighs protection of the conditions of life.

This enabling of access takes shape through active steps undertaken by government, such as the Royalty Relief Act, but also through weakening state regulatory capacities by depriving the regulators of the means to do so. The reduction in the percentage of the federal budget dedicated to what might be characterized as "environmental-protective functions" is shown in Figure 3.1. The declining priority of funding for the Department of the Interior is shown in Figure 3.2.

In both, note the significant declines occurring from 1979 to 1982. The DOI shows a small recovery in 1983–84 before declining again through

Figure 3.1 Natural resource and environmental outlays as percent of federal total

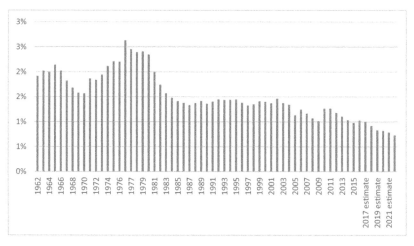

Source: www.whitehouse.gov/omb/budget/Historicals, table 3.2

1985. The Natural Resource and Environment outlays show a steady decline all the way to 1987.

Anne Gorsuch had a similarly tumultuous and brief stint as Director of the Environmental Protection Agency, and one that was emblematic of neoliberal aspirations to clear the way to unfettered use and abuse of air, water, and land in the pursuit of profit. Her commitment to pushing aside the environmental regulatory "burden" on industry had been demonstrated during her tenure in the Colorado state legislature, where she was a member of the "House Crazies"—a group of strongly conservative legislators with an agenda of aggressive deregulation. There, she presided over the State Affairs Committee which came to be known as "the killing field" for regulatory bills, including an important bill regulating the disposal of hazardous waste. One state health official who had monitored the committee hearings on the bill commented, with a certain degree of (possibly performative) naivety about the tight entanglements of elite rule, "I don't think they were in anyone's pocket. They obviously had very deep personal convictions about the problems of overregulation. It's just that this led them to do exactly what industry wanted" (Russakoff, 1983).

Gorsuch's dedication to putting the state's resources in the service of industry caught the new Reagan administration's attention, and in 1981 she was brought in as head of the EPA. There, she continued, in her own words, to "follow orders" (Burford & Greenya, 1986) until she ran afoul of allegations of corruption and contempt of Congress for refusing to turn over Superfund records and was forced to resign (Sullivan, 2004).

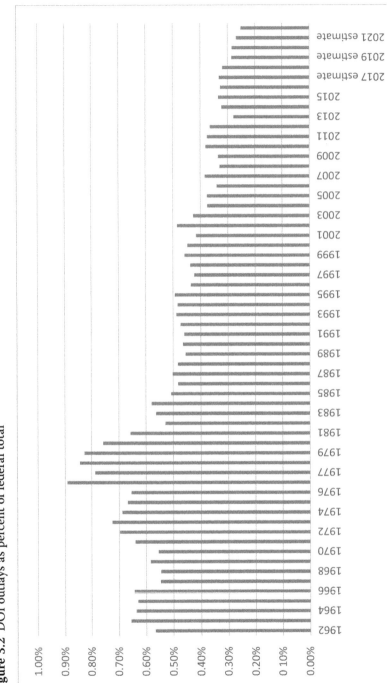

Figure 3.2 DOI outlays as percent of federal total

Source: www.whitehouse.gov/omb/budget/Historicals, table 4.1

A 1981 story in *The Washington Post* reported that under Gorsuch's direction,

> Budget cuts at the Environmental Protection Agency will strip 3,200 person-nel of their jobs by the end of 1983, eliminating 30 percent of the agency's 10,380 employees at a cost of $17.6 million just for severance pay. The cuts are so massive that they could mean a basic retreat on all the envi-ronmental programs of the past 10 years, according to agency sources and administration critics. At the same time, divisions between ... Gorsuch and career agency staff over her approach to policymaking have all but reached open warfare. (quoted in Dennis & Mooney, 2017)

Gorsuch came out of the starting blocks at a furious and unsustainable pace. Nonetheless, despite her short tenure and inglorious termination, the course she set has not changed. The neoliberal assault on legal structures that regulate capital's access to nature—either directly by setting aside land for preservation purposes, by limiting access to air, water, and land as waste dumps, or by providing opportunities for the input of regular citizens in land-use planning—have continued in the same direction since, only at a more gradual and punctuated pace. Again, a quick look at EPA funding over the years tells part of the story (Figure 3.3).

As we gained greater understanding of the scale of environmental degradation in the late 1960s and 1970s, the EPA was granted more funding, up until 1979, when it began a sharp decline, continuing a slower, step-like reduction until today. By 2018, when scientists understand us to be in the grip of a civilizational crisis as a result of ecological destruction (Ripple et al. 2017), the estimated priority of the EPA for the federal government had returned to where it was in 1968. While Watt and Gorsuch were only short, bright blips in the history of neoliberal transformations of the state's mediation of capital's (and thus all of our) relationship with nature, their aborted, radical agenda of using the state to open more spaces up to extraction with fewer obligations or limits, has continued in a slower, more uneven, and less spectacular way. Environmental victories on the expansion of public lands, protected areas, and the regulation of pollution—most notably greenhouse gases—have been notable, but are again under severe pressure from the muscular neoliberalism of the Trump administration, which we address in the final chapter.

Making markets

Neoliberalism is, as we have discussed, about more than destroying or eroding regulatory protections. It is at least as much of a creative process

Figure 3.3 EPA outlays as percent of federal total

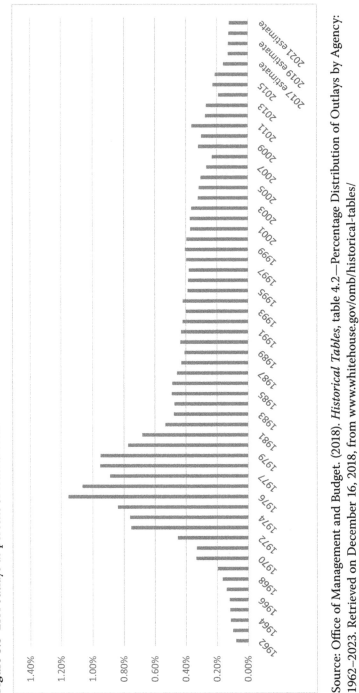

Source: Office of Management and Budget. (2018). *Historical Tables*, table 4.2—Percentage Distribution of Outlays by Agency: 1962–2023. Retrieved on December 16, 2018, from www.whitehouse.gov/omb/historical-tables/

as it is a destructive one. Neoliberalism sets out to remake economies, political subjectivities, relations of power, legal systems, and it sets out to fundamentally reorganize the entanglement of nature and society. Neoliberalism does not result in a neglect of "the environment," any more than it results in a neglect of the state. First of all, every social formation or regime of accumulation implies a specific organization of nature. There is no "neglect," even if there is no explicit recognition of the ways in which societies remake and are (eventually) structured by nature, and even as species are wiped out, landscapes are transformed, and greenhouse gases accumulate to dangerous levels. Neoliberal actors are forced to confront the degradation of air, water, soil, species diversity, and climate stability, partly because of successful social movements demanding that they do so, but more so because of the risks and costs generated by neoliberal transformations of the non-human world. Processes like species extinction and climate change, while caused primarily by the dynamics of capitalism, also pose threats to its continued functioning, as accumulation relies on things like genetic diversity, climate stability, and existing coastal infrastructure—all of which are now either horrendously diminished or under grave threat.

However, neoliberal agents confront this not with the intent of accommodating our economic system to the flourishing of life, but with the intent of effectively subsuming nature under the logic of capital. This involves nothing short of a transformation of all aspects of the non-human world into commodities in the full sense, or attributing to them value, in the strictly capitalist sense. Concepts like "natural capital," and "ecosystem services," that reflect and effect that transformation, that fundamentally reconstitute nature, both ideationally and materially, began to be introduced in the 1980s, and institutionalized at the level of policy beginning in the 1990s.

The first instance of this is the now widely known process of generating various markets in environmental goods, such as pollution prevention. Rather than have governments engage in the allegedly costly, technically difficult, and hard-to-enforce regulation of pollution, the neoliberal solution to sub-optimal pollution has been to create markets for the right to pollute. That is, rather than directly regulating what comes out of smokestacks and effluent pipes, or mandating particular kinds of "clean tech" for use in industry, the neoliberal approach is to create, and then trust in, markets to deliver equivalent reductions. These kinds of markets have mutated and proliferated so that there are many such markets or their cousins ranging from the bizarre to the increasingly mundane. The most widely known and with the highest stakes are probably markets in pollution entitlements, like carbon markets, but there are also markets for a variety of what have been labeled "ecosystem services"—most commonly having to do with carbon absorption, hydrological services like water filtration and retention, and biodiversity services, like habitat conservation or enhancement. Some of these are for compliance with legal restrictions (so the state is still needed to pass the laws enabling the markets), and some of them are voluntary, enabling individuals, organizations, or firms to "offset" or internalize environmental costs.

To give a flavour for how offset markets work, we can look at the Queensland market in koala offsets. In Australia, home of the iconic, seldom-conscious koala bear, the Queensland government has established a policy for koala habitat. The major threat to the koala is habitat destruction. Once their habitat is lost to (frequently suburban) development, they encounter a hostile new terrain of cars, dogs, and swimming pools that they are frequently fatally incapable of navigating. Koalas also experience habitat loss—including loss of food and shelter—as a major stressor, and, when stressed, koalas tend to get chlamydia. This is an unfortunate stress-reaction, but such is the lot of the koala. Recognizing this, if a development proponent wants to build something that negatively affects koala habitat, the Queensland law specifies that they must first of all make every effort to mitigate the damage to habitat. Damage that is "unavoidable" (taking as "unavoidable" the construction of, say, an outlet mall or more housing for the population of South East Queensland, which is growing at one thousand people per day (Queensland Government, 2017)) must be offset by the rehabilitation, establishment and protection of koala habitat elsewhere in the same local government area. For every non-juvenile koala habitat tree taken out by the development, three must be planted in the offset site, and they must "be reflective of the species that are endemic to the site and be planted at densities that will produce a mature density reflective of the regional ecosystems present on the site" (Queensland Department of Environment and Heritage Protection, 2013, 13). The damage done by the developer is ostensibly "offset" by increases to equivalent habitat down the road, paid for by the proponent. While there is a certain tragic-comic dimension to the koala offset, offsets are coming to take a larger and larger role in policy designed to address the environmental damage resulting from development, recreation, and industry, and they are subject to a bedevilling set of uncertainties.

A crucial institutional milestone along this neoliberal road was laid in the US as a response to increasing awareness of acid rain. As the US public started to notice their lakes and forests dying as a result of acid precipitation, sulfur dioxide (SO_2) emissions, primarily from coal-fired electricity generation, and nitrogen oxides (NOx), primarily from transportation, were identified as the chief culprits. Numerous bills came before Congress through the 1980s to regulate these emissions, but they were beaten back by the Reagan administration working in coalition with eastern coal-country Democrats. (MacKenzie, 2009) It was not until 1990 that the idea to create a market in sulfur dioxide emissions permits took hold and, in many senses, that grip continues to shape international efforts to address greenhouse gas emissions—to which we will return. Drawing on a buildup of neoclassical techniques for the monetary valuation of work performed by the non-human world (later conceptualized as "ecosystem services" provided by "natural capital") that had taken off in the 1960s, and a much earlier shift from understanding non-human contributions to production through the lens of use value, to the lens of exchange value (Gómez-Baggethun et al., 2010), policy makers were enabled and encouraged to conceive of nature as an assemblage of service-providing assets, each of which could be assigned a net present value based on the exchange value of their associated stream of services. In the case of sulfur dioxide, the key asset was the atmosphere's capacity to absorb pollution. The creation of a market for entitlements to that capacity required government to take a series of steps. First and foremost, it had to establish a maximum aggregate level of sulfur dioxide emissions, which it did in the Clean Air Act Amendments of 1990. Second, it had to allocate permits equivalent to that maximum among major polluters. This it did by handing them out, rather than auctioning them. Firms were then allowed, beginning in 1995, to buy and sell these permits, so that firms for whom reducing emissions was relatively cheap could make deep cuts and sell their surplus permits, while those for whom it was relatively expensive could purchase them. Fines of $2000 per ton for emitting above the level allowed by a firm's permits encouraged compliance. (See, for a full description of the market's design, Schmalensee & Stavins, 2012.)

There were indeed substantial reductions in sulfur dioxide emissions after 1995. A great deal of this, though, is attributable to factors other than the sulfur dioxide market. Emissions were falling fairly sharply before the market scheme came into effect. From 1970 to 1990, emissions in the US and Canada combined (with the US making up by far the lion's share of the total) fell from 35 to 24 million metric tons—a 31 percent reduction (Smith et al., 2011, p. 1109). From 1990 to 2010, during the trading program, emissions fell by a similar amount, from 15 to just over 5 million metric tons. From 2010 to 2015, emissions continued to fall, even after the sulfur dioxide market collapsed in 2012 (Shmalensee & Stavins, 2012; US Energy Information Administration, 2017). Much of the reduction during the cap-and-trade years resulted from reduced rail freight rates, enabling power-generators to substitute low-sulfur coal from the Powder River Basin for the much higher-sulfur coal of Appalachia.

Despite this, and the market's collapse, the scheme's apparent success in the 1990s solidified the case for market-based tools. According to two analysts of the program, "By the close of the twentieth century, the SO2 allowance trading system had come to be seen as both innovative and successful. It has become exceptionally influential, leading to a series of policy innovations in the United States and abroad to address a range of environmental challenges, including the threat of global climate change" (Schmalensee & Stavins, 2012, p. 2). It was the US's insistence in the 1997 negotiations resulting in the Kyoto Protocol that led to the inclusion (and centrality) of carbon trading in the deal (which, despite the US's non-ratification of the Protocol remains a core aspect of the Paris Agreement—the Kyoto Protocol's successor) and the launching of the EU's highly troubled and ineffective Emissions Trading System (the EU-ETS).

While the EU-ETS remains the most mature and, in terms of emissions traded, by far the largest carbon trading system in the world, it is in a state of dramatic oversupply of carbon allowances (a combined product of recession, soft rules on the use of imported international credits, and industrial lobbying on the basis of threats to competitiveness) and has had very little if anything to do with reductions in EU-wide emissions. Sandbag, a non-profit advocate of carbon markets, provided an analysis following the second phase of the system's operation (2008–12), stressing that recession and direct regulation were responsible for all but a "negligible" portion of the drop in emissions (Morris, 2013). Further analysis by Bel and Joseph supports this finding (Bel & Joseph, 2015). By 2017, ETS-covered emissions had actually begun to rise again in Europe, as lignite coal became a more important part of power generators' energy mix, and as stubborn industrial emissions rose (Sandbag, 2018). This despite Brussels attempting to prop up the carbon price and rebalance the market's 2–3 billion ton allowance oversupply with a plan to "backload" the system by postponing the auctioning of new allowances until 2019–20.

Though cap-and-trade systems have lost some of their initial lustre, such schemes are still proliferating. The International Emissions Trading Association, for example, offers analyses of 19 distinct carbon emissions trading systems (International Emissions Trading Association (IETA), 2017). Much more significantly in terms of the neoliberal reconstitution of our relationship with non-human nature, the core concept of the sulfur dioxide market innovation—that nature could be conceived of as a divisible, commodifiable assemblage of service-providing assets—remains at the core of the neoliberal reorganization of nature. Markets in Ecosystem Services (MES) and Payments for Ecosystem Services (PES) are the primary institutional manifestations of this neoliberal nature in which ecological functions are identified, access to those functions is allocated and traded (in the case of MES), and stewards are compensated financially for restoring or protecting functionality (in the case of PES).

This, of course, is not as simple as having an idea and then changing the world. Enacting this neoliberal dream requires the development of a whole host of new technologies and techniques of accounting, mapping, and measuring, all of which enable the shift from an ideational *reconceptualization* of what nature is to its slow, material *reconfiguration* and articulation within the logic of capital. As Jessica Dempsey (2016) details in the case of biodiversity markets, this is not an easy process, and in her estimation one that is likely to remain a capitalist utopia. Very little private money is going into these markets as of yet, and the labor required to generate the commodities in question is almost entirely socialized (philanthropic, government, or non-governmental organization).

Nature as an asset

The mythical figure at the heart of advocacy for this reconfiguration is *homo economicus*—that battered and debunked pillar of introductory economics. While behavioral economics has essentially done away with the empirical basis for belief in *homo economicus*, neoliberalism has always understood that *homo economicus* is a figure which doesn't actually exist but which should be created. As Margaret Thatcher famously quipped in response to a question about her government's radical new economic policies, "Economics are the method; the object is to change the heart and soul" (Butt, 1981). By this she meant that the goal of her government was to reorient people's focus from collective duties and obligations to individual ones. The goal of neoliberalism is to create within people an inwardly focused arithmetic impulse, ceaselessly calculating individual costs and benefits of actions and potential actions. People must be disciplined into understanding themselves as entrepreneurs of their own lives, requiring them to view the worlds they inhabit as assemblages of potential value. Friendships and relations become value-enhancing (or -detracting!) social networks; learning becomes an accumulation of human capital, targeted at achieving maximum return; dwellings and places become real estate investments. The utopia is one in which the universe becomes a stream of net present-value calculations, and we their navigators. Of course, this requires pricing. *Homo economicus* is utterly lost without prices to respond to. A thing without a price, so goes the argument, is a non-thing.

This line of thought is well captured in various initiatives to put prices on ecological functions. One of the most prominent of these was The Economics of Ecosystems & Biodiversity, an initiative hosted by the United Nations Environment Programme. The project of valuing and integrating Ecosystem Services in economic decision making originated with the G8+5 (the "+5" being Brazil, Mexico, India, China, and South Africa) meeting of environmental ministers in Potsdam, in 2007. The Potsdam Initiative pledged to chart the global economic benefits of biodiversity. Essentially, the environment ministers of this powerful group of nations conceded that they needed to make the case that life on the planet had to justify its existence relative to the values that could be otherwise created by its destruction. While initially, again, aimed at "making the case for conservation," the valuation techniques are now being turned towards the establishment of markets in biodiversity which enable speculation, risk management, and profit opportunities for developers, land owners, and traders. The TEEB project, headed by a former Managing Director and Head of Deutsche Bank's Global Markets in India, now tags itself with the mission of "making nature's values visible." It is a revealing tagline. Implicit in the tag is that they are making those values visible to those who matter, and who have so far been prevented from seeing these values by the lack of currency symbols floating above them.

In one report, for example, TEEB suggests that €21.7 million annually is saved through the sequestration of damaging carbon (damaging to the tune of €70 per ton of carbon dioxide equivalent) by restored peatlands (Forster, 2010). Hawaiian coral reefs, meanwhile, have a 50-year net present value of $10 billion. The vast bulk of this is in the form of "cultural services"—largely tourism (Van Beukering & Cesar, 2010). In the logic of capitalism, then, corals are worth saving until an alternative use for the environments that support them is discovered to produce greater value. Similarly, "a global economic assessment of 63 million hectares of wetlands estimated their value at $3.4 billion per year" (Brander & Schuyt, 2010, p. 1).

Such a construction of peatlands, coral reefs, and wetlands builds on the concept of "natural capital," associated with economists like Herman Daly and Robert Costanza (Costanza & Daly, 1992). Natural capital, which actively reconstructs nature as a bundle of assets that provide flows of value, was initially intended to be a kind of "teaching tool" for policy makers; a way of allowing them to visualize, in terms they could understand, the scale of destruction being visited upon the non-human world. However, according to ecological economist Richard Norgaard (2010, p. 1219), "The eye-opening metaphor ... soon rose to become a central framework for scientifically assessing ecosystem change."

The numbers generated in such exercises may seem solid, and big enough to bolster the case for saving corals and peatlands. However, the logic of natural capital and initiatives like TEEB leaves us helplessly trapped within the ruthless decision-making framework of the Summers Memo (referred to earlier), in which the value of all things is captured exclusively by its market-established price. Life, death, flourishing, degradation, survival, and extinction are meted out on the basis of (imputed) exchange value. The head of the TEEB, in a public lecture on valuing nature, asserted (apparently uncontroversially) that "economics has become the currency of policy." Further, he claimed that if the "economic invisibility of nature persists," then we will continue to destroy biodiversity without even noticing (Sukhdev, 2011). No doubt we are continuing to destroy biodiversity, but of course we do notice. Communities living in and from

of animal feed into bodyweight, the capacity of fossil fuels to flow, or their spatial concentration), it aims to shift from simple appropriation of nature, to its reconfiguration and capitalization. Just as human bodies under factory production become appendages of the machines they tend, bound to their pace and rhythm, so nature is reorganized with the intent of overcoming its initial material limits (Boyer, 2015). Humans have been doing this for a very, very long time, of course, through a huge variety of means, from landscape-wide burning by indigenous societies practiced to induce the growth of particular plants and to attract game, to selective breeding of plants and animals for particular traits. Humans in the reproduction of their existence actively reorganize nature. We are its producers as well as its inhabitants. However, under neoliberalism, the real subsumption of nature—its recreation in the image of capital and in the service of value—plunges more deeply into living things and becomes more totalizing. Through the "real subsumption of nature," biological life is being transformed in a variety of ways into surplus value (Cooper, 2017).

The biotech revolution is at the heart of this, and from the level of the microbe up to familiar livestock or even until recently wild-caught species, huge investments are moving into channeling evolution and reconfiguring life in the service of accumulation. Some of this represents another example of the appropriation of the dynamic, transformative, and self-reproductive force of life for capital, and some of it arises as a profit-friendly response to the ecological consequences of intensive, industrialized production. With the biotech revolution, we come full circle to the neoliberal dream of "every molecule on earth" being privately owned. The generative principles of life (the capacity for self-reproduction) become property, protected globally by agreements on the enforcement of intellectual property rights such as the TRIPS (Trade Related Intellectual Property) agreement of the World Trade Organization.

Take, for example, the AquAdvantage Salmon—the first genetically modified animal for human consumption. Clausen & Longo (2012) detail the sad history of the decline of wild salmon as that species became increasingly defined in commodity terms, and the corresponding shift from managing salmon for use value (as was the practice with many coastal First Nations) to managing to maximize exchange value. Various interventions aimed at overcoming the limits of salmon production (the availability of suitable spawning streams, and seasonality, for example) have been attempted historically to moderate population decline, mostly based on the proliferation of hatcheries, but adding eventually the newish innovation of industrial aquaculture. However, aquaculture itself was confronted with a number of significant snags and limits (and it still is), amongst which was the relatively poor efficiency of the conversion from feed to salmon bodyweight, and the resultingly large ecological footprint of farmed salmon. The AquAdvantage, which is a proprietary fish owned by AquaBounty Technologies, combines the Atlantic Salmon with genetic material from the ocean pout and the (Pacific) Chinook Salmon. This genetic reassembly enables the AquAdavantage Salmon to grow to adult size in 18 months, rather than the usual three years. Rather than taking salmon "as is," capital sees salmon as inefficient production machines, and turns its attention to enhancing it—"really subsuming" it—by improving its metabolic rate. This in turn is alleged to reduce the ecological footprint of aquaculture (since less feed—frequently derived from other fisheries—is needed to produce the same amount of salmon meat). Clausen and Longo call into question this alleged benefit, suggesting that the more likely result will be a continued upward increase in the quantity demanded of salmon, driven by the lower production costs of the AquAdvantage, and thus an overall increase in the fish-feed requirements of the industry. They also raise serious criticisms of the continued environmental and social concerns that come along with industrial salmon farming over and above their depletion of global fisheries (salmon farming currently consumes about 40 percent of global fish oil). While continuing to externalize the costs of aquaculture onto nearby First Nations communities and onto the environment, capital's focus must be on increased productive efficiency—resulting in what Clausen and Longo term "the tragedy of the commodity," in contrast to Hardin's alleged "tragedy of the commons." Fisheries, they argue, are much more heavily affected by the former than they are the latter.

However, the important question of whether or not the AquAdvantage Salmon, or the now defunct "Enviropig" (a pig genetically altered to produce much less phosphorus in its manure), function as advertised is perhaps secondary to the increasingly deep reach of capital's drive for efficiency, and its implication for how we understand and relate to non-human life. Biological processes are often more efficient, if properly channeled and tuned, than are machine processes. Animals and plants, having been subject to husbandry and breeding practices for centuries (or millennia), are easily reimagined as machines themselves, producing exchange value in a variety of forms. Kenneth Fish (2013) relates the case of Webster and Peter, "two goats engineered (in a partnership between the US Army, the Canadian Department of National Defense, and Nexia Biotechnologies) with a gene from an orb-weaving spider. The Bele goats produced 'silky milk' containing dragline spider-silk proteins. The goal was to weave the silk into BioSteel, a flexible, lightweight material five times stronger than steel" (2013, p. 4). Fish continues to enumerate the surprising ways in which animals and plants have been transformed into biological factories:

There were other goats—not to mention the cows and rabbits—producing human therapeutics in their milk, and chickens producing pharmaceuticals in their egg whites. ... Fields of safflower were growing with human genes in their oil bodies, and plants were in development that would produce plastics and other materials. And of course tiny transgenic bacteria had been plugging away since the 1980s, supplying the multi-billion dollar a year market for human insulin. (2013, p. 4)

Each of these "technologies" (and here again we see the ease with which that boundary is crossed) is proprietary. It is a living being whose method of generation is owned, and which exists for the sole purpose of producing privatized exchange value through the appropriation and ownership of its biological processes. In principle, we are not far from simple livestock husbandry. Most of the same claims can be made of any cow, which converts low-value feed into high-value protein to be sold for the benefit of the farmer. However, capitalism, unregulated and heavily subsidized by public funding and research, no longer takes the biology, instincts, or metabolic processes of the non-human as given, nor must it abide by the generational temporality of breeding practices. Non-human life is now manufactured for the purpose of manufacturing. Its value—or more accurately the value of the intellectual property its existence represents—is derivative of the exchange value it can be predicted to produce. Nature is rendered nakedly as capital.

Neoliberal nature and human flourishing

What, then, are we to take from these neoliberal transformations of nature? What does the neoliberal reconfiguration of the nature–society tangle mean for the possibility of human development and flourishing? One cannot with any degree of confidence discount the possibility that, in allowing neoliberal politics and reason to constitute nature, we will render it inhospitable or uninhabitable. There is, first of all, the raw and urgent question of what a warmer planet might look like. The consequences of a world that is 4 degrees Celsius warmer—the world to which we are currently heading by many estimates (see, for example, climateaction-tracker.org)—are indeed uncertain (particularly since that 4 degrees is an average global warming, masking considerable variation), but the models and what we've already seen so far of the consequences of changing climate suggest the foreclosure of a great deal of human potential. While the dangers of the often negative political consequences of giving in to "catastrophism" (despondency, apathy, authoritarianism) present one set of hazards, so too does ignoring or soft-pedaling the alarm bells being sounded by natural and systems scientists. Climate change has been a long time in the creation, but its signals have become much louder in the neoliberal age, and every shred of evidence we have so far suggests that neoliberalism, acutely aware of the issue, is utterly incapable of generating the kind of transformative change required if we are to face its challenge.

Capital's response began with (and in some parts of the world continues with) an organized campaign to deny the issue, morphing later into an attempt simply to introduce sufficient doubt to prevent political action (McCright & Dunlap, 2000; Oreskes & Conway, 2010). Capital continues—even while forced eventually into recognizing the reality of anthropogenic climate change—to work diligently and with all of its considerable organizational power behind the scenes to thwart effective climate action (Carroll & Daub, 2015). As the neoliberal dynamic of redistributing wealth and power upward continues, the disparity in organizational power between the super-rich and the rest of us also spreads (Hacker & Pierson, 2010). It is a widely recognized phenomenon (International Panel on Climate Change, 2014) that the rich are likely to be the last to feel the negative effects of climate change. Their ability to build privatized "climate proofed" spaces and dwellings is robust. An article in the design magazine *Dwell*, to take just one illustrative example, profiles a Queens, NY, couple who, following the wreckage of Hurricane Sandy, redesigned their about-to-be-built beachfront vacation home on Long Island to be more climate-resilient, raised (as per the Federal Emergency Management Agency's flood regulations) 14 feet above sea level, and wrapped in a hurricane-resistant armour-cladding. In claiming that the 2500-square-foot second home is "all about minimalism," the owners revealed not a shred of ironic awareness (Hopping, 2017). This kind of perfectly individualistic, *sauve qui peut* response to climate change is bound to be the first and possibly only reaction of the rich to rising sea levels and increasingly extreme weather—continuing to contribute to the problem while mobilizing resources to shield from the effects. Urbanists have begun to talk about "climate gentrification" (Keenan, 2017), wherein previously undesirable, but higher-elevation neighborhoods in counties like Miami-Dade are seeing a rise in property values as the rich move back from the waterfront. The same phenomenon, according to people like Jesse Keenan at the Harvard Graduate School of Design, is likely to occur for any properties coming to be classified as low-exposure, whether that exposure is to flood, wildfire, or hurricane (Schouten, 2017). The inequalities that are part-and-parcel of neoliberalism are not only horrific on their own terms but skew the experience of environmental hazard one way, and decision-making power the other in such a way as to scupper the prospects of an adequate political response to climate change. The only reasonable, non-utopian reaction to this from below is full-scale rebellion on every possible front.

There is additionally a more insidious consequence to neoliberalism's shaping of the relationship between society and non-human nature. As neoliberal forms of reason and calculation come to dominate even our "progressive" conversations about how we might possibly deal with climate change, we turn to what are perceived as politically palatable market-based tools—cap and trade (emissions trading) systems, markets in species habitat or nitrogen fixation. All of the latter require the conceptual and material remaking of nature as a set of distinct, divisible, alienable, and ultimately commodifiable assets. This is a fiction beyond even what Polanyi might have imagined, requiring a massive new wave of remappings, accountings, monitoring, certification, and verification in order to render nature and its "parts" as commodities credible enough for sale and purchase.

One of the charges frequently leveled at the Left during the political height of the 2008 financial crisis was that it had a failure of imagination: it had no viable model to compete with the one that produced the gross swindle of the crisis and the bailouts. Looking at this from a Polanyian perspective, our capacity to bring questions of production, need, and reproduction back into the political sphere, our capacity to re-embed production and exchange within the spheres of politics and society has atrophied under neoliberalism. The move towards making nature visible through its valuation and capitalization is part of a long-term tendency towards foreclosing on non-capitalist modes of decision-making. While this may seem a small thing in relation to the likelihood of impending climate catastrophe, it is not. Humans' relationship to non-human life, and even to landscapes, will be deeply, deeply impoverished should it be entirely mediated by capitalist valuation, and should access to the natural world be restricted through a pay-to-play regime of privatized spaces and experiences. The ability to enjoy public space, cared for in common; to develop oneself through interaction with the other kinds of life, with clean waters, clean soil, and clean air; to experience moments outside of the structures of contract or the authoritarian spaces of employment; and to conceive of the "web of life" as something to which we owe ethical and moral consideration, rather than as something either worthy of existence or not depending on its capacity to generate exchange value; these things are precious, and we argue central to long-term human flourishing. Should we fail in many local struggles to reconfigure the nature–society tangle in non-capitalist terms, outside of neoliberal reason, we have no hope of attaining even more pragmatic environmental goals like the preservation of biodiversity, reducing the spread of substances toxic to human and non-human life, clearing the oceans of plastics, preventing the draw-down of our aquifers, and maintaining the fertility of soil. If, as the UN's Food and Agriculture Organization claimed in 2014, the latter is reaching a serious crisis point (at current rates of degradation, we have about sixty years of topsoil left, according to the Food and Agriculture Organization of the United Nations (Arsenault, 2015)), the most pragmatic and essential form of interaction between human and non-human life—feeding ourselves—becomes a massively uncertain prospect. Without soil, the prospects for human flourishing vanish to a pinpoint.

Notes

1 Credit-Suisse estimates, however, that even where trigger events have occurred (Katrina, for example, or Fukushima), diversified cat bond portfolios lost only about 4 percent of their value.
2 This example is drawn from an actual cat bond circular, issued by MetroCat Re in partnership with GC Securities and Goldman Sachs in 2016. A list of cat bond offerings is conveniently available at the website of Artemis, a Bermuda-based information and analysis shop specializing in risk-transfer: www.artemis.bm/deal_directory/.
3 This appropriation of Coase is performed with the significant and selective omission of some crucial small print involving transactions costs which qualify the author's conclusions significantly.
4 Extractive interests in the US West have a long history of such efforts stretching back to the creation of federal public lands, notably including the Sagebrush Rebellion that spawned following the passage of the Federal Land Policy and Management Act in 1976.
5 The Clean Water Act was a series of sweeping amendments to the 1948 Federal Water Pollution Control Act.

References

ALEC. (2012). *Disposal and Taxation of Public Lands Act.* Retrieved July 13, 2017, from American Legislative Exchange Council: www.alec.org/model-policy/disposal-and-taxation-of-public-lands-act/.

Arsenault, C. (2015). *Only 60 Years of Farming Left if Soil Degradation Continues.* Retrieved September 17, 2007, from Scientific American: www.scientificamerican.com/article/only-60-years-of-farming-left-if-soil-degradation-continues/.

Bel, G., & Joseph, S. (2015). Emissions Abatement: Untangling the Effects of the EU-ETS and the Economic Crisis. *Energy Economics,* 49, 531–539.

Block, W., & Nelson, P. (2016). *Water Capitalism: The Case for Privatizing Oceans, Rivers, Lakes, and Aquifers.* Lanham, MD: Lexington Books.

Boyd, W., Prudham, S., & Schurman, R.A. (2001). Industrial Dynamics and the Problem of Nature. *Society and Natural Resources,* 14(7), 555–570.

Boyer, M. (2015). *Nature Materialities and Economic Valuation: Conceptual Perspectives and Their Relevance for the Study of Social Inequalities.* Berlin: Research Network on Interdependent Inequalities in Latin America. Retrieved from DesiguALdades.net.

Brander, L., & Schuyt, K. (2010). *Benefits Transfer: The Economic Value of World's Wetlands.* Geneva: The Economics of Ecosystems and Biodiversity.

Burford, A., & Greenya, J. (1986). *Are You Tough Enough?* Columbus, OH: McGraw Hill.

Butt, R. (1981). Mrs. Thatcher: the First Two Years (Interview with Margaret Thatcher), May 1. *The Sunday Times*. Retrieved December 14, 2017, from www.margaretthatcher.org/document/104475.

Butts, G. (1979). The Status of Exotic Big Game in Texas. *Rangelands*, 1(4), 152–153.

Cannon, L. (2003). *Governor Reagan: His Rise to Power.* New York: Public Affairs.

Carroll, W., & Daub, S. (2015). Why Corporate Power Is a Problem at the Climate Crossroads. Parkland Institute Blog. Retrieved November 25, 2018, from www.parklandinstitute.ca/why_corporate_power_is_a_problem_at_the_climate_crossroads.

Carson, R. (1962). *Silent Spring.* Boston: Houghton Mifflin.

Clark, B., & York, R. (2005). Carbon Metabolism: Global Capitalism, Climate Change, and the Biospheric Rift. *Theory and Society*, 34(4), 391–428.

Clausen, R., & Clark, B. (2005). The Metabolic Rift and Marine Ecology: An Analysis of the Ocean Crisis Within Capitalist Production. *Organization and Environment*, 18(4), 422–444.

Clausen, R., & Longo, S. (2012). The Tragedy of the Commodity and the Farce of AquAdvantage Salmon (R). *Development and Change*, 43, 229–251.

Coase, R. (2013 [1960]). The Problem of Social Cost. *Journal of Law and Economics*, 56(4), 837–877.

Coggins, G.C., & Nagel, D.K. (1989). The Legal Legacy of James G. Watts' Tenure as Secretary of the Interior on Federal Land Law and Policy. *Boston College Environmental Affairs Law Review*, 17, 473–550.

Colorado College State of the Rockies Project. (2016). *New Survey Separates Rhetoric from Reality When It Comes to Mountain West Voters' Support for National Public Lands.* Retrieved August 5, 2017, from Colorado College: www.coloradocollege.edu/dotAsset/10b5e54f-bd80–4b72–9390-cde2161bcefd.pdf.

Cooper, M. (2017). Open Up and Say "Baa": Examining the Stomachs of Ruminant Livestock and the Real Subsumption of Nature. *Society and Natural Resources*, 30(7), 812–828.

Costanza, R., & Daly, H. (1992). Natural Capital and Sustainable Development. *Conservation Biology*, 6, 37–46.

Dempsey, J. (2016). *Enterprising Natures: Economics, Markets, and Finance in Global Biodiversity Politics.* Hoboken: Wiley Blackwell.

Dennis, B., & Mooney, C. (2017). Neil Gorsuch's Mother Once Ran the EPA. It Didn't Go Well, February 1. *The Washington Post*. Retrieved June 10, 2017, from www.washingtonpost.com/news/energy-environment/wp/2017/02/01/neil-gorsuchs-mother-once-ran-the-epa-it-was-a-disaster/?utm_term=.6d34e362f23c.

Easterbrook, G. (2009). Privatize the Seas. *The Atlantic*, July/Aug, Retrieved May 13, 2017 from www.theatlantic.com/magazine/archive/2009/07/privatize-the-seas/307544/.

Fish, K. (2013). *Living Factories: Biotechnology and the Unique Nature of Capitalism.* Montreal and Kingston: McGill-Queen's University Press.

Forster, J. (2010). *Peatlands Restoration in Germany: A Potential Win-Win-Win Solution for Climate Protection, Biodiversity Conservation, and Land Use.* Geneva: The Economics of Ecosytems and Biodiversity.

Foster, J.B. (1999). Marx's Theory of Metabolic Rift: Classical Foundations for Environmental Sociology. *American Journal of Sociology*, 105(2), 366–405.

Foster, J.B. (2000). *Marx's Ecology*. New York: Monthly Review Press.

Furor Over Memo at World Bank. New York Times, Feb 7, 1992, p. 2.

Gómez-Baggethun, E., de Groot, R., Lomas, P.L., & Montes, C. (2010). The History of Ecosystem Services in Economic Theory and Practice: From Early Notions to Markets and Payment Schemes. *Ecological Economics*, 69, 1209–1218.

Gramling, B., & Freudenberg, B. (2010). Pay, Baby, Pay, April 30. *Pacific Standard*. Retrieved October 20, 2017, from https://psmag.com/economics/pay-baby-pay-3633.

Gramling, B., & Freudenberg, W. (2012). A Century of Macondo: United States Energy Policy and the BP Blowout Catastrophe. *American Behavioral Scientist*, 56(1), 48–75.

Guidestar. (2017). *Mountain States Legal Foundation*. Retrieved from Guidestar: www.guidestar.org/profile/84–0736725.

Hacker, J., & Pierson, P. (2010). Winner-Take-All Politics: Public Policy, Political Organization, and the Precipitous Rise of Top Incomes in the United States. *Politics and Society*, 38(2), 152–204.

Hirt, P. (1996). *A Conspiracy of Optimism: Management of the National Forests Since World War Two*. Lincoln: University of Nebraska Press.

Hopping, L. (2017). Shore Bet: Can Smarter Materials and Better Engineering Mitigate the Risks of Living near the Sea?, March/April. *Dwell*, 48–58.

Hudson, M. (2011). *Fire Management in the American West: Forest Politics and the Rise of Megafires*. Boulder: University of Colorado Press.

International Emissions Trading Association (IETA). (2017). *The World's Carbon Markets: A Case-Study Guide to Emissions Trading*. Retrieved December 14, 2017, from International Emissions Trading Association: www.ieta.org/the-worlds-carbon-markets.

International Panel on Climate Change. (2014). *Climate Change 2014: Impacts, Adaptation, and Vulnerability*. New York: Cambridge University Press.

Keenan, J.M. (2017). Sea Level Rise & Climate Gentrification: Why Relying on Building Code Reform and Insurance Markets Is Short-Sighted. In N. Clark (ed.), *Sea Level Rise and the Future of Our Coastal Settlements: Evolving Concepts in Urban and Cultural Adaptation to Changing Environments*. Rome: UNESCO.

Ketcham, C. (2014). *This Land Was Your Land*, February 4. Retrieved July 15, 2017, from The American Prospect: http://prospect.org/article/land-was-your-land.

Klement, J. (2016). *Catastrophe Bonds: Anything but a Catastrophe for Investors*. Retrieved June 7, 2017, from Credit-Suisse.com: www.credit-suisse.com/microsites/next/en/financial-literacy-expertise/articles/catastrophe-bonds-anything-but-a-catastrophe-for-investors.html.

MacKenzie, D. (2009). Making Things the Same: Gases, Emission Rights and the Politics of Carbon Markets. *Accounting, Organizations, and Society*, 34, 440–455.

MacLean, N. (2017). *Democracy in Chains: The Deep History of the Radical Right's Stealth Plan for America*. New York: Viking Books.

Marx, K. (1845). *The German Ideology*. Retrieved from Marxists.org: www.marxists.org/archive/marx/works/1845/german-ideology/ch01a.htm.

Marx, K. (1981a). *Capital* (Vol. 3). London: Penguin.

Marx, K. (1981b). *Capital* (Vol. 1). London: Penguin.

Marx, K. (1994 [1864]). *Marx & Engels Collected Works* (Vol. 34: Economic Works of Karl Marx 1861–1864). Trans. B. Fowkes. London: Lawrence & Wishart. Retrieved August 12, 2017, from www.Marxists.org.

McCright, A., & Dunlap, R. (2000). Challenging Global Warming as a Social Problem: An Analysis of the Conservative Movement's Counter-Claims. *Social Problems*, 47(4), 499–522.

McGowan, C.J., Kwok, R.K., Engel, L.S., Stenzel, M.R., Stewart, P.A., & Sandler, D.P. (2017). Respiratory, Dermal, and Eye Irritation Symptoms Associated with Corexit™ EC9527A/EC9500A following the Deepwater Horizon Oil Spill: Findings from the GuLF STUDY, September. *Environmental Health Perspectives*, 125(9). doi:https://doi.org/10.1289/EHP1677.

Middleton, R. (2007). Texotics, April. *Texas Parks and Wildlife Magazine*. Retrieved June 12, 2017, from https://tpwmagazine.com/archive/2007/apr/ed_3/.

Moore, J. (2015). *Capitalism in the Web of Life: Ecology and the Accumulation of Capital*. New York: Verso.

Morris, D. (2013). *New Emissions Data Builds Pressure to Rescue Europe's Failing Emissions Trading Scheme*, April 2. Retrieved June 14, 2017, from Sandbag: https://sandbag.org.uk/2013/04/02/new-emissions-data-builds-pressure-to-rescue-europes-failing-emissions-trading-scheme/.

Nash, R.F. (2014 [1967]). *Wilderness and the American Mind*. 5th edn. New Haven: Yale University Press.

NOAA. (2016). *The Tuna–Dolphin Issue*. Retrieved August 11, 2017, from National Oceanic and Atmospheric Administration: https://swfsc.noaa.gov/textblock.aspx?Division=PRD&ParentMenuId=228&id=1408.

Norgaard, R. (2010). Ecosystem Services: From Eye-Opening Metaphor to Complexity Blinder. *Ecological Economics*, 69(6), 1219–1227.

O'Connor, J. (1991). On the Two Contradictions of Capitalism. *Capitalism, Nature, Socialism*, 2(3), 107–109.

O'Connor, J. (1998). *Natural Causes: Essays in Ecological Marxism*. New York: Guilford Press.

Oreskes, N., & Conway, E. (2010). *Merchants of Doubt*. New York: Bloomsbury.

Ostrom, E. (2002). Common-Pool Resources and Institutions: Toward a Revised Theory. In B.L. Gardener & G.C. Rausser (eds), *Handbook of Agricultural Economics* (Vol. 2, pp. 1315–1339). Amsterdam: Elsevier.

Pilon, R. (1995). *Property Rights and Environmental Protection*, June 27. Retrieved from Cato Institute: www.cato.org/publications/congressional-testimony/property-rights-environmental-protection.

Polanyi, K. (1944 [1957]). *The Great Transformation*. Boston: Beacon Press.

Public Opinion Strategies/FM3. (2014). *Memorandum from POS/FM3 to Interested Parties, re: Western Voter Attitudes Towards Management of Public Lands*, September 23. Retrieved September 9, 2017, from American Progress: https://cdn.americanprogress.org/wp-content/uploads/2014/09/2014-Western-Voter-Attitudes-Toward-Management-of-Public-Lands_analysis.pdf.

Queensland Department of Environment and Heritage Protection. (2013). Queensland Environmental Offsets Policy. Retrieved November 30, 2018, from https://environment.des.qld.gov.au/assets/documents/pollution/management/offsets/offsets-policyv1-3.pdf.

Queensland Government. (2017). Koala Threats. Retrieved November 29, 2018, from https://environment.des.qld.gov.au/wildlife/koalas/koala-threats.html.

Republican National Committee. (2016). *Republican Platform: America's Natural Resources: Agriculture, Energy, and the Environment.* Retrieved September 9, 2017, from www.gop.com: www.gop.com/platform/americas-natural-resources.

Ripple, W. J., Wolf, C., Newsome, T. M., Alamgir, M. G. M., Crist, E., Mahmoud, M. I., Laurance, W, F., and 15,364 scientist signatories from 184 countries. (2017). World Scientists' Warning to Humanity: A Second Notice. *BioScience,* 67(12), 1026–1028.

Robbins, J. (2017). *With Trump, A Full-Scale Assault on Protections for U.S. Public Lands,* May 31. Retrieved June 4, 2017, from Yale Environment 360: http://e360.yale.edu/features/with-trump-a-full-scale-assault-on-protections-for-u-s-public-lands.

Robbins, W. (1982). *Lumberjacks and Legislators: Political Economy of the U.S. Lumber Industry 1890–1941.* College Station: Texas A&M Press.

Ruple, J. A. (2016). *Alternatives to the Transfer of Public Lands Act.* University of Utah, S.J. Quinney College of Law. Salt Lake City: Wallace Stegner Center for Land, Resources, and the Environment.

Russakoff, D. (1983). Denver Allies Became Keepers of the Rules They Had Attacked, March 3. *The Washington Post.* Retrieved July 10, 2017, from www.washingtonpost.com/archive/politics/1983/03/03/denver-allies-became-keepers-of-the-rules-they-had-attacked/109df6dc-81a4–4a08-b478-e1853a7cee5d/?utm_term=.830ed3e971fd.

Sandbag. (2018). *New Data: EU ETS Emissions Rise for First Time in Seven Years,* April 3. Retrieved April 4, 2017, from Sandbag: https://sandbag.org.uk/project/eu-emissions-rise-for-first-time-in-7-years/.

Schmalensee, R., & Stavins, R. (2012). *The SO2 Allowance Trading System: The Ironic History of a Grand Policy Experiment.* Cambridge, MA: National Bureau of Economic Research. Retrieved January 12, 2017, from www.nber.org/papers/w18306.

Schouten. (2017). *"Climate Gentrification" Could Add Value to Elevation in Real Estate,* December 28. Retrieved September 21, 2017, from CBS Moneywatch: www.cbsnews.com/news/climate-gentrification-home-values-rising-sea-level/.

Smith, S., van Ardenne, J., Klimont, Z., Andres, R., Volke, A., & Delgado Arias, S. (2011). Anthropogenic Sulfur Dioxide Emissions: 1850–2005. *Atmospheric Chemistry and Physics,* 11, 1101–1116.

Spencer, J., Boccia, R., & Gordon, R. (2014). *Environmental Conservation Based on Individual Liberty and Economic Freedom,* January 14. Retrieved August 17, 2017, from The Heritage Foundation: www.heritage.org/environment/report/environmental-conservation-based-individual-liberty-and-economic-freedom.

Streep, A. (2017). *Three Million Acres of Public Lands Are off the Market— For Now,* February 2. Retrieved February 2, 2017, from Outside Online: www.outsideonline.com/2154196/public-lands-safe-for-now.

Sukhdev, P. (2011). *Put a Value on Nature!* Retrieved from Ted.com: www.ted.com/talks/pavan_sukhdev_what_s_the_price_of_nature.

Sullivan, P. (2004). Anne Gorsuch Burford, 62, Dies; Reagan EPA Director, July 22. *The Washington Post*. Retrieved June 13, 2017, from www.washingtonpost.com/wp-dyn/articles/A3418–2004Jul21.html.

Taylor, D.E. (1997). American Environmentalism: The Role of Race, Class and Gender in Shaping Activism 1820–1995. *Race, Gender, and Class*, 5(1), 16–62.

US Department of the Interior, US Fish and Wildlife Service, and US Department of Commerce, US Census Bureau. (2011). *National Survey of Fishing, Hunting, and Wildlife Associated Recreation*. Washington DC: US Department of Interior.

US Energy Information Administration. (2017). *Today in Energy*, February 3. Retrieved December 4, 2017, from US EIA: www.eia.gov/todayinenergy/detail.php?id=29812.

US Government Accountability Office. (2007). GAO-07-676R Oil and Gas Royalties. Washington, DC: GAO, p. 2. Retrieved November 29, 2018, from www.gao.gov/new.items/d07676r.pdf.

Van Beukering, P., & Cesar, H. (2010). *Economic Valuation of the Coral Reefs of Hawai'i*. Geneva: The Economics of Ecosystems and Biodiversity.

Weisman, S.R. (1983). Watts Quits Post; President Accepts with "Reluctance.", October 10. *The New York Times*. Retrieved November 9, 2017, from www.nytimes.com/1983/10/10/us/watt-quits-post-president-accepts-with-reluctance.html?pagewanted=all.

Wildlife Partners LLC. (N.d.). History of Exotic Wildlife in Texas. Retrieved July 10, 2017 from www.wildlifepartners.com.

Williamson, J. (2012). *Memorandum from the Wyoming Office of the Attorney General, Water and Natural Resources Division to Jerimiah L. Rieman, Natural Resource Policy Advisor, re: Utah Transfer of Public Lands Act*. Retrieved June 15, 2017, from http://trib.com/ag-memo-on-taking-back-federal-lands/pdf_3ee3b765–09b8–5ba7–9d12–5f6ad934d692.html.

Zinke, R. (2016). *Memorandum for the President, re: Final Report Summarizing Findings of the Review of Designations under the Antiquities Act*. Retrieved February 5, 2017, from assets.documentcloud.org: https://assets.documentcloud.org/documents/4052225/Interior-Secretary-Ryan-Zinke-s-Report-to-the.html.

4

Health: US exceptionalism

The ability to live a full and flourishing life is severely constrained by poor health, and made literally impossible by death. For those suffering through the trials of chronic illness or with diminished physical capacity, a flourishing life is that much more difficult to realize. Retired janitor Geraldine Mayho suffers a bewildering array of undiagnosed ailments, from headaches to stomach aches and heart problems. The closest she has probably come to an accurate diagnosis was a doctor's note claiming that she suffered from exposure to "toxic substances." Six female relatives, who all live nearby, have been diagnosed with, or died from, breast cancer. One of her sons is infertile and another daughter died at 30 (Zanolli, 2017). It is probably safe to say that had Mayho and her family not suffered these health tragedies, their life would have been more flourishing. Mayho lives in Louisiana, the poorest state in the union, in "cancer alley," a 150-mile stretch between Baton Rouge and New Orleans that is home to 150 petrochemical and chemical facilities. It also has the highest cancer mortality rate in the US (Katz, 2012, p. 102). Unfortunately, Mayho's story is not an anomaly in the US.

The US has the worst health indicators among wealthy industrialized nations by almost all measures, and, prior to President Obama's Affordable Care Act (ACA) enacted in 2010, was the only industrialized nation without some form of universal healthcare insurance. US life expectancy is, according to the 2016 United Nations Human Development Index, 79.2 years, behind 36 other countries, including Costa Rica, Cuba, and Lebanon. In terms of mortality rates for children under five, it ranks a worrying forty-fourth just behind Bahrain and Hungary (United Nations, 2016). The US was ranked fourth highest out of 34 countries in potential life years lost through premature death. People in the US have higher rates of chronic disease than in other wealthy nations. Among the comparably rich countries, Americans had the second highest risk of dying from non-communicable disease and the fourth highest risk of dying from communicable (infectious) disease in 2008. The US also has relatively high rates of disease and disability (Woolf & Aron, 2013, p. 26). According to the OECD, in 2011 the United States ranked tenth highest out of the 34 countries for ischemic heart disease mortality. Most of the countries with higher rates than the United States were Eastern European countries such as Poland, Russia, and the Czech Republic. The US had the seventh highest rate of overall cancer incidence out of 40 nations in 2011 (although it fares much better in terms of cancer mortality rates) (OECD, 2011).

These results are not because of underfunding of the US healthcare system. The US spends more on healthcare in absolute and relative terms than any other affluent economy. In 2015 the US spent $9500 per person on health expenditure from all sources, the most in the OECD. The second highest, Switzerland, spent a much more modest $7,500. Relative to the overall size of the economy, the US spent 17 percent of its GDP on healthcare, again the highest among OECD nations. Switzerland, again in second place, only spent 12 percent (OECD, 2017). The question for the US is why it spends so much and achieves so little compared to other nations.

This chapter is about how class and power in the United States have determined its health outcomes and healthcare system. The core argument is that disease and death in all nations, including the US, are predominately structured and influenced by social and economic imperatives, not by irresistible laws of nature that are independent of socially determined political and economic factors (Cairns, 1971; Cassel, 1976; Chernomas, 1999; Chernomas and Donner, 2004; Dubos, 1965; Galdston, 1954; Navarro et al., 2003; Poland et al., 1998; Wilkinson, 1996). The specific evolution of neoliberal US capitalism has shaped these social conditions that influence health outcomes and the healthcare system that evolved to deal with them. It follows, then, that improving health in the US will require a change in the system of power, and in turn the conditions in which people live and work, as well as a restructured healthcare system.

In an international health context, the neoliberal capitalist system in the US should be viewed as a cautionary tale. As a result of the ability of social democratic countries to win redistributive policies, including an egalitarian healthcare system, and regulatory checks on business activities, people in these countries have superior health results (like lower infant mortality and longer life expectancy) than the US (Navarro et al., 2003; Raphael and Bryant, 2004; Birn et al., 2009). The wide variation of political and economic structures that exist between the social demo-cratic and neoliberal nations, among which the US is most likely the wealthy nation closest to the neoliberal end of the spectrum, suggests that, while the capitalist system does have inherent trends, there is still considerable scope for class politics—the conflict and collaboration of classes and groups—in each country to alter the conditions that create health problems and the health systems that deal with their outcomes.

The economic determinants of health

The historical record suggests that relatively poor health and early death are heavily influenced by economics and politics. This is the central thesis of what has become known as the Social Determinants of Health or Political Economy of Health, which argue that the way in which the economy operates, an individual's place in it, and the social and political systems that go with it, have a strong influence on health outcomes. In the words of a leading text on the subject, "a political economy of health approach uncovers how personal, household, social, political, and economic conditions interrelate at various levels to produce particular health circumstances and outcomes" (Birn et al., 2009, p. 140). According to Lester Breslow, former Director of Public Health for the State of California and UCLA professor of public health, "With all due respect to genetics and to theories that attribute chronic disease to senescence, it would be more rewarding to examine the changes that have occurred over the past half century in man's diet, habits, forms of work, and physical surroundings" (cited in Dubos, 1965).

An early scholar in this tradition, Thomas McKeown, argued that it was income gains, and the corresponding increase in nutrition, not medical cures, that were responsible for defeating the epidemics of infectious disease that ravaged populations until the early 1900s. His most telling piece of evidence was that medical interventions, like vaccines, arrived after the decline in infectious disease rates (McKeown and Record, 1962; McKeown et al., 1975; McKeown, 1976a; McKeown, 1976b; McKeown, 1979). Economic historian Robert Fogel's research using height and weight data came to similar conclusions, finding that almost the entire reduction in mortality during the 1800s was due to improved nutrition (Fogel 1997; Fogel 2004).

The findings of McKeown and Fogel were qualified by other researchers, not because of their downplaying of the importance of the medical solutions but because their focus on income gains was seen as too narrow. Other researchers have pointed out that it is not merely income gains that defeated infectious disease but, crucially, the uses to which those income gains were put. For example, massive public health projects like sewer systems, fresh drinking water, and swamp drainage improved the conditions in which people lived, as did broader health measures, like occupational safety and health regulations, fledgling social welfare, and child labor laws (Szreter, 1988; Szreter, 2002a; Szreter, 2002b; Szreter, 2003, Szreter, 2004a; Szreter, 2004b). Similarly, health outcomes started to improve only once income gains started to be distributed broadly among the population, highlighting the importance of the distribution of income as opposed to merely income growth. In keeping with the general thesis of this book, we argue that the extent to which the majority of the population will benefit from income gains depends crucially on the power relationships between workers and their employers as outlined in Chapter 2. In early industrial capitalism in the US, both the political and judicial arms of the state acted time and again to suppress the claims of workers and supported those of capital. This was true when troops were used to ensure that replacement workers could safely be used to break strikes, and when workers were denied compensation for injuries in the courts. Infectious disease was prominent when political and economic structures favored capital at the expense of labor so blatantly that it left a large portion of the working population virtually at death's door. In the US, as in other countries, economic growth was channeled to working class incomes, civic improvements, and better working conditions only when the populace became sufficiently mobilized that they created pressure for a redistribution of the income towards these purposes. It was resistance by labor that created a more liveable workday, child labor laws, a higher wage and the resulting improvements in nutrition and housing that improved health outcomes in the early 1900s (Chernomas & Hudson, 2013).

If we take seriously the idea that the environment in which people work and live has a crucial impact on their health, then neoliberal policies are literally unhealthy. In analyzing how the US policy environment impacts health, it is possible to make two different comparisons. The first is that US economic policy has historically been closer to the neoliberal end of the spectrum than that of almost all other nations. The second is that, as we highlighted in other chapters, the US has adopted increasingly neoliberal policies since 1980. As a result, the US is a relatively neoliberal country in a relatively neoliberal period. If our twin claims that, first, the economic determinants of health are important and that, second, neoliberal policies create worse determinants of health, it follows that the US should have worse health measures relative to other countries and that this gap has worsened after 1980.

Let us start with demonstrating that the economic determinants of health are important. To some, this may be stating the obvious. A person growing up in poverty, unable to afford nutritious food, living in sub-standard housing and navigating a neighborhood filled with environmental hazards is less likely to enjoy rude health than someone reveling in more welcoming living conditions. Broad evidence about the importance of living conditions certainly comes from the increase in life expectancy as countries' incomes increase. However, it might be worth highlighting how particular economic and social conditions can lead to adverse health outcomes.

Poorer people have poorer health. Wealthier people have a lower incidence of high blood pressure and of cholesterol, and tend to live longer. In a 2008 study of 16 developed nations, every one showed that mortality decreased with income for both men and women. This result held for virtually all causes of death. Most of the illnesses responsible for the decreases in longevity of the poor were not correctable with health interventions, placing the emphasis clearly on societal conditions rather than revising the medical system. Poorer children grow up in more challenging environments, including increased crowding, poorly maintained schools, and inferior housing. They also grow up in more stressful psychosocial contexts, with greater crime, violence, and family turmoil. Studies have found that this more challenging upbringing leads to increased levels of stress, and to deficits in academic achievement, which increase as children age, and then translate into lower occupational success (Evans et al., 2011). People with higher education levels tend to earn higher incomes and have greater occupational success. In the US, the risk of stroke is 80 percent lower for those with some university education than those without a high school diploma. People who had not completed high school had an incidence of diabetes of 13.2 percent compared to adults with a bachelor's degree, at 6.4 percent. Once people reach 25, college graduates live five years longer than those who do not finish high school. If every person in the US were to have the mortality rate of those who attended (not even graduated) university, it would save seven times as many lives as all biomedical advances (Woolf, 2011, p. 1902). The incidence of cardiac arrest in four big US cities is almost double in the poorest 25 percent of neighborhoods than in the richest quartile (Reinier et al., 2011). In the US, between 2001 and 2014, the difference in life expectancy between the richest 1 percent and poorest 1 percent of men was 14.6 years. For women the gap was 10.1 years (Chetty et al., 2016). As Harvey Brenner confidently declared, "It is now among the firmest of epidemiological findings ... higher income has been routinely shown to be a significant inverse predictor of morbidity and mortality" (2005, p. 1215).

Even for those not living in poverty, health outcomes deteriorate as income inequality increases. A study examining health indicators, such as mortality, health status, and activity limitation, of both children and adults found a clear health gradient between the wealthiest, middle, and lowest income groups (Braverman et al., 2010). Income inequality is strongly associated with a variety of health measures such as age-adjusted death rates, low birth weight, crime rates, and incarceration rates (Poland et al., 1998, p. 790). In the tribute to equality *The Spirit Level*, one of the many scores on which more equal societies outperform less equal ones is on health (Wilkinson and Pickett, 2009). In the US, people live four years longer in more equal states. Internationally, looking at 23 wealthy countries, infant mortality is lowest among countries that have the lowest income inequality (Navarro et al., 2003). A study attempting to explain the improved health performance of Canada relative to the United States over the last 50 years concluded that Canada's greater income equality and public healthcare provision were the two dominant factors (Hertzman and Siddiqi, 2008). The loss of common purpose, perceptions of unfairness, disrespect, and lack of trust that evolve from inequality of income may in turn result in inequalities in health outcomes. Even health results that would seemingly be the result of lifestyle choices are heavily influenced by the broader economic context in which people live. Recent research has linked obesity to economic insecurity. Obesity is one-third higher in countries like the US and Canada than it is in countries like Norway and Sweden. The weight difference was not due to Scandinavians' greater love of sport, or increased availability of fast food in the US. Rather, the authors find that it is the stress of life in an economic environment without a social safety net that contributes to obesity in the Anglo nations (Offer et al., 2010). People live longer and enjoy healthier lives where income inequality is the smallest.

The kind of work people do also affects their health even beyond its crucial role in providing income. Negative health results appear more frequently for those at the lower end of the labor spectrum. In contrast to popular belief, stress is not an executives' disease, despite the supposed pressure at the top of the corporate hierarchy. Poor health results related to stress are linked to frustration and lack of control in the work environment, and these are found much more often at the lower ends of the job hierarchy than they are higher up. In fact, stress exists in higher proportions among the lower echelons of organizations. Evidence suggests that those who can make decisions actually have less stress, while those who have less autonomy over their work life generate increased adrenal hormones and fat energy. This associates work stress with high-effort, low-reward conditions. Jobs that rank high on an effort-to-reward scale are associated with a variety of poor health results, but are most strongly associated with increased incidence of coronary heart disease, especially among middle-aged males (Marmot et al., 2006, p. 116). Stress hormones can make the blood "sticky" and may eventually over long periods of time degrade the immune system, make tumors grow faster and harden the arteries (Epstein, 1998). High-demand and low-control jobs have been linked to increases in coronary heart disease, as well as increased incidence of psychological strain and more minor illness, even when the classic "behavioral" factors are taken into account (Marmot et al., 2006, p. 107). Between 1997 and 2001, professionals in England and Wales lived an average of 8.4 years longer than manual workers (Cutler et al., 2006, p. 99). Further, the number of health-related problems is higher for manual workers, and these unequal results persist even when the differences in behavior of the two groups (professionals eat better—again begging the question why this is the case) are taken into consideration (Cutler et al., 2006, p. 113). A clerk, stuck in a stressful routine, who is subject to another's authority, suffers from a very different sort of stress than an executive who has too many appointments in a day where they will exercise significant authority.

"Behavioral" choices like smoking or diet influence health outcomes. Although what you eat is clearly a choice, it is misleading to refer to these decisions without reference to the context in which they are made. To take one, particularly topical, decision, dietary choices are influenced and constrained by income, time pressure and food availability, so it is more complicated than simply suggesting that people should choose a small quinoa salad rather than the fried onion ring burger. In the US, changes in diet have had conflicting effects on health. On one hand, the reduction in cholesterol has contributed to a decline in coronary heart disease. However, this beneficial effect is being partially offset by negative impact of the increase in the body-mass index of the US population (Ford et al., 2007). Given the link between diet and chronic disease, recent trends in US food consumption have experts concerned about an obesity "epidemic." Since the 1990s, total calories, saturated fat and absolute fat consumption in the US have all increased rapidly for both adults and children (Dubois, 2006, p. 142). However, these trends vary considerably for different groups in society. Higher-income groups have healthier diets (Dubois, 2006, p. 143). As a result, low-income earners have higher rates of diet-related diseases than those who have more money (Thirlaway and Upton, 2009, p. 58). The proliferation of obesity certainly disproportionately affects the poor (Drewnowski and Specter, 2004; Dixon, 2009; Drewnowski, 2009; Popkin, 2009). The reason for this is not simply that the poor eat poorly. Rather, it is the combined result of food affordability and availability in the context of profound income inequality, which gives rise to what one study referred to as "the neoliberal diet" (Otero et al., 2015). When the cheapest food is high-calorie and nutritionally poor, diet is less an individual choice and more a structural feature of the economic landscape.

The cost of different types of food in the US is not inevitable. Nor is it the result of market forces. Rather it is the result of the policy environment surrounding food production. In Chapter 1, we argued that neoliberalism is more than merely the withdrawal of the state to leave the logic of the market as the dominant mechanism for production and distribution, although this is certainly part of it. Rather neoliberalism also involves intervening on the side of business in a variety of ways. In food production this manifests itself in the insertion of the government through widespread subsidization of particular kinds of agriculture coupled with the withdrawal of the state from its protective role of regulatory oversight. In food production, the state is particularly heavily involved in subsidizing animal feed, sugar, and fat, all of which are prominent inputs into a high-calorie, fast-food diet (Freeman, 2007, p. 2245). Corn and soybeans are also highly subsidized, which has resulted in their use in processed food, including high-fructose corn syrup (Otero, Pechlaner, Liberman, & Gürcan, 2015). According to the Union of Concerned Scientists, if government shifted funding to promoting fruits and vegetables, it could prevent around 127,000 deaths per year from cardiovascular diseases and save $17 billion in annual national medical costs (Union of Concerned Scientists, 2013).

The second neoliberal component in food production is the withdrawal of regulation. To take just one example, artificial food coloring and flavoring are popular in the food industry because they are a low-cost method of creating visual appeal. For example, food coloring is used to make oranges more orange. The bright colors made possible by dyes are especially popular in food targeted at children. Over 17 million pounds of food dyes were produced in the US in 2005 for goods as diverse as candy, baked goods, and beverages. Of the nine food dye colors permitted in the US in 2013, Norway bans three, Finland two, and France and Austria one each (Kim, 2013). The prevalence of food additives like dyes comes despite nagging worries among many in the scientific community that they have links to cancer. One review of the literature claims "artificial dyes may be involved in chemical induced carcinogenesis due to their mutagenic properties" (Irigaray et al, 2007, p. 651). A 2015 study that quantified the amount of dyes contained in US processed foods found that they were present in surprisingly high amounts, making it quite likely that children were consuming a larger quantity than had been subject to testing and considered safe (Stevens et al., 2015). Similarly, carcinogens are present in many foods including growth hormones (such as Carbadox, used in pork production, and Revlar, used in beef production) and nitrites used in preserved meats such as hot dogs to keep them looking pink and fresh longer. The nitrites combine with amines which are naturally present in the meat to form N-Nitrosodimethylamine, classified by the International Agency for Research on Cancer as a probable human carcinogen. Studies have linked consumption of hot dogs more than once per week to increased brain cancers and leukemia in children. Children whose mothers ate hot dogs more than once per week while they were pregnant have also been found to have increased rates of cancer (Epstein 1998, pp. 574–576).

Yet, in keeping with the neoliberal tenet of reducing regulation that increases costs to firms, the agency tasked with ensuring that food and drugs are safe for human consumption, the Food and Drug Agency (FDA), has been whittled down substantially starting in the early 1980s. Like other protective regulatory agencies (such as the Environmental Protection Agency, which was discussed in Chapter 3) a wide range of tactics were used to limit the scope of regulatory oversight of the FDA. Agencies were populated with political appointees, especially during the Republican years, which usually resulted in a head ideologically opposed to the very mandate of the particular organization. Budgets were slashed, limiting their ability to monitor and enforce their regulatory mandate. The FDA budget was cut by 30 percent between 1981 and 1984, and its enforcement orders declined by 88 percent (Blyth, 2002, pp. 181–185). In 2006, a subcommittee reviewing the FDA Science Board concluded that the agency was "not prepared to meet regulatory responsibilities," due to "insufficient workforce capacity and capability" in part because after inflation its budget was $300 million less in 2007 than it was in 1998 (Reuben, 2010, p. 20). Under neoliberalism, regulatory agencies relied much more heavily on collaborative relationships with the industries they were supposed to be supervising. The trend of businesses influencing the activities of regulatory agencies became so prevalent that one study argues that it is the "modus operandi of at least a large proportion of corporations in the United States" (Bohme et al., 2005, p. 338). A study examining nutrition-related health problems in the US found that much of the blame could be traced to the fact that the "food industry seems to exert a big influence on the development of food policies" (Dubois, 2006, p. 138).

The controversy surrounding Vioxx, a drug used to treat chronic pain, is an infamous example of the dangers of this trend. It was pulled from the market because it increased the risk of heart attack and stroke. The scientist whose research exposed the dangers of Vioxx, Dr David Graham, who worked in the FDA's Office of Drug Safety, estimated that "Vioxx killed some 60,000 patients—as many … as died in the Vietnam War" (Herper, 2005). During the 1990s, the Clinton administration allowed the drug companies to fund drug trials for the FDA. This was touted as having industry foot the bill for testing from which it benefits. Yet Graham argued that it also created a conflict of interest because the funder of safety research has a vested interest in the outcome. Graham's research on the dangers of Vioxx was not welcomed by his employers at the FDA. His supervisors described his work as "scientific rumor," and his director called the study "junk science" in an attempt to defend both the safety of Vioxx and the industry-friendly testing process at the FDA that had declared the drug safe (Graham, 2004). Graham's prescription for FDA reform is to restore the independence of publicly funded testing. "People should turn to Congress and demand a drug safety system that is free from corporate influence—and a distinct center for drug safety" (Herper, 2005).

Finally, health is impacted by the environment in which people live. Chapter 3, which examines the neoliberal response to environmental issues more generally, argues that neoliberalism has resulted in a deterioration of the capacity and willingness to confront ecological issues. This has resulted in an increase in exposure to health-decreasing environmental hazards, from the local dangers of polluted sites to hazards associated with specific products like lead, to those that travel far and wide like airborne pollutants. People in the US are being exposed to an increasing number of chemicals that cause tumors in animals. At least 29 of these chemicals are produced in quantities of at least one million pounds per year. The International Agency for Research on Cancer investigated 880 industrial substances between 1972 and 2003 to determine the likelihood that they were carcinogenic. It classified 89 of these as definite, a further 64 to be likely, and another 264 as possible carcinogens (Clapp et al., 2007, p. 638).

In one telling example of the prevalence of chemicals, Andrea Martin, who died of cancer, was a participant in a study on Biomonitoring by the Center for Disease Control, led by researchers from Mt. Sinai School of Medicine in 2003. Martin had at least 95 toxic chemicals in her system, 59 of which were cancer-causing. Martin said at the time, "I was shocked at the breadth and variety of the number of chemicals. I was outraged to find out that without my permission, without my knowledge, my body was accumulating this toxic mixture." The chemicals in her body were accumulated in the common acts of consuming everyday products and living a very average life in California (Malkan, 2003). In another example, PBS journalist Bill Moyers and eight other volunteers were tested for the presence of chemicals, pollutants, and pesticides in their blood and urine. None of the volunteers worked in jobs that would obviously place them at risk of contamination or worked with chemicals, yet they had an average of 91 compounds in their bodies, most of which did not even exist 75 years ago. More worryingly, on average, 53 of the chemicals were linked to cancer in humans or animals (Environmental Working Group, 2003).

Further, although considerable uncertainty exists linking specific chemicals to particular health problems, there is more general evidence that increased exposure to pollutants increases the risk of cancer. To provide just one example from the US, a survey of 500,000 people showed that residents in areas with the worst air pollution were about 30 percent more likely to develop lung cancer than those in cities with clean air (Davis, 2007, p. 229). Similarly, children in high-traffic areas had higher rates of leukemia (Irigaray et al, 2007, p. 648). Studies have also linked increases in prostate, kidney, testis, breast, and lung cancers to increased exposure to industrial chemicals (Faber and Krieg, 2002, p. 279). These studies are only a small sample of the growing evidence that links environmental conditions with negative health impacts.

In keeping with the neoliberal trends analyzed elsewhere in this book, the 2010 report by the President's Cancer Panel argued that the regulatory oversight of chemicals in the US is compromised by, among other issues, inadequate funding and staffing, weak regulations, and undue industry influence (Reuben, 2010, p. ii). Perhaps at an even more fundamental level, one of the ways in which this has manifested itself is a lack of effort in understanding the link between production methods, environmental exposures, and health. To take cancer as one example, detecting the environmental links to cancer has been given a very low funding priority, especially compared to studies that focus on genetic causes. In 2008, only 14 percent of the National Cancer Institute budget was spent on occupational or environmental research (Reuben, 2010, p. 5). The President's Cancer Panel also expressed concern over the number of new chemicals and the extent to which these have been tested for safety. By 2010 "only a few hundred of the more than 80,000 chemicals in use in the United States have been tested" (Reuben, 2010, p. ii). As a result, exposures to cancer-causing agents and the manner in which different contaminants interact to impact health remain virtually unstudied.

The health impacts of environmental problems are not distributed evenly across income groups. It is most often the less affluent members of the working class who live in hazardous proximity to adverse environmental conditions. In Massachusetts, 368 communities were ranked based on their exposure to environmental hazards from a wide variety of industrial sources. All but one of the 15 most "intensively burdened towns" had an average household income of under $40,000. There was also a pronounced racial gradient. Only 20 towns in Massachusetts had a non-white population of over 15 percent. Yet of these 20 towns, nine were among the 15 most burdened. The study concludes that "the communities most heavily burdened with environmentally hazardous industrial facilities and sites are overwhelmingly low-income towns and/or communities of color" (Faber and Krieg 2002, p. 286). Another study in Tampa found that persons in poverty lived in neighborhoods located closer to sites on the toxic release inventory (Stuart, Mudhasakul, & Sriwatanapongse, 2009). Similarly, a study looking at US census tracts concluded that people living under the poverty line had higher exposure to airborne particulate matter (Bell & Ebisu, 2012).

Public health is improved when food is safer and the environment in which we live contains fewer pollutants. Health results are much worse for those at the lower ends of both the workplace and the income hierarchy. Finally, for high-income countries, higher levels of inequality are associated with poorer health results. Given these facts, it is little surprise that the US ranks poorly in health outcomes. Beginning in the late 1970s, the political and economic structure in the US was dramatically transformed in response to falling corporate profitability in a manner that worsened every one of these factors.[1]

Evidence seems to suggest that the relatively neoliberal US not only fares worse than other countries when it comes to health, but that during its more neoliberal period it has fallen further behind and health inequalities within the US have become more pronounced. Turning first to growing inequality within the US, one study created a county-level "deprivation index" consisting of 11 indicators based on education, occupation, wealth, income distribution, unemployment, poverty, and housing. It found that, between the early 1980s and 2000s, there was a larger difference in the index between the most and least deprived countries. Although infant mortality has fallen in the US during this period, the gap between most and least deprived has grown. The infant mortality rate of the most-deprived group was 1.43 times the least deprived in 1980 but by 2000 it had increased to 1.63 times. Life expectancy at birth in 1980–82 for the least-deprived group was 2.8 years longer than for the most-deprived group but by 1998–2000 it had increased to 4.5 years (79.2 to 74.7 years). Importantly, the authors of the study explicitly connect the neoliberal contraction of protective public spending at the local level to the growing gap in deprivation levels. "County-level deprivation levels are strongly associated with lower local government spending on a variety of infrastructural resources (such as public safety, fire protection, social and welfare services, education, affordable housing, and employment)" (Singh & Siahpush, 2006, p. 977). This widening health gap did not end in the early 2000s. Between 2001 and 2014 the life expectancy for those in the top 5 percent of income earners increased by 2.34 years for men and 2.91 years for women. By contrast life expectancy in the bottom 5 percent remained virtually unchanged, increasing only by 0.32 years for men and 0.04 years for women (Chetty et al., 2016). The health gap between income groups is also higher in the US than in other nations (Woolf & Aron, 2013, p. 35).

A considerable stir was caused when life expectancy actually fell in the US between 2014 and 2015. The decline was not particularly large, from 78.9 to 78.8 years, but it is extraordinary given that life expectancy usually falls only in times of serious crisis, like the AIDS epidemic in the US or the economic collapse in Russia following the fall of communism (Squires, 2017). Also in stark contrast to both historical and international trends, the mortality (deaths per 1000) and morbidity (incidence of disease) rates of white, non-Hispanic US adults between 45 and 55 increased by a half a percent a year between 1998 and 2013. This increase was particular to both this ethnicity and this age demographic. Older white non-Hispanics and Hispanic whites between 45 and 55 and over 55 had declines in mortality consistent with historical and international trends. The study that uncovered this worrying trend estimated that, if the mortality rate had declined at its historical rate from 1979 to 1998 of 1.8 percent per year, rather than increasing, 488,500 deaths would have been avoided between 1999 and 2013 (Case & Deaton, 2015).

This startling finding begged an explanation. One account focused on the increase in "deaths of despair" among the white, low-income population. Deaths by drug, alcohol and suicide for the white, non-Hispanic 50–54 population increased from around 30 per 100,000 to 80 between 1990 and 2015. Further, while these causes of death increased only very slightly for the 50–54 age group with a four-year college degree during this period, they increased most dramatically for those with a high-school degree or less (Case & Deaton, 2017). The average mortality rate from these three causes between 2006 and 2014 was 36 per 100,000 for the least economically distressed counties but 49 per 100,000 in the most distressed. Further, many of the counties with the highest mortality rates experienced significant declines in manufacturing employment over the last several decades (Monnat, 2016). As concerning as the "death by despair" hypothesis may be, it represents only a partial explanation for the increase in white working-age mortality. Taking a broader cohort of 25–64-year-old, working-age whites, excess deaths due to causes other than substance abuse and suicide also increased at an alarming rate, from almost 0 per 100,000 in 2000 to over 35 by 2015. The conclusion is that the increase in "deaths by despair" has coincided with worsening trends for a wide variety of heath conditions (Squires, 2017).

In the beginning of the chapter we showed that health in the US lags behind other wealthy nations. Although this is a longstanding deficit, it has been growing worse during the neoliberal period. Although life expectancy increased in the US between 1980 and 2006, it did so more slowly than in almost every other high-income country (Woolf & Aron, 2013, p. 22). In comparison with 21 other high income countries, the life expectancy at birth for US males ranked fourth from the bottom in 1980 but fell to the very last by 2007. For women, the US ranked around the middle of the 21 nations in 1980 but fell to the bottom in 2006. This result holds even after the higher US infant mortality rate is taken into account. For example, life expectancy at age 50 (the age you are expected to live to once you reach age 50) increased by 2.5 years in the US, but by an average of 3.9 years in nine other high-income countries between 1980 and 2007. Over-50 life expectancy in Japan increased by 6.4 years during this period. In 1980 the US over-50 life expectancy ranked around the middle of the rich country ranking but by 2007 it had dropped into the bottom 20 percent (Woolf & Aron, 2013, pp. 36–38).

Learning from others: improving the economic determinants of health

The contemporary US is more unequal, its employment conditions more precarious, and its environmental oversight less stringent than the pre-1980 US. It is also broadly true that places where income and resources (such as healthcare, education and family-supportive services) are more equally distributed have better health outcomes (Navarro et al., 2004, p. 222). It follows that improving the economic and social environment in which people live in the US would drastically improve people's health. Although other nations face pressure from many of the same neoliberal trends as the US, they were historically further away from the neoliberal end of the economic policy spectrum and better able to resist the neoliberal trends over the last three decades. As a result, their nations are more equal, have stronger universal public services, like education, more generous social welfare policies and tougher regulations.

The difference between the US and Europe's regulation of chemicals is a telling example. In contrast to the limited US regulatory regime surrounding chemicals in food and the environment, the European Union implemented the Registration, Evaluation and Authorization of Chemicals (REACH) directive. The REACH directive represents an upheaval in the basic philosophy of chemical regulation, flipping the American presumption of "innocent until proven guilty" on its head by placing the burden of proof on manufacturers to prove chemicals are safe, using what is known as the "precautionary principle" (Sachs, 2009). REACH contains several improvements over the way chemicals are treated in the US. All substances sold in Europe have to be registered, which requires increasingly stringent toxicity testing with the quantity of the product sold. According to one evaluation, it is, so far, the "largest effort in history to collect comprehensive toxicity data for chemicals." Without the toxicity data, the product is not allowed to be sold in Europe (Sachs, 2009). The chemical industry has complained about how much REACH would cost to implement. Industry studies estimated the cost at $19 billion (€13 billion) over eleven years, but other organizations put forward much lower estimates. Even an upper-range cost of $1.4 billion per year, almost that provided by the industry study, would represent only 0.2 percent of yearly revenues of the European chemical industry. Further, in implementing REACH, the European Union anticipates that many of the costs would be offset over time by profits generated from safer alternatives. More importantly, the European Union estimated that the health benefits would add up to around €50 billion over the 30 years following REACH's implementation (Commission of the European Communities, 2003).

As we highlighted in Chapter 2, during the neoliberal period the US has increasingly withdrawn social protection that maintains people's non-work incomes. In that chapter we focused on the switch from the AFDC to TANF but that same trend affected a wide variety of programs. The US was not alone in clawing back these kinds of protections, but they started at a lower level than most other countries, and the declines have often been more marked. If the condition in which people live is an important determinant of their health then these changes should have negative health impacts. Evidence suggests this is the case. A study comparing the differences in life expectancy between the US and 17 other OECD countries estimated that, if the US increased the level of its welfare state spending (defined as the generosity and coverage of unemployment insurance, sickness benefits, and public pension programs) to the average of the other nations in the study, life expectancy in the US would increase by 3.77 years (Beckfield & Bambra, 2016). Elizabeth Bradley and Lauren Taylor, of Yale University, took the economic determinants of health seriously and broadened the definition of health spending to include "social services, like rent subsidies, employment-training programs, unemployment benefits, old-age pensions, family support and other services that can extend and improve life." They found that, in 2005, the US devoted 29 percent of GDP to health and social services combined, while comparator countries (Sweden, France, the Netherlands, Belgium and Denmark) spent 33 percent to 38 percent of their GDP. In addition, the US is one of only three countries to spend the majority of its health and social services budget on healthcare, narrowly defined, rather than social services. Bradley and Taylor found that countries with low social spending relative to healthcare had lower life expectancy and higher infant mortality than peer countries that reversed these priorities. They conclude, "It is Americans' prerogative to continually vote down the encroachment of government programs on our free-market ideology, but recognizing the health effects of our disdain for comprehensive safety nets may well be the key to unraveling the 'spend more, get less' paradox. Before we spend even more money, we should consider allocating it differently" (Bradley & Taylor, 2013).

Health outcomes are the products of historically specific, socially determined production and distribution conditions. In the US these conditions have deteriorated under neoliberal capitalism. A 2008 report by the World Health Organization Commission on the Social Determinants of Health argues that health is shaped by the conditions in which "people grow, work, live and age." As the World Health Organization points out in its executive summary, "social justice is a matter of life and death" (World Health Organization, 2008).

Improving health requires changing these conditions. Other countries have done so. The US should improve the regulatory capacity of agencies that protect people's health, similar to the REACH policy in Europe. It should create a more egalitarian society using a combination of taxes, social welfare-policies, and labor-market measures to increase access to services by those lower down on the income distribution.

These policies are ambitious because they would mark a profound reversal of current US policy. There is little evidence on the horizon that a nation that has failed to pass any meaningful progressive legislation since the mid-1980s is about to start now. However, they are also realistic, having been enacted in other nations. These already existing alternatives are more effective, efficient, and egalitarian than the policies currently in place in the US. These policies would unquestionably represent a 180-degree turn from the general direction of US policy over the last forty years. Yet, continuing down the slippery slope that is current US economic and health policy will result in worsening health and earlier mortality. The food people eat, the environment in which they live, and the conditions of their work would continue to cause the health of people in the US, especially those at the lower ends of the socio-economic spectrum, to fall further behind other nations. While no healthcare system could possibly compensate for these problems, the current system in the US is singularly poorly equipped to do so.

The Affordable Care Act: neoliberal healthcare

Healthcare focuses on the production and distribution of specific goods and services that are seen as being directly related to health status (Evans, 1984, p. 3). The healthcare system in most countries is a mixture of different types of ownership. In the United Kingdom, the National Health Service established in 1948 was a single-payer, universal healthcare system, where hospitals were owned by the state. In Canada, hospitals are independent non-profits, where basic medical services are paid for and financed by the state through universal public insurance. In the United States, hospitals are run by for-profit corporations, non-profits, and even the state through the Veterans Administration. Health insurance is provided through the public Medicare and Medicaid programs, private companies, often through employers, and out-of-pocket payments.

There are two key differences between the US and the rest of the industrialized world. First, the US has relied far less on a government-led or regulated plan of universal insurance coverage. In every other industrialized country there is a guarantee that, no matter how the rest of the healthcare system is owned and organized, its citizens will have complete coverage for necessary physician and hospital services. All of these other nations have deliberately removed access to healthcare from the realm of the market. The logic behind this, at its most fundamental level, is that access to medical services should not be determined by an individual's ability to pay either directly for the health services or through insurance premiums. The second difference is that the US relies more heavily on the private, for-profit sector to deliver its healthcare than other wealthy nations.

We have already seen that the amount spent on healthcare per person (or as a percentage of GDP) is highest in the US system that relies more heavily on the market. Part of the reason for this increased overall cost is spending on health insurance administration. In contrast to a publicly funded single-payer insurance system (like Canada), the US system of private insurance is unnecessarily expensive. The administrative costs (the amount above that paid out for medical care) of insurance made up 5.9 percent of total healthcare costs in the US compared with 1.9 percent in Canada. Further, within the US, the overhead of private insurance was 11.7 percent compared with 3.6 and 6.8 percent for publicly administered Medicare and Medicaid respectively (Woolhandler et al., 2003; see also Himmelstein and Woolhandler, 2008). Other studies have found that administrative costs account for nearly half of the difference between the share of resources allocated to the health sector in the two countries (Himmelstein and Woolhandler, 1986; Fuchs and Hahn, 1990; Himmelstein et al., 1996). According to the US General Accounting Office (GAO), "If the US were to shift to a system of universal coverage and a single payer, as in Canada, the savings in administrative costs would be more than enough to offset the expense of universal coverage" (1991, p. 6).

Canada also offers universal insurance, so the entire population is covered for basic hospital and physician services, unlike the US system which, prior to the ACA, left around 40 million Americans uninsured. The greater access of the Canadian population to medical care has been credited with part of its superior health outcomes relative to the US. Canadian patients with cystic fibrosis live an average of ten years longer than American patients. The authors who found this result argue that the difference is likely caused by "uninsurance" in the US (Stephenson et al., 2017). The US has a higher rate of prematurity and lower birth weight than Canada. A higher percentage of women receive no prenatal care in the first trimester in the US (16 percent) than in Canada. Better access to healthcare in Canada explains a great deal of the Canadian superiority in heart disease over the US. Canada has a lower age-adjusted death rate from all cancers (except colorectal) than the US. The difference in comparable preventable hospitalization rates between rich and poor neighborhoods is much greater in cities in the US than in publicly insured Canada (Billings et al., 1996). Finally, health inequalities between the top 10 percent and bottom 10 percent of the income earners are greater in the US than in Canada (Himmelstein and Woolhandler, n.d.). A particularly sweeping study comparing the two nations found that people in the US were less likely to have a regular doctor, had more unmet health needs, and were more likely to go without needed medicine. In addition, disparities in health between income groups were more pronounced in the US (Lasser et al., 2006). Even more convincingly, all of these Canadian advantages appeared only after the passage of national health insurance in that country.

Outside the realm of health insurance, the costs in the rest of the US healthcare system are also higher than in other countries. This is because in other countries much of the purchasing is either centralized in the hands of the state (as in Canada) or regulated (Germany) (Marmor et al., 2009, p. 487). A study on heart surgery found that it was 83 percent more expensive in the US than in Canada. Despite the higher US costs, there was no difference in hospital mortality and Canadians remained in the hospital for 17 percent longer (Eisenberg et al., 2005). Another review of studies comparing health outcomes in the two countries found that healthcare spending per patient was 89 percent higher in the US than in Canada because of Canada's single-payer system for physician and hospital care (Guyatt et al., 2007). These increased healthcare costs are not associated with superior results. According to the Guyatt et al. (2007) review, Canada "produces health benefits similar, or perhaps superior, to those of the US health system."

Overall, the US health system fares poorly in comparison to the system in other nations, including the single-payer system of Canada. The Commonwealth Fund produces one of the few systematic comparisons of healthcare systems in different countries. Every year it ranks countries according to quality of care, administrative efficiency, access, equity (difference between high and low income) and outcomes. In this ranking, the US has scored consistently at the very bottom of all 11 countries in the study (Schneider et al., 2017).

The US healthcare system is more expensive, less equitable and less accessible than those in other nations. Yet, despite a number of serious efforts to transform the healthcare system, its private, market-oriented emphasis remains. What accounts for this? The political economy of healthcare in the US has been driven by two longstanding trends. The first is the widespread public dissatisfaction with lack of access and affordability of the existing system. Polling data show that the US population repeatedly favored a universal, comprehensive health program, even if it resulted in higher taxes, but this has not been translated into political action (Navarro, 1989). In 2007, seven separate polls showed that the majority of people in the US were in favor of a universal government plan. For example, a 2007 Associated Press poll found that 54 percent of respondents answered "yes", while 44 percent answered "no" to the question: "Do you consider yourself a supporter of a single-payer healthcare system, that is a national health plan financed by taxpayers in which all Americans would get their insurance from a single government plan, or not?" Similar results were found in polls conducted by the National Small Business Association (60 percent in favor), and CBS (55 percent in favor) to name a couple of the other examples. In the run-up to Obama's healthcare plan a *New York Times* poll found that 72 percent of the population preferred a public plan (Hilzenrath, 2009).

The second trend, pushing to maintain the private, for-profit, nature of the system, is driven by a particular segment of the business class, perhaps best described by a term first used in Barbara and John

Ehrenreich's (1971) *The American Health Empire*—the Medical Industrial Complex (MIC). The MIC has been fairly consistent in its opposition to public intrusion into the healthcare system in any form other than subsidization. The health insurance industry, for example, has been predictably hostile to any significant encroachments into its very profitable business. As the healthcare system becomes more corporatized, it is likely to increasingly resist proposals for nationalization of profitable sectors. For example, profit-making hospitals currently benefit from private health insurance, and would obviously oppose any reduction in the number of for-profit hospitals (Starr, 1982, p. 448). The American Medical Association has not been in favor of a single-payer public plan, preferring instead to recommend that people "purchase the health insurance of their choice", with some financial assistance for low-income families. In a submission to the Senate Finance Committee in 2009, it wrote "The introduction of a new public plan threatens to restrict patient choice by driving out private insurers, which currently provide coverage for nearly 70 per cent of Americans" (Pear, 2009). Although the MIC is not a completely homogeneous group with respect to its interests in state intervention, it is a fairly accurate generalization that the MIC is in favor of government subsidies that increase the profits of private firms but opposes any state role in owning, regulating or negotiating prices in the industry.

After World War II, citizens in other industrial countries demanded and received various forms of universal healthcare, while reform efforts in the US were defeated (with the important exceptions of Medicare and Medicaid) because of a concerted effort by the MIC. The twin, and conflicting, trends of the power of the MIC against the increasing dissatisfaction of Americans with the health system confronted Obama and his effort to reform healthcare in the US through the ACA (Chernomas and Hudson, 2013).

Obama's healthcare plan

Obama began his healthcare reform strategy with the most efficient and accessible single-payer system in mind and wound up with one orchestrated by the medical-industrial-complex. Campaigning in 2003 he claimed:

> I see no reason why the United States of America, the wealthiest country in the history of the world, spending 14 percent of its gross national product on healthcare, cannot provide basic health insurance to everybody … everybody in, nobody out—a single-payer healthcare plan, a universal healthcare plan. That's what I'd like to see. But as all of you know, we may not get there immediately. Because first we've got to take back the White House, we've got to take back the Senate, and we've got to take back the House.

By 2008 the Senate and House were Democratic and Obama was president. The fact that President Obama chose to reduce the number of uninsured through the complicated, privately led, ACA rather than a public scheme reflects a particularly neoliberal compromise between the strength of the MIC and the groundswell of discontent with US healthcare. A Canadian-style public single insurer was never seriously considered although it might have been an obvious solution. Indeed, a proposal by a small group of Democrats to create a public insurer that would compete with private industry (a discarded plank in the Obama presidential campaign of 2008) died a rapid death facing opposition from Republicans, the insurance industry, and conservative Democrats (Marmor and Oberlander, 2010, p. 2).

As was the case in previous instances when a serious transformation of the healthcare system has been considered in the US, the MIC swung into political action in order to limit or channel the reform in its favor. One obvious way to influence political decisions is to donate to politicians. Obama's election campaign received $19.5 million from the healthcare industries, far more than the $7.4 million given to his Republican opponent John McCain. Of course, Obama was not alone in receiving funding from the MIC. Max Baucus, chairman of the Senate Finance Committee (which drafted the Senate's healthcare legislation) received $2 million between 2005 and 2010 from the healthcare sector. In return, he met 20 times with representatives of the MIC in 2009, while public interest groups were granted only 12 meetings. In all, the MIC donated $28 million to various politicians between 2009 and 2010 (Tomasky, 2010, p. 14). Lobbying activity by the MIC also spiked during the debate about healthcare reform. At its apex in 2009, for every single member of the House and Senate there were six healthcare lobbyists, some 3300 in all. The 25 highest-spending organizations in healthcare lobbying spent a combined $288 million in 2009. One of the strongest opponents of healthcare reform, the US Chamber of Commerce, spent $71 million in the last quarter of 2009 alone. PhRMA, the largest drug lobbyist, spent $26 million. This money did appear to pay some dividends. Until doctors, nurses, and medical students supporting public insurance threatened a public demonstration at the White House Healthcare Summit, it did not contain a single participant advocating a single-payer, universal system to provide a counterpoint to the tide of MIC opinion (Bernstein, 2009). Lobbying on healthcare is not left to outsiders. When Baucus met with healthcare representatives, two of the lobbyists in the meeting were former chiefs of his staff, David Castagnetti and Jeffrey Forbes. Of the 165 people whom PhRMA employed to lobby for its various interests, 137 have had government experience (Tomasky, 2010, p. 12). Of course, lobbying was done by those who supported healthcare reform as well. The American Association of Retired People, which favors expanding coverage, even when it was proposed that some of the money for this would come from cuts to Medicare, spent $21 million in 2009. The American Federation of Labor and Congress of Industrial Organizations contributed a much more modest $2 million lobbying in support of healthcare reform (Tomasky, 2010, p. 12). The third arrow in the MIC political influence quiver was advertisements to influence public opinion. Six large insurance companies pooled between $10 and $20 million for television ads opposing meaningful healthcare reform that might damage the industry (Tomasky, 2010, p. 12).

The US government passed the ACA in 2010. It was backed by President Obama to provide insurance for more people and control healthcare spending. Its final provisions were a bit complicated, to put it mildly, but the rudiments of the bill were that the first goal would be addressed by forcing all of those not eligible for Medicare or Medicaid to purchase private insurance, and the second, through some cost-containment measures in the government-funded programs.

More people were insured by expanding Medicaid and making private insurance more easily available. All those who earned less than 138 percent of the federal poverty level were eligible for Medicaid. Although this would be entirely federally funded, individual states could opt out of this provision. Further, income became the only criterion for coverage, as opposed to the exclusion of single adults without children that was the case previously. Those who did not qualify for Medicaid, did not have employer-based plans, and had incomes below 400 percent of the poverty level purchased subsidized private insurance on health benefit "exchanges" set up and run at either the state or federal level. Individuals were "forced" to buy insurance in the sense that they would face a tax penalty if they refused. There was also a range of provisions to encourage firms to offer insurance to their workforce. The specific provisions differed depending on the size of the firm. For example, firms with under 50 employees received tax credits if they provided coverage for their employees, but were not required to provide employer-based health insurance.

In exchange for the emphasis on private insurance in the Obama reform, insurance companies would face some restrictions on their operations. Insurance companies were prevented from dropping people when they became ill. They were not able to refuse coverage or charge higher rates to those with existing conditions. They were obliged to keep young adults on their parents' plan until they reached 26 (many had previously dropped them at 19).

There was far less in the ACA that might contribute to the second goal of controlling healthcare costs. Within the Medicare system, the ACA legislated a reduction in spending increases by limiting payments to hospitals and private insurers. Outside Medicare, the cost-containment measures were more limited. Private insurers faced a limit on how much revenue could be spent on non-medical costs. In addition, a "Cadillac tax" was imposed on the most expansive, and expensive, health insurance plans. The hope was that this would cut the number of high-end plans that supposedly offered "luxury" care with benefits often of low value. These stopgap measures were made necessary by the refusal of the ACA to take a more systemic approach to cutting costs. Other wealthy countries spend much less than the US, primarily because the government has a much broader role.

The ACA was sufficiently favorable to pharmaceutical companies that PhRMA spent $100 million on ads that supported Obama's reforms. This simultaneously highlights how Obama chose to craft reform that would benefit the MIC and how its influence dramatically reduced the likelihood of any but the most marginal changes to the US healthcare system. According to Robert Reich, the labor secretary in the Clinton administration, "The White House made a Faustian bargain with big pharma and big insurance, essentially scuttling ... profit-squeezing mechanisms in return for these industries' agreement not to oppose healthcare legislation with platoons of lobbyists and millions of dollars of TV ads" (cited in McGreal, 2009). Even so, the largely MIC-friendly ACA was too much reform for many. No Republicans voted for the bill because it increased health costs to many businesses, taxed "Cadillac" insurance, and increased government healthcare subsidies. They framed the modest ACA reforms as a "government takeover" of medicine that would result in "death panels" and "pulling the plug on grandma" (Marmor and Oberlander, 2010, p. 1). A more radical restructuring of the industry, involving a more meaningful role for government, would have attracted even stronger opposition from Republicans and alienated many Democrats.

The ACA contained some positive changes to US healthcare. The greatest accomplishment of the ACA was that it expanded health insurance to many previously uncovered people. Estimates on the number of people insured as a result of the ACA vary, depending on both the methods of the study and the time frame chosen, from somewhere between seven and sixteen million. The percentage of uninsured adults fell from 20 percent in 2010 to 16 percent in 2014. Further, the expansion has been especially pronounced among those, like low-income individuals, who have historically been uninsured in the greatest numbers. According to a study in *the New England Journal of Medicine*, "these changes are meaningful and unprecedented in the U.S. healthcare system" (Blumenthal et al., 2015, p. 2451).

Yet many of the previous problems remained. Unlike most other nations, where insurance is universal, many people remained uninsured either because the subsidized insurance was still too expensive (but they were not eligible for the expansion of Medicaid, or in a state that refused the expansion) or they were sufficiently confident in their continued rude health that they would opt to pay the penalty rather than purchase insurance (Marmor and Oberlander, 2010, p. 4). Further, many of the insured still faced discouragingly high costs that limited their use of healthcare. People with insurance often still paid substantial deductibles and co-payments. Indeed, insurers often offer a tradeoff where more affordable premiums are linked with higher out-of-pocket expenses for the insured, which could limit their access to medical services (Blumenthal et al., 2015). In addition, the problems related to relying primarily on insurance provided by employers still remained, as both a growing cost for firms and a disincentive for workers to leave jobs with good insurance plans.

Part of the reason that the ACA has not had a greater impact reducing the number of insured is that states could opt out of the expansion of Medicaid. As of 2015, 28 states and the District of Columbia had opted in. The divergence in ACA Medicaid take-up provides an opportunity to contrast the health outcomes for people in opt-in and opt-out states. A study that compared low-income individuals who obtained insurance through the Medicaid expansion in Arkansas and Kentucky with those in Texas, which opted out of the Medicaid expansion, found that those in the opt-in states had superior access to primary and preventative care, paid lower out-of-pocket costs, had better medication compliance and improved self-reported health (Sommers et al., 2017).

The ACA was also predicted to save the government some money. The CBO was asked to review the fiscal impact of the ACA when the Republicans in the House proposed its elimination with the inflammatorily named Repealing the Job-Killing Healthcare Law Act, and estimated that the ACA would reduce federal deficits by $143 billion between 2010 and 2019. Although the ACA was predicted to increase spending by $788 billion on things like increased Medicaid coverage and subsidies for employer insurance, it was also predicted to reduce spending on Medicare and generate revenue primarily through increasing the Hospital Insurance Payroll Tax and fees on manufacturers and insurance companies (Congressional Budget Office, 2011, p. 4).

There is more uncertainly around the impact of the ACA on healthcare spending more generally. As we have pointed out the US spends more on healthcare than any other wealthy nation. Between 2000 and 2010 per capita spending was increasing by 5.6 percent per year. However, in the three years following the implementation of the ACA, the rate of growth fell to 3.2 percent annually (Blumenthal et al., 2015). There is considerable debate about the extent to which this reduction, which began before the 2010 introduction, can be attributed to the ACA. There are other competing explanations, such as the income constraints created by the 2008 recession. However, it is probably safe to conclude that the ACA did not contribute to a massive increase in spending (Blumenthal et al., 2015).

Obama's ACA was the latest example of how the conflict over US healthcare has so often played out in favor of the MIC. The US population would benefit from expanding access and lowering costs. The fact that access was improved should not be downplayed. Millions who were previously without health insurance were insured. Yet, this was done in a manner that was very favorable to the MIC. A single-payer public system, and even a public competitor to private insurance, was never seriously considered, even when it was the obvious solution to the twin problems of access and cost escalation. The ACA did attempt to deal with the inequitable access to a healthcare system that relied heavily on private, for-profit insurance and delivery. Yet, it attempted to do so in a manner that depended on, and in many ways benefited, the private insurance market. Public insurance was extended only to low-income earners who were, predictably, minimal purchasers of private insurance. Further, the ACA had provisions subsidizing individual and employer purchases of private insurance. Finally, the ACA marked a successful resistance to any large-scale public intrusion into the arena of for profit insurance and delivery. A dramatic restructuring of the US healthcare system, not the tinkering reforms of the ACA, is required if the US is to genuinely improve its medical system.

Conclusion

The domination of US healthcare by the medical industry has resulted in an unresolved contradiction. What is desired by the industry has not been satisfactory to the general public. The starting assumption of the Obama administration was that universal coverage would never be achieved if it were opposed by the political and financial clout of the MIC, so a proposal had to be crafted from which the MIC would benefit. As was the case with neoliberal environmentalism discussed in Chapter 3, the ACA was a pro-market, pro-business, pro-profit, method of accommodating legitimate public displeasure with the results of a pro-market, pro-business, pro-profit healthcare system. This might explain why the ACA has focused on expanding coverage in a manner that, although it constrains private insurance companies in some ways, improves their revenue base by expanding the number of people who buy private insurance and rules out any public option. It also explains why cost control measures are fairly weak. The 2010 ACA does nothing to change the decade-old conclusion of one health researcher: "What has become clear is that the unique problems the U.S. medical-industrial complex has created are rooted in the subordination of the state and civil society to corporate interests" (Estes et al., 2000, p. 1827).

Note

1 These trends are supported by research on "austerity" policies in other countries. See, for example Stuckler & Basu (2013).

References

Bartlett, B. (2011). What Your Taxes Do (and Don't) Buy for You. *New York Times*, June 7. Retrieved July 13, 2017, from http://economix.blogs.nytimes.com/2011/06/07/health-care-costs-and-the-tax-burden/.

Beckfield, J., & Bambra, C. (2016). Shorter Lives in Stingier States: Social Policy Shortcomings Help Explain the US Mortality Disadvantage. *Social Science and Medicine*, 171, 30–38.

Bell, M., & Ebisu, K. (2012). Environmental Inequality in Exposures to Airborne Particulate Matter Components in the United States. *Environmental Health Perspectives*, 120, 1699–1704.

Bernstein, M. (2009) Propaganda and Prejudice Distort the Health Reform Debate, April 22. *Health Affairs*. Retrieved July 15, 2017, from http://healthaffairs.org/blog/2009/04/22/proganda-and-prejudice-distort-the-health-reform-debate/.

Billings, J., Anderson, G., & Newman, L. (1996). Recent Findings on Preventable Hospitalizations. *Health Affairs*, 15(3), 239–249.

Birn, A.-E., Pillay, Y., & Holtz, T. (2009). *Textbook of International Health: Global Health in a Dynamic World*. New York: Oxford University Press.

Blumenthal, D., Abrams, M., & Nuzum, R. (2015). The Affordable Care Act at 5 Years. *The New England Journal of Medicine*, 372, 2451–2458.

Blyth, M. (2002) *Great Transformations: Economic Ideas and Institutional Change in the Twentieth Century*. Cambridge: Cambridge University Press.

Bohme, S., Zorabedian, J., & Egilman, D. (2005). Maximizing Profit and Endangering Health: Corporate Strategies to Avoid Litigation and Regulation. *International Journal of Occupational and Environmental Health*, 11(4), 338–348.

Bradley, E., & Taylor, L. (2013). *The American Healthcare Paradox: Why Spending More Is Getting Us Less*. New York: Public Affairs.

Braverman, P. A., Cubbin, C., Egeter, S., Williams, D. R., and Pamuk, E. (2010). Socioeconomic Disparities in Health in the US: What the Patterns Tell Us. *American Journal of Public Health*, 100(1).

Brenner, H. (2005). Commentary: Economic Growth Is the Basis of Mortality Rate Decline in the 20th Century—Experience of the United States 1901–2000. *International Journal of Epidemiology*, 35.

Cairns, E. (1971). *The Biological Imperatives*. New York: Holt, Rinehart & Winston.

Case, A., & Deaton, A. (2015). Rising Morbidity and Mortality in Midlife among White Non-Hispanic Americans in the 21st Century. *Proceedings of the National Academy of Sciences of the United States of America*, 112(49), 15078–15083.

Case, A., & Deaton, A. (2017). *Mortality and Morbidity in the 21st Century*. Washington, DC: Brookings Institution.

Cassel, E. (1976). *The Healer's Art*. Philadelphia: J.B. Lippincott.

Chernomas, R. (1999). *The Social and Economic Causes of Disease*. Ottawa, ON: Canadian Centre for Policy Alternatives.

Chernomas, R., & Donner, L. (2004). *The Cancer Epidemic as a Social Event*. Winnipeg, MB: Canadian Centre for Policy Alternatives–MB.

Chernomas, R., & Hudson, I. (2013). *To Live and Die in America*. London: Pluto Press.

Chetty, R., Stepner, M., Abraham, S., Lin, S., Scuderi, B., Turner, N., ... Cutler, D. (2016). The Association Between Income and Life Expectancy in the United States, 2001–2014. *Journal of the American Medical Association*, 315(16), 1750–1766.

Clapp, R., Howe, G., & Jacobs, M. (2007). Environmental and Occupational Causes of Cancer: A Call to Act on What We Know. *Biomedicine and Pharmacotherapy*, 61(10), 1–37.

Commission of the European Communities. (2003). *Regulation of the European Parliament and the Council Concerning the Registration, Evaluation, Authorisation and Restrictions of Chemicals (REACH)*. Brussels: Commission of the European Communities.

Congressional Budget Office. (1991). *Universal Health Insurance Coverage Using Medicare's Payment Rates*. Washington DC: US Government Printing Office.

Congressional Budget Office. (2011). *Letter to Honorable John Boehner, Speaker of the House, January 6: Review of the H.R. 2, The Repealing the Job-Killing Healthcare Law Act*. Retrieved July 17, 2017, from www.cbo.gov/ftpdocs/120xx/doc12040/01–06-PPACA_Repeal.pdf.

Cutler, D., Deaton, A., & Lleras-Muney, A. (2006). The Determinants of Mortality. *Journal of Economic Perspectives*, 20(3), 97–120.

Davis, D. (2007). *The Secret History of the War on Cancer*. New York: Basic Books.

Dixon, J. (2009). From the Imperial to the Empty Calorie: How Nutrition Relations Underpin Food Regime Transitions. *Agriculture and Human Values*, 26(4), 321–333.

Drewnowski, A. (2009). Obesity, Diets and Social Inequality. *Nutrition Reviews*, 67 (Issue Supplement), 36–39.

Drewnowski, A., & Specter, S.E. (2004). Poverty and Obesity: The Role of Energy Density and Energy Costs. *American Journal of Clinical Nutrition*, 79(1), 6–16.

Dubois, L. (2006). Food, Nutrition and Population Health: From Scarcity to Social Inequalities. In J. Heymann (ed.), *Healthier Societies: From Analysis to Action*. Oxford: Oxford University Press.

Dubos, R. (1965). *Man Adapting*. New Haven, CT: Yale University Press.

Ehrenreich, B., and Ehrenreich, J. (1971). *The American Health Empire: Power, Profits and Politics*. New York: Vintage.

Eisenberg, M.J., Filion, K. B., Azoulay, A., Brox, A. C., Haider, S., and Pilote, L. (2005). Outcomes and Cost of Coronary Artery Bypass Graft Surgery in the United States and Canada. *Archives of Internal Medicine*, 165(13), 1506–1513.

Environmental Working Group. (2003). *Summary of Chemicals Found in EWG/Commonweal Study #1, Industrial Chemicals and Pesticides in Adults*. Retrieved February 8, 2018, from www.ewg.org/sites/humantoxome/participants/participant-group.php?group=bb1.

Epstein, H. (1998). Life and Death on the Social Ladder, July 16. *New York Review of Books*, 45(12). 574–576.

Estes, C., Harrington, C., and Pellow, D. (2000) Medical-industrial complex. In E. Borgatta and R. Montgomery (eds), *Encyclopedia of Sociology*. Farmington Hills, MI: Gale Group.

Evans, G., Brooks-Gunn, J., & Klebanov, P. (2011). Stressing Out the Poor: Chronic Physiological Stress and the Income-Achievement Gap. *Community Investments*, 23(2), 22–27.

Evans, R. (1984). *Strained Mercy: The Economics of Canadian Healthcare*. Toronto: Butterworths.

Faber, D., & Krieg, E. (2002). Unequal Exposure to Ecological Hazards: Environmental Injustices in the Commonwealth of Massachusetts. *Environmental Health Perspectives*, 110(2), 277–288.

Fogel, R. (1997). New Findings on Secular Trends in Nutrition and Mortality: Some Implications for Population Theory. In M.R. Rosenzweig & O. Stark (eds), *Handbook of Population and Family Economics*. New York: Elsevier Science, North Holland.

Fogel, R. (2004). *The Escape from Hunger and Premature Death, 1700–2100*. Cambridge: Cambridge University Press.

Ford, E., Ajani, U. A., Croft J. B., Critchley, J. A., Labarthe, D. R., Kottke, T. E., Giles, W. H., and Capewell, S. (2007). Explaining the Decrease in U.S. Deaths from Coronary Disease, 1980–2000. *New England Journal of Medicine*, 356, 2388–2398.

Freeman, A. (2007). Fast Food: Oppression Through Poor Nutrition. *California Law Review*, 95(6), 2221–2259.

Fuchs, V., & Hahn, J. (1990). How Does Canada Do It? A Comparison of Expenditures for Physicians' Services in the United States and Canada. *New England Journal of Medicine*, 323(13), 884–890.

Galdston, I. (1954). *The Meaning of Social Medicine*. Cambridge, MA: Harvard University Press.

General Accounting Office (1991). *Canadian Health Insurance: Lessons for the United States, Ref. No. HRD-91–90*. Washington, DC: US Government Printing Office.

Graham, D. (2004). Blowing the Whistle on the FDA: An Interview with Dr. David Graham. *Multinational Monitor*, 25(12). Retrieved November 27, 2018, from www.google.ca/url?sa=t&rct=j&q=&esrc=s&source=web&cd=1&cad=rja&uact=8&ved=2ahUKEwjlkKbE3fXeAhVCqVQKHf93CgQQFjAAegQICRAB&url=http%3A%2F%2Fmultinationalmonitor.org%2Fmm2004%2F122004%2Finterview-graham.html&usg=AOvVaw24Mx_x8tud8aRpR4pdmt66.

Guyatt, G. et al. (2007). A Systematic Review of Studies Comparing Health Outcomes in Canada and the United States. *Open Medicine*, 1(1), e27–36.

Herper, M. (2005). David Graham on the Vioxx Verdict, August 19. *Forbes*. Retrieved February 6, 2018, from www.forbes.com/2005/08/19/merck-vioxx-graham_cx_mh_0819graham.html#152f9d005698.

Hertzman, C., & Siddiqi, A. (2008). Tortoises 1 Hares 0: How Comparative Health Trends between Canada and the United States Support a Long Term View of Health Policy. *Healthcare Policy*, 4(2), 16–24.

Hilzenrath, D. (2009). Health Insurance Lobby Cherry-Picks Data in Fight against Public Plan, July 22. *Washington Post*.

Himmelstein, D., Lewontin, J., & Woolhandler, S. (1996). Who Administers Who Cares? Medical Administrative and Clinical Employment in the United States and Canada. *American Journal of Public Health*, 86(2), 172–178.

Himmelstein, D., & Woolhandler, S. (1986). Cost without Benefit: Administrative Waste in U.S. Healthcare. *New England Journal of Medicine*, 314(7), 441–445.

Himmelstein, D., & Woolhandler, S. (2008). Privatization in a Publicly Funded Healthcare System: The US Experience. *International Journal of Health Services*, 38(3), 407–419.

Himmelstein, D., & Woolhandler, S. (n.d.). Recent Attacks on Single Payer Health Reform: Ideology Masquerading as Scholarship. *Single Payer FAQ*. Retrieved July 13, 2017, from www.pnhp.org/facts/single-payer-faq#response-papers.

Irigaray, P., Newby, J. A., Clapp, R., Hardell, L, Howard. V., Montagnier, L., Epstein, S., and Belpomme, D. (2007). Lifestyle-Related Factors and Environmental Agents Causing Cancer: An Overview. *Biomedicine and Pharmacotherapy*, 61(10), 640–658.

Katz, R. (2012). Environmental Pollution: Corporate Crime and Cancer Mortality. *Contemporary Justice Review: Issues in Criminal, Social, and Restorative Justice*, 15(1), 97–125.

Kim, S. (2013). *11 Food Ingredients Banned Outside the U.S. That We Eat*, June 26. Retrieved July 11, 2017, from ABC News: http://abcnews.go.com/Lifestyle/Food/11-foods-banned-us/story?id=19457237.

Lasser, K., Himmelstein, D., & Woolhandler, S. (2006). Access to Care, Health Status, and Health Disparities in the United States and Canada: Results of a Cross-National Population-Based Survey. *American Journal of Public Health*, 96(7), 1300–1307.

Malkan, S. (2003). Chemical Trespass: The Chemical Body Burden and the Threat to Public Health. *Multinational Monitor*, 24(4) 8+.

Marmor, T., & Oberlander, J. (2010). The Health Bill Explained at Last, August 19. *New York Review of Books*.

Marmor, T., Oberlander, J., & White, J. (2009). The Obama Administration's Options for Health Care Cost Control: Hope Versus Reality. *Annals of Internal Medicine*, 150(7), 455–489.

Marmot, M., Siegrist, S., & Theorell, T. (2006). Health and the Psychosocial Environment at Work. In Marmot, M. and Wilkinson, R. (eds), *Social Determinants of Health*. Oxford: Oxford University Press.

McGreal, C. (2009). Revealed: Millions Spent by Lobby Firms Fighting Obama Health Reforms, October 1. *The Guardian*. Retrieved July 16, 2017, from www.theguardian.com/world/2009/oct/01/lobbyists-millions-obama-healthcare-reform.

McKeown, T. (1976a). *The Role of Medicine*. London: Nuffield Provincial Hospitals Trust.

McKeown, T. (1976b). *The Modern Rise of Population*. London: Edward Arnold.

McKeown, T. (1979). *The Role of Medicine: Dream, Mirage or Nemesis?* 2nd edn. Oxford: Basil Blackwell.

McKeown, T., & Record, R. (1962). Reasons for the Decline of Mortality in England and Wales during the Nineteenth Century. *Population Studies*, 16(2), 94-122.

McKeown, T., Record, R., & Turner, R. (1975). An Interpretation of the Decline of Mortality in England and Wales during the Twentieth Century. *Population Studies*, 29(3), 391–422.

Monnat, S. (2016). *Deaths of Despair and Support for Trump in the 2016 Presidential Election*. State College, PA: The Pennsylvania State University, Department of Agricultural Economics, Sociology and Education Research Brief 12/04/16.

Navarro, V. (1989). Why Some Countries Have National Health Insurance, Others Have National Health Services and the United States Has Neither. *Social Science and Medicine*, 28(9), 887–898.

Navarro, V., Burrell, C., Benach, J. et al. (2003). The Importance of the Political and the Social in Explaining Mortality Differentials Amongst Countries of the OECD, 1950–1998. *International Journal of Health Services*, 33(3), 419–494.

Navarro, V., Doran, T., Burström, B, et al. (2004). Summary and Conclusions of the Study. In V. Navarro (ed.), *The Political and Social Contests of Health*. Amityville, NY: Baywood.

OECD. (2011). *Health at a Glance 2011: OECD Indicators*. Retrieved July 18, 2017, from http://dx.doi.org/10.1787/health_glance-2011-en.

OECD. (2017). *Health Expenditures and Financing*. Retrieved July 5, 2017, from OECD.Stat: http://stats.oecd.org/Index.aspx?DataSetCode=SHA.

Offer, A., Pechey, R., & Ulijaszek, S. (2010). Obesity under Affluence Varies by Welfare Regimes: The Effect of Fast Food, Insecurity, and Inequality. *Economics and Human Biology*, 6(3), 297–308.

Otero, G., Pechlaner, G., Liberman, G., & Gürcan, E. (2015). The Neoliberal Diet and Inequality in the United States. *Social Science and Medicine*, 142, 47–55.

Pear, R. (2009). Doctors' Group Opposes Public Insurance Plan, June 11. *New York Times*.

Poland, B., Coburn D., Robertson, A., and Eakin, J. (1998). Wealth, Equality and Healthcare: A Critique of a 'Population Health' Perspective on the Determinants of Health. *Social Science and Medicine*, 46(7), 785–798.

Popkin, B. (2009). *The World Is Fat: The Fads, Trends, Policies, and Products that Aare Fattening the Human Race*. New York: Avery.

Raphael, D., & Bryant, T. (2004). The Welfare State as a Determinant of Women's Health: Support for Women's Quality of Life in Canada and Four Comparison Nations. *Health Policy*, 68(1), 63–79.

Reinier, K., Thomas, E., Andrusiek, D. L, Aufderheide, T. P. et al. (2011). Socio-economic Status and Incidence of Sudden Cardiac Arrest. *Canadian Medical Association Journal*, 183(15), 1705–1712.

Reuben, S. (2010). *Reducing Environmental Cancer Risk: President's Cancer Panel 2008--2009*. Washington, DC: US Department of Health and Human Services.

Sachs, N. (2009). Jumping the Pond: Transnational Law and the Future of Chemical Regulation. *Vanderbilt Law Review*, 62(6), 450–462.

Schneider, E., Sarnak, D., Squires, D., Shah, A., & Doty, M. (2017). *Mirror, Mirror 2017: International Comparison Reflects Flaws and Opportunities for Better U.S. Healthcare*. Retrieved July 15, 2017, from The Commonwealth Fund: www.commonwealthfund.org/interactives/2017/july/mirror-mirror/.

Singh, G., & Siahpush, M. (2006). Widening Socioeconomic Inequalities in US Life Expectancy, 1980–2000. *International Journal of Epidemiology*, 35(4), 969–979.

Sommers, B., Maylone, B., Blendon, R., Orav, E., & Epstein, A. (2017). Three-Year Impacts of the Affordable Care Act: Improved Medical Care and Health among Low-Income Adults. *Health Affairs*, 36(6), 1119–1128.

Squires, D. (2017). *The Shortening American Lifespan*, January 4. Retrieved July 11, 2017, from The Commonwealth Fund: www.commonwealthfund.org/publications/blog/2017/jan/shortening-american-lifespan.

Starr, P. (1982). *The Social Transformation of American Medicine*. New York: Basic Books.

Stephenson, A., Sykes, J., Stanojevic, S. et al. (2017). Survival Comparison of Patient Survival of Patients with Cystic Fibrosis in Canada and the United States: A Population-Based Cohort Study. *Annals of Internal Medicine*, 166(8), 537–546.

Stevens, L., Burgess, J., Stochelski, M., & Kuczek, T. (2015). Amounts of Artificial Food Dyes and Added Sugars in Foods and Sweets Commonly Consumed by Children. *Clinical Pediatrics*, 54(4), 309–321.

Stuart, A., Mudhasakul, S., & Sriwatanapongse, W. (2009). The Social Distribution of Neighborhood-Scale Air Pollution and Monitoring Protection. *Journal of Air Waste Management Association*, 59, 591–602.

Stuckler, D., & Basu, S. (2013). *The Body Economic: Why Austerity Kills*. New York: Basic Books.

Szreter, S. (1988). The Importance Of Social Intervention in Britain's Mortality Decline 1850–1914: A Reinterpretation of the Role of Public Health. *Social History of Medicine*, 1(1), 1–38.

Szreter, S. (2002a). Rethinking McKeown: The Relationship between Public Health and Social Change. *American Journal of Public Health*, 92(5), 722–725.

Szreter, S. (2002b). The State of Social Capital: Bringing Back in Power, Politics, and History. *Theory and Society*, 31(50), 573–621.

Szreter, S. (2003). The Population Health Approach in Historical Perspective. *American Journal of Public Health*, 93(2), 421–431.

Szreter, S. (2004a). Industrialization and Health. *British Medical Bulletin*, 69, 75–86.

Szreter, S. (2004b). Author Response: Debating Mortality Trends in 19th Century Britain. *International Journal of Epidemiology*, 33(4), 705–709.

Thirlaway, K., & Upton, D. (2009). *The Phycology of Lifestyle: Promoting Healthy Behaviour*. London and New York: Routledge.

Tomasky, M. (2010). The Money Fighting Healthcare Reform, April 8. *New York Review of Books*, 17(6). Retrieved November 27, 2018, from www.nybooks.com/articles/2010/04/08/the-money-fighting-health-care-reform/.

Union of Concerned Scientists. (2013). *The $11 Trillion Reward: How Simple Dietary Changes Can Save Lives and Money, and How We Get There*. Cambridge, MA: Union of Concerned Scientists.

United Nations. (2016). *Human Development Report 2016*. United Nations. Retrieved July 5, 2017, from http://hdr.undp.org/en/data#.

Wilkinson, R. (1996). *Unhealthy Societies*. London: Routledge.

Wilkinson, R., & Pickett, K. (2009). *The Spirit Level: Why More Equal Societies Almost Always Do Better*. New York: Bloomsbury.

Woolf, S. (2011). Public Health Implications f Government Spending Reductions. *Journal of the American Medical Association*, 305(18), 1902–1903.

Woolf, S., & Aron, L. (2013). *U.S. Health in International Perspective: Shorter Lives, Poorer Health.* Washington, DC: The National Academies Press.

Woolhandler, S., Campbell, T., & Himmelstein, D. (2003). Costs of Healthcare Administration in the United States and Canada. *New England Journal of Medicine*, 349(8), 768–775.

World Health Organization. (2008). *WHO Commission on the Social Determinants of Health.* Geneva: World Health Organization.

Zanolli, L. (2017). "Cancer Alley" Residents Say Industry Is Hurting Town: "We're Collateral Damage", June 6. *The Guardian.* Retrieved July 5, 2017, from www.theguardian.com/us-news/2017/jun/06/louisiana-cancer-alley-st-james-industry-environment.

5

Education: public good or finishing school?

Introduction

Since you are presumably actually reading this book, and not merely scanning its pages before settling it on your shelves, nestled between Ayn Rand's *Fountainhead* and Dan Brown's *DaVinci Code*, to impress visitors, it is probably safe to assume that literacy, and even numeracy, are not overwhelming obstacles in your daily life. Imagine if that were not the case. Imagine not being able to read street signs, drug prescriptions or even a ballot. A National Center for Education Statistics adult literacy survey found that 14 percent of American adults had "below basic" levels of literacy, which meant that they could not "locate easily identifiable information in short, commonplace prose texts" or follow "written instructions in simple documents" (National Center for Education Statistics, 2005; Thomas et al., 2008). While functional illiteracy is at the extreme low end of educational capabilities, even those with considerably more formal education often do not possess the skills necessary to lead what we have described as a flourishing life. The same study indicated that only 25 percent of college graduates could successfully use "printed and written information to function in society, to achieve one's goals, and to develop one's knowledge and potential" (Lederman, 2005).

The idea that all children should go to school is a relatively recent one. It was not so long ago that an education was the privilege of the elite. Only families of substantial means could afford to forgo children's contribution to the family income and pay for the costs of schooling. For those from less well-to-do families, education was cut short by an early entrance into the dark, satanic mills or long days in the field. In this context, education serves to reinforce income and class divisions from one generation to the next. Talent and ability are wasted as education is disproportionately restricted to those fortunate enough to have rich parents.

The idea of education as a great equalizer was at the heart of Massachusetts politician Horace Mann's advocacy of public schools in the 1800s. According to Mann, universal public education was crucial in equalizing the opportunities between rich and poor: "education, then, beyond all other divides of human origin, is a great equalizer of conditions of men—the balance wheel of the social machinery" (Cremin, 1957). This optimistic view of the social leveling abilities of education drove Mann's implementation of the first public school system in the country. It is true that greater proficiency in literacy and numeracy are associated with better labor market returns. Those with college degrees earn more than those without (Hout, 2012). Among OECD countries, workers scoring at the top level of literacy earn 61 percent more than those at the lowest level. Predictably given the labor market inequalities outlined in Chapter 2, the returns to educational proficiency in the US are higher than most other nations. The percentage change in wages associated with an increase in literacy in the US is the second highest in the entire OECD (OECD, 2013, p. 232).

Yet Mann also had a limited view of the role of education. For Mann, the principal role of schooling was to provide students with the skills that they would need to more fully participate in the labor force. Of course, this not only benefits the students by increasing their potential future income, it also supports employers by providing workforce training paid for by the public purse rather than the corporate dollar. In the terminology of more radical analysts of the role of education, school plays a crucial role in the social reproduction of the labor force and legitimizing the social and economic system (Brathwaite, 2017).

Around the turn of the twentieth century, another education reformer, John Dewey, had a more expansive view of schooling. For Dewey, schooling was far more than a training ground for future workers. Rather, schooling was about personal growth and preparing future citizens to meaningfully participate in a democratic society. Dewey thought that more than merely preparation for life, schooling was life. He argued that education should be run as a functioning example of democracy, encouraging collective decision making at schools (Dewey, 1916). This broader role for education in creating a citizenry capable of understanding and communicating complicated ideas, receptive to new concepts, and able to critically evaluate competing philosophies has been championed by more recent scholars. Linguistics scholar Noam Chomsky, for example, argued that education should produce people capable of "creative and independent thought and inquiry, challenging perceived beliefs, exploring new horizons and forgetting external constraints" (Chomsky, 2011).

There is evidence that, on average, those who are more literate and numerate are more active participants in their society. According to a 2013 study of OECD nations, adults who score at the highest levels of literacy are twice as likely to engage in volunteer activities as those with the lowest proficiency. This is likely because those with greater proficiency have a stronger sense that they "have something to offer," and are more aware of the conditions of others around them. Similarly, on average in the OECD nations, adults at the lowest level of literacy are more than two times as likely to claim that they have no impact on what the government does compared to those in the highest literacy level. The study argues that higher skill levels are needed to understand complex political issues facing a country and access information on current affairs (OECD, 2013, pp. 239–40). The increased capacity of people also provides broader benefits to society as a whole. In fact some estimates for the US suggest that the social gains to college education may be higher than the private gains of increased income (Hu & McMahon, 2010; Hout, 2012).

Mann's equality of access for skills of the marketplace could be considered a necessary but not sufficient role for education. Providing the basic requirements to participate in the labor market to all citizens is certainly superior to only providing those skills to some, or even worse, to none. However, education should strive for something greater. As Dewey suggested, a sufficient role for education would be one that fosters the skills one needs for self-development, for understanding society and meaningful participation in democracy (Macpherson, 1977).

By international standards the US education system fares much better than its health system. Its results are not rock bottom among affluent nations. Rather, US educational levels are below average and exhibit high inequality. Among the OECD nations, the US population aged between 16 and 65 scored "significantly below average" in literacy, numeracy, and "problem solving in technology rich environments." It tied for the seventh lowest literacy score of the 21 nations (along with Germany), third lowest on numeracy, and sixth lowest on problem solving (OECD, 2013, p. 96). The US also has the largest gaps in proficiency by parental background, indicating that educational differences are more intergenerationally persistent in the US than in other OECD countries. The US has the lowest average literacy proficiency score for people whose parents did not attain an upper secondary education. It also has the largest gap in literacy scores between those who have at least one parent with tertiary education and those who have no parents with an upper secondary education (OECD, 2013, p. 113).

Unfortunately, the impact of neoliberalism on education has undermined Dewey's self-development role. Although neoliberal education explicitly attempts to focus education more narrowly on the skills of the marketplace, it does so in a manner that also discards Mann's entreaty that high-quality education should be accessible to all. As we shall see, neoliberalism has had different impacts on tertiary (beyond high school) and K-12 (high school and below) educational experiences. However, there are some important commonalities in how neoliberal ideas have impacted all education. First, the desire to lower taxes has limited government's ability to fund all levels of education, a trend that was exacerbated when many state governments responded to the decline in revenues from the economic collapse of 2007 by cutting spending to balance their budgets. Second, the neoliberal principle that the private sector is more efficient than the public sector, and its commitment to creating more opportunities for profits, have resulted in a dramatic restructuring of educational funding and delivery. Third, the conviction that competition and individual choice are necessary for incentives and innovation has transformed the manner in which educational institutions are organized at all levels (Tabb, 2002, p. 29; Schultz, 2005; Hursh, 2007).

K-12

As with many of the other neoliberal timelines in this book, the transformation of education from kindergarten through grade 12 started under the Reagan administration in the early 1980s. In 1983, the Reagan administration's commission on education published *A Nation at Risk*, which put forward two overarching narratives that would reappear in many of the subsequent discussions of education. First, public education has failed to provide students with the skills required to compete in a new, competitive global world. Second, students needed to be held to a high standard and taught a more challenging curriculum (Brathwaite, 2017, p. 433). These principles were repeated under President George W. Bush's No Child Left Behind (NCLB) policy. Commenting on the success of NCLB in a speech, President Bush argued that "the education system must compete with education systems in India and China. If we fail to give our students the skills to compete in the world of the 21st century, the jobs will go elsewhere. That's just a fact of life" (Quoted in Hursh, 2007, p. 499). It was not only Republican presidents that followed this logic. President Obama's heroically named 2009 "Race to the Top" program (RTTT) contained many of the neoliberal elements championed in NCLB and used many of the same competitive admonishments. For example, RTTT forces state governments to compete for federal funds according to their willingness to implement educational reforms, including linking teacher evaluation and pay to test scores.

The state of K-12 education in the US

Before embarking on a tour of the education system in the US it is worth pointing out that, like the healthcare system, there is a great deal outside the classroom that impacts educational performance. Just as there are political-economy determinants of health, so too there are political-economy determinants of education. As we pointed out in Chapter 2, among affluent nations, the US has a high degree of inequality and poverty. Predictably, students from poorer backgrounds face a greater barrage of challenges and are more likely to struggle than those who grow up in comfortable homes. For example, in 2016, 10 percent of the students in the New York public school system experienced at least one spell of homelessness during the school year. Homeless students face obvious challenges that make educational success much more difficult. Students living in shelters had the highest rates of absenteeism. The pass rate on English tests for homeless students is only about half that of their peers in permanent homes (Harris, 2017). However, it is also true that the education system, and the neoliberal changes to it, do a particularly poor job in the US in reducing these disparities.

This is not to say that things are not improving over time. The high-school completion rate of 18-to-24-year-olds (not currently enrolled in high school or below) increased from 82.8 percent in 1972 to 89.8 percent in 2009 (Chapman et al., 2011, p. 46). Dropout rates have also fallen from 14.6 percent in 1972 to 8.1 percent in 2009. The graduation rates (which is different from high-school completion) of freshmen within four years at public high schools increased from 72.6 percent in 2002 to 75.5 percent in 2009 (Chapman et al., 2011, p. 52). There was still a considerable gap between the four-year graduation rates of low-income students and the national average in 2015. The public high-school graduation rate in the US was 83.2 percent, but for low-income students it was only 76.1 percent (US Department of Education, 2016). Although it was still very high by 2009, the gap between the dropout rates of the rich and the poor has also been falling. In 1975 the dropout rate was 15.7 percent for low-income students and 2.6 percent for those from high-income households. By 2009 it had fallen to 7.4 percent for low-income families and 1.4 percent for high-income (Chapman et al., 2011, p. 34).

Although the US is also not quite the overspending outlier in education that it is in health, it is still at the higher end of the spending spectrum for OECD nations. Despite a 4 percent reduction in spending per student between 2010 and 2014, the US spent $12,000 per student in 2014, the fourth highest in the OECD, about on par with Sweden, Denmark, Belgium and the UK (OECD, 2017, p. 6). The US ranks further down when comparing teachers' salaries to those of other nations. In absolute terms, US teachers earn more than the OECD average. However, teachers in the US earn only between 55 and 59 percent of the income of similarly trained workers. For secondary-school teachers, that number is 58 percent, second lowest in the OECD, behind only the Czech Republic (OECD, 2017, p. 7).

For this money, the US produces fairly mediocre results, at least in terms of international rankings of cognitive abilities. The Program for

International Student Assessment (PISA), organized by the OECD, measures 15-year-old students' reading, mathematics, and science literacy. In the 2015 report, the US ranked twenty-fourth in reading, twenty-sixth in science, and fortieth in math, a ranking that has remained fairly consistent since 2006 (National Center for Education Statistics, 2016). The PISA study also categorizes student results by an index of economic, social and cultural status. For US students ranked in the bottom quarter of this index, the average PISA reading and math scores (462 and 431 respectively) were below the OECD average (493 and 490). US students in the top quarter of the index scored well above (540 in reading and 517 in math) the OECD average (National Center for Education Statistics, 2016). Students from more privileged backgrounds fare considerably better than their less favorably placed counterparts.

There is a perception that part of this gap is caused by underfunded public schools for many and lavish private schools for the elite. It is certainly true that tuition fees at non-sectarian private schools have escalated to a level that would stretch all but the highest budgets. In 2000 the average tuition fee was $15,500 per student (in 2015 dollars). By 2012 it had increased to $22,370 (National Center for Education Statistics, 2015a). However, only a small, and declining, percent of students attend private schools. In 1995, private schools accounted for 11.7 percent of total enrolment, but by 2013 only 9.8 percent of students went to private school (National Center for Education Statistics, 2015b).

US spending on public education increased during the neoliberal period. Total expenditures per public elementary and secondary student increased from $9757 to $12,509 in constant dollars between 1991 and 2014, an increase of 28 percent. However, more recent trends are more alarming. Since the economic crisis, funding has decreased as both states and local governments have responded to declining revenues by cutting spending. Total spending per student in public schools in 2014 was down 8 percent from $13,567 in 2008 (National Center for Education Statistics, 2016). The overall decline in public education spending masks some important differences by state. Since 2008, of the 45 states for which consistent data are available, 31 have decreased constant dollar funding per student for public education, some, like Arizona (23 percent) and Alabama (21 percent), by considerable amounts. Other states have taken a very different approach to education spending, increasing their real funding per student. Illinois, for example increased its real per student funding by 10 percent during this period and North Dakota (which has been enjoying an oil boom) by 90 percent (Leachman et al., 2016).

The differences in spending since 2008 reflect the inequalities in the US public education system. Unlike most nations, which have more centralized arrangements, public education is funded almost entirely by state and local governments in the US. In 2013, local governments paid for 45 percent, states 46 percent and the federal government 9 percent (Leachman et al., 2016). As a result, per-student public spending varies considerably between different states. In 2013 New York spent a high of $19,818 while Utah penny-pinched its students with a low of $6555 (US Census Bureau, 2015). Because nearly half the funding for public schools comes from local taxation, large differences in funding are created by localities' willingness and ability to levy taxes, so even within states there are large inequalities between different school districts. This disparity has been longstanding. In 1998, in Vermont the top-spending 5 percent of school districts spent an average of $15,186 per student while the bottom 5 percent spent only $6442. In Illinois, these figures were $11,507 for the highest spending districts and $5260 for the lowest (Biddle & Berliner, 2002). Unsurprisingly, as the income of residents falls, school district funding decreases. In school districts with funding of $4000 per student or lower, the average poverty rate was 22 percent in 1998. In districts where funding was more than $13,000 the average poverty rate was 6.4 percent. As a result, some fortunate students receive funding of $15,000 or more per year, while less fortunate others get by with under $4000 (Biddle & Berliner, 2002).

The tremendous inequalities in student funding have created a lively debate about the extent to which increasing the funding for lower-income students will increase their educational performance. It is certainly true that students from poorer school districts, with lower funding levels, perform worse academically than those from richer districts. In the late 1990s, the two best-scoring districts in an international academic test were Naperville, Illinois, and a district from Chicago's North Shore. Both were among the best funded, with the lowest poverty rates in the country. Both had scores that would rank among the best national school systems in the world. The two districts with the lowest scores were Miami-Dade in Florida and Rochester, NY, both of which were poorly funded and had a high poverty rate. Students in these districts had achievement scores that were similar to Turkey, Jordan, and Iran, the worst-ranking nations in the study (Biddle & Berliner, 2002).

However, as we mentioned in the beginning of this section, this may be due to factors outside the education system. As a result of a lawsuit known as Abbott v. Burke, New Jersey was forced to increase state funding to education in its poorest school districts. By 2016 funding per student in these districts was among the highest in the state. The Camden district, for example, was spending $23,000 per student. Yet test scores and graduation rates showed little improvement. In Camden, one-third of the seniors did not graduate on time and more than 90 percent of high-school students were not considered proficient in the language arts or math (Turner, 2016). This anecdotal evidence is supported by a number of studies suggesting that there is little connection between education spending and academic success (Hanushek, 1997; Hanushek & Lindseth, 2009; Coulson, 2014).

While it is certainly true that broader societal inequalities play a major role in educational success and the education system has a staggering task in remedying the disadvantages of poorer students, it seems counterintuitive to suggest that the levels of resource inequality in the US school system do not disadvantage students in low-funding districts, most of which are in areas of low income (Condron & Roscigno, 2003). In one school in Philadelphia's William Penn School District, the classrooms are so poorly heated that the teachers provide blankets for students. According to student Jameria Miller, "The cold is definitely a distraction." Miller, who has also studied in more affluent districts, with better-funded schools, lamented that "it's never going to be fair. They're always going to be a step ahead of us. They'll have more money than us, and they'll get better jobs than us, always" (Turner et al., 2016). Schools in poorer districts suffer from a host of resource issues, which may help explain their unequal outcomes, despite some authors' claims that increasing funding is not linked to better academic achievement. These schools have larger classes, fewer, older books, and fewer qualified teachers, none of which should be expected to improve student achievement (Darling-Hammond, 2004; Clotfelter, Ladd, & Vigdor, 2010; Brathwaite, 2017).

Few are arguing for throwing money randomly at school districts in the hope that some of it will stick to something helpful, but increased spending targeted at attracting and keeping high-quality teachers, appropriately heated classrooms, and up-to-date instructional materials should improve the educational experience. So, too, should common-sense attempts to alleviate the most obvious disadvantages of poverty. For example, if students are coming to school suffering from poor health and nutrition, funding directed at alleviating those problems may be more effective than a new textbook (Turner, 2016). There is certainly ample empirical evidence to counter the "money does no good" theory, at least for low-income students. For example, a massive 2016 study, looking at fifteen thousand students over the thirty-year period from 1955 to 1985, found that poor children who attended schools that received a 10 percent increase in inflation-adjusted per-pupil spending before they started their 12-year education were 10 percentage points more likely to complete high school than other poor children. The study also tracked their adult earnings and found that the low-income children who went to the better-funded schools had 10 percent higher earnings and were 6 percentage points less likely to be poor (Jackson et al., 2016) (for other studies that find a positive relationship between funding and achievement see: Biddle, 1997; Wenglinsky, 1997; Elliott, 1998; Harter, 1999; Payne & Biddle, 1999). Another study compared the math scores of students in poorly and well-funded public schools. It found that the better-funded schools had a lower gap in academic achievement between students from high and low socio-economic status than did poorly funded schools (Wenglinsky, 1998). More broadly, the states that spent more on public education between 1970 and 1995 had greater equality (as measured by Gini coefficients) in the year 2000 than states that spent less (Behr, Christofides, & Neelakantan, 2004).

Compared to other nations, funding of K-12 education in the US is fairly high. However, for this spending, educational results are fair to middling at best. Part of the explanation for this is the unequal economic context from which students come. Another part of the explanation is that school funding is very uneven, meaning that for some school districts, most often those in poorer areas, there is legitimate talk of a crisis in public education funding that has been exacerbated by states' fiscal cutbacks after the 2008 economic collapse. As a result, the very students who already start off at a disadvantage due to the high levels of income inequality and poverty in the US find themselves further hindered by the limited funding of the public schools they are more likely to attend, while those students with the advantages of being born into a high-income household enjoy the benefits of well-funded schools. The third part of the explanation for the modest K-12 results in the US is that it has applied neoliberal ideas to running education.

Neoliberalism in the K-12 school system

The neoliberal trend of reducing taxing and spending has hit to varying degrees in different districts and states. So, too, has the attempt to reform how education is delivered along neoliberal lines. Neoliberalism, when applied to education, opens up the sector to private firms while stressing the importance of choice, accountability, and labor-market flexibility. In practice, this has been operationalized by several key changes to how schooling is organized and taught since the 1980s. The first change revolves around accountability, which has been interpreted as measuring student, teacher, and school achievement in a uniform and consistent manner through standardized testing. Second, these test scores then provide crucial information for parents to select between schools under the assumption that the competition for students will create excellence in education. Third, the alleged bureaucratic sluggishness of publicly administered schools was replaced with schools run by private-sector groups of varying stripes. Finally, as a method of cost reduction teachers have come under attack under the misleading language of transferring power from unions to parents.

In 2015, eleven teachers in Atlanta were convicted of racketeering, among other crimes, after they were found guilty of cheating on standardized tests. The scale of the cheating was remarkable: "answer sheets were altered, fabricated, and falsely certified. Test scores that were inflated as a result of cheating were purported to be the actual achievement of targets through legitimately obtained improvements in students' performance." Although the teachers were found culpable, the indictment made it very clear that the real guilty party was the system of rewards and punishments linked to test scores instigated by former Superintendent of the Year Beverly Hall, in which employees who missed targets were either fired or threatened with termination while those who surpassed the goals received financial rewards. "Over time, the unreasonable pressure to meet annual APS [Atlanta Public Schools] targets led some employees to cheat" (Strauss, 2015).

This was not supposed to be the outcome of standardized testing. According to NCLB, standardized testing was supposed to provide an objective measure of student performance between classrooms, schools, and districts. The concern was that an A in one school may not mean the same as an A in another. Indeed, there was some worry that an A in some schools may not even prepare students adequately for college (Hursh, 2007). But standardized testing was not merely used to assess how students were performing. Rather, test scores were linked to a variety of rewards and punishments by federal and state governments. For example, in NCLB, test scores were linked to Adequate Yearly Progress (AYP) targets that would trigger consequences well beyond the usual student stress over passing a grade or graduation (although student success did depend on success in standardized testing). Success or failure in meeting the AYP goals meant that schools would receive extra resources, face reorganization, or even face closure. Districts were threatened with the loss of federal funds. Teachers and other employees meeting AYP targets received bonuses, while those who failed could face demotion or firing.

There is an inevitable tension between the dual goals of standardized testing: to provide accurate assessment of student achievement and act as an incentive for teachers, schools, and districts. As one report on standardized testing perceptively noted, "as the stakes associated with a test go up, so does the uncertainty about the meaning of a score on the test" (Nichols & Berliner, 2005). If test scores are going to be used to reward and punish actors in the schools, it creates an inevitable incentive to manipulate the scores. This can be, and, as the Atlanta case clearly shows, has been, accomplished by outright cheating on the tests, but it can be done in much more subtle methods that compromise the goals of education as well.

In New York, standardized testing, and the NCLB-inspired rewards and punishments, were introduced in the mid-1990s. As in Atlanta, cheating and manipulation were a problem. Students had to pass a set of exams in a handful of subjects in order to graduate. Until 2010, teachers graded the exams of their own students and were responsible for regrading tests that were just below a pass. Economists studying the tests found that in 40 percent of the tests in which scores were near the cutoffs (6 percent of all the exams) the grades were inflated (Dee, Dobbie, Jacob, & Rockoff, 2016). Studies on how teachers and schools have changed their behavior as a result of the emphasis on testing found that teachers would "teach the test" at the expense of more diverse, interesting styles of learning. Teachers also focused more effort on students whose abilities were just below the pass level of the test, while limiting their attention on students who would be much more certain to either pass or fail. Part of the evaluation in New York was based on student performance in exit exams. Schools responded to this by encouraging poorly performing students to leave the school before the exam either by transferring to another school or by completing high school through the General Educational Development degree (Hursh, 2007).

More generally, the emphasis on standardized testing and accountability can be expected to have four effects of dubious academic value: reallocation of resources to subjects, questions, and students most important to passing the test; alignment of material to more closely reflect the test questions; coaching students specifically for the test, for example practice on past test questions; and cheating (Koretz, 2009; see also Au, 2009). It is important to stress that none of these responses should be expected to improve the actual educational experience of the student. Rather, they are designed to make the student, school, and district appear to be better educated according to the narrow metric of standardized testing. No other results should be expected from the use of a standardized metric as an arbiter of reward and punishment in education, as they are predicted perfectly by Goodhart's Law, which posits that, when used for purposes of control, such metrics cease to be reliable, since "they do not measure performance itself, distort what is measured, influence practice towards what is being measured and cause unmeasured parts to get neglected" (Elton, 2004, p. 121). Even more broadly, as former PBS education journalist John Merrow noted, if the goal of the education system is to produce citizens capable of fully participating in democratic decision making, then the emphasis on standardized testing is particularly poorly thought out (Merrow, 2017).

A crucial part of applying neoliberal ideas to schools is providing parents with the right to choose. The language of "choice," key to market-resonant understandings of the good life, is a vehicle for two important aspects of neoliberal politics. One is that it positions teachers' unions as the enemy of choice, attempting to weaken them. With dwindling private sector union rates, teachers form an important pillar of the labor movement in the US more broadly, so undermining teachers' unions is understood by conservatives as an effective assault on workers' power nationally. The other is that it helps open the vast, publicly funded US educational system up as a source of profit for the private sector. Companies like the failed Edison Inc., or the current for-profit educational giant K12, have long been promising to revolutionize learning, bring innovative new technologies, and transform American education while turning a profit. Their records on these fronts are not very strong, but private businesses have not given up the dream of channeling public educational funds into their pockets. Charter schools, as one visible example of this, not only promote school choice but also move the ownership and control of schools outside the public sector. Charter schools are so named because they sign a contract, or charter, with the government promising to deliver certain educational objectives in return for payment. Charters are publicly funded, and, therefore, admission is free, but they can be selective in the students they admit (although not on the basis of race or gender). The key difference is that charters are owned and run not by the government educational authority but by independent institutions that range from non-profits to for-profit corporations. Advocates of charter schools argue that they free education from the overly bureaucratic apparatus of the public education system and the worker-focused influence of teachers' unions. Further, because the charter specifies measurable outcomes, schools are more accountable and can even have their charter revoked if they do not deliver (Brathwaite, 2017).

The idea that publically funded schools do not need to be run by the government has a long history. In 1955, Milton Friedman argued that because education, especially in its early years, has strong positive effects on a democratic society and should be available to all without income acting as a barrier, government should pay for children's education. However, that did not mean that they should necessarily deliver educational services. Friedman, a critic of most things not private, argued for a voucher system that would allow parents to choose between competing schools. The only real necessary roles for the state were to ensure that children went to school and establish a set of standards by which schools must abide (Friedman, 1955).

The evidence on the impact of charter schools on educational outcomes is mixed. Research conducted on charter schools in Massachusetts suggests that they have had some positive impacts. In low-achieving, non-white, poor, urban areas, student achievement improved more at charter schools than other public schools. Non-urban charters, on the other hand, appear to reduce student achievement. The authors of the study attribute much of the success of the urban charters to their use of the "No Excuses"[1] educational approach rather than the inherent benefits of charter schools themselves (Angrist et al., 2013). A later study by many of the same authors reached even more positive conclusions. Compared to regular public school pupils, students at charter schools were more likely to pass their high-school graduation exam, qualify for a college scholarship from the state, and attend a four-year rather than a two-year post-secondary institution (Angrist et al., 2016).

Studies on charter schools in other states have come to much less positive conclusions. In a script straight out of *The Shock Doctrine*, Louisiana implemented an especially aggressive charter-school push after Hurricane Katrina swept through (Hursh, 2007). In the weeks following the hurricane, the Urban Institute published a report that called for a massive restructuring of public education in the state with an emphasis on vouchers and charter schools. The state certainly used the disaster as an excuse to dismantle the existing system of public schools, especially the influential teachers' union. Louisiana let all its 4500 public school teachers go and dramatically restructured its school administrative apparatus. By 2010, 61 of 88 public schools were charters (Lipman, 2011).

In a 2010 interview, US Secretary of Education under President Obama, Arne Duncan candidly claimed that "the best thing that happened to the education system in New Orleans was Hurricane Katrina. That education system was a disaster. And it took Hurricane Katrina to wake up the community to say that we have to do better. And the progress that it made in four years since the hurricane is unbelievable" (Bruce, 2010). While he was certainly correct that the wake of a hurricane provided the void into which charter-school reform could be pushed, his claims about the progress of those reforms were made well before the evidence was in. In a major study of the Louisiana Scholarship Program, a voucher program that pays for low- and middle-income public school children to attend other schools, results were not encouraging. The study took advantage of a lottery format in which the private schools that received more applicants than they could enroll admitted students through a lottery. The study compared students moving from public to private through the lottery to those who did not. Students who moved from the public to private schools scored worse in both reading and math in their first two years after the move. The results were dramatic. Students starting in the fiftieth percentile while at public school fell 24 percentile points below the control group in math. Further, the move from public to private failed to improve student scores on what might be described as broader citizenship measures of student self-esteem and political tolerance (Mills et al., 2016).

Another study of Ohio's Educational Choice Scholarship voucher program was similarly ambiguous. The study was conducted by the conservative Thomas B. Fordham Institute, an advocate for school choice, and funded by another voucher proponent, the Walton Family Foundation. The study concluded that the voucher program had produced "a mixed bag" (Figlio & Karbownik, 2016, p. 39). On one hand students eligible for the Educational Choice vouchers showed improved performance. However, students who actually participated in the voucher system by moving from a public to a private school had test results that were "unambiguously negative" in both reading and math compared to remaining in public school (Figlio & Karbownik, 2016, p. 34).

In the midst of the debate about student achievement, there is another undercurrent to the debate about vouchers and charter schools. Schools are not only a place in which the next generation, more or less successfully, acquires the skills necessary to be both workers and citizens. The conditions under which students learn are also the conditions under which teachers work. Advocates of vouchers and charter schools often see these reforms as an effective method of eliminating what they see as the cumbersome, bureaucratic weight of teachers and their unions dragging down the education system. The logic is very much in line with the neoliberal claim about performance and competition. Schools should be able to punish poorly performing teachers and reward those who succeed (with performance bonuses for example). Further, innovative teaching methods and curriculum design should not be thwarted by intransigent teachers, reluctant to change. This argument has survived despite evidence that school districts with strong unions are better able to keep good teachers and more successful at dismissing poor performers (Han, 2016). The percent of charter schools that were unionized declined from 12 to 7 percent between 2009 and 2012 while the percentage that used "performance based compensation" increased from 19 to 37 percent (Rebarber & Zgainer, 2014, p. 3). By contrast, 68 percent of public-school teachers were unionized in 2012 (Bureau of Labor Statistics (BLS), 2014). The differing unionization rate is one reason that teachers, who once were fairly open to the idea of school choice, have become increasingly opposed (Carey, 2017). Unionization of the teaching staff is also only one indication of the more general issue of the role of teachers in schools. In the US, the relatively low salaries of teachers compared to similarly educated workers are indicative of the role that teachers are expected to play. In the US, teachers are required to obtain a Bachelor's degree, which is less education than is required in many affluent nations. The average teaching load in the US is 30 hours per week, which is 50 percent higher than in many other countries (Brown, 2011). High professional standards, generous compensation, secure tenure and teacher control over the classroom are very much at odds with both the general neoliberal tenet of labor-market flexibility and the educational priorities of standardized testing and rigid curriculum.

The issues we have raised about standardized testing, school choice and alternative forms of ownership should not be confused with an uncritical endorsement of the old public-school system. While the US school system was (and still is) required to do some extraordinarily heavily lifting to create anything approaching equality of opportunity considering the overwhelmingly unequal context in which it operates, like the health system, it was always a bit understrength for the task. The US is distinctive in the extent to which it seeks to use the education system as a major pillar of its welfare system (Katz, 2010), charged not only with direct delivery of healthcare and nutrition to children in poverty but with creating the conditions for social mobility. Unfortunately, the education system is neither a suitable vehicle nor adequately resourced to handle the weight of poverty and inequality produced by US capitalism. Differences in funding between rich and poor districts were especially to blame for exacerbating inequalities. So, while public education could, and should, fulfill a role in which all students are provided with the opportunity to flourish, in the US it has "historically been saturated with inequalities and exclusions" (Lipman, 2011). However, the neoliberal reforms outlined above move the education system in entirely the wrong direction.

Nations that perform better than the US (in the sense that they deliver better educational outcomes at lower cost) take a very different approach. Finland, for example consistently spends under $10,000 per student (compared to over $12,000 in the US) on non-tertiary education (OECD, 2017). Despite this lower spending per student, Finland ranks much higher than the US in international testing, as shown in Table 5.1. Further, the difference between the weakest and strongest students is the smallest in the world (Taylor, 2012).

Finland's approach to education could not be more different from that in the US. Rather than an emphasis on standardized testing, students in Finland only take one mandatory standardized test, when they are 16. They usually don't get homework until their teenage years. They have an egalitarian system where all children, regardless of ability, are taught in the same room. Students get the freedom of a 75-minute recess (compared to an average of 27 in the US) (Taylor, 2012). Teachers are better paid, better qualified, and worked less intensely. Teachers have required to have a Master's degree. To ensure that there is an adequate supply of qualified instructors, their education is fully funded. All teachers are unionized and their unions are invited to provide much more input into the way in which education is structured and delivered in the classroom. Teachers spend about twenty hours a week in the classroom. Science classes are capped

Table 5.1 PISA rankings 2015

	Math	Reading	Science
Finland	13	4	5
United States	40	24	26

Source: National Center for Education Statistics, 2016

at 16 students (Brown, 2011). High-school teachers with 15 years of experience get paid 102 percent of other college graduates (in the US this is around 60 percent) (OECD, 2017). Finally, the education system in Finland is completely state-funded.

The adverse impacts of neoliberal reforms on education have caused one of its original, high-profile supporters to dramatically reconsider her position. Diane Ravitch was the assistant secretary of education in the George H. W. Bush administration and a member of the National Assessment Governing Board during the Clinton presidency. During her terms in office she supported NCLB, charter schools, standardized testing, and school choice. However, in her 2010 book *The Death and Life of the Great American School System* Ravitch argues that all these changes have resulted in US children not receiving a full education (Ravitch, 2010a). As she succinctly summarized, "the evidence says No Child Left Behind was a failure, and charter schools aren't going to be any better" (Ravitch, 2010b).

Post-secondary education

Neoliberalism has also caused a dramatic transformation in the landscape of post-secondary education. Berkeley, regarded by many as the nation's finest public university, and one of the so-called "public Ivies" (along with UCLA, Michigan, North Carolina, and Virginia) is a cautionary case study about the perils of this new educational environment. In 1991, the state's share of the Berkeley operating budget was 47 percent. By 2011, state funding was only 11 percent of the budget (de Vise, 2011). In response to the declining state funding, Berkeley increased tuition fees, so that they made up 30 percent of revenue in 2015. According to an open letter by Chancellor Nicholas Dirks, this was a small part of the "new normal" at the institution that would also include changes to the university's course offerings and employment conditions, greater fund raising, and increased on-line offerings (Kelderman, 2016).

As part of the fund raising drive, Berkeley signed a lucrative but controversial deal with BP in 2007 to create the Energy Biosciences Institute (EBI). This $500 million project was designed to fund research on alternative energy sources and reducing the impact of energy consumption on the environment. In a press release, Berkeley Vice Chancellor for Research, Beth Burnside, declared that "in launching this visionary institute, BP is creating a new model for university-industry collaboration" (Sanders, 2007). Notwithstanding the supposedly "visionary" nature of this new partnership, the funding relationship highlighted some of the problems with increased dependence on corporate-funded research. First, there were concerns about the independence of the research. As Jennifer Washburn, the author of *University, Inc.* (Washburn, 2005), noted in an op-ed in the *Los Angeles Times*, BP seemed to have a great deal of control over who would staff the new institute, and who would control the research. BP would "propose" that the director and senior positions be filled by either BP employees or people appointed by BP, who could then be expected to wield considerable influence over the direction of research through their control of the institute's finances. BP would also co-own the intellectual property created by the institute. Even Berkeley acknowledged that these terms "deviate from standard policy" (Washburn, 2007). In addition to questions surrounding the independence of the research, the funding levels were also subject to BP's discretion. In an ironic twist, the cost of BP's calamitous Gulf of Mexico oil spill in 2010 (alongside falling gasoline prices) forced a belt-tightening re-examination of corporate spending priorities, resulting in BP pulling about one-third of its funding for the EBI and its goal of reducing the impact of energy extraction on the environment, in 2015. Larger cuts were slated for the remaining two years of the deal (Neumann, 2015).

Evaluating the Berkeley–BP deal requires a consideration of the role of post-secondary education in our society. Like K-12 schooling, post-secondary education should have a dual role. It should fulfill the Mann criteria of accessible training for the labor market. This not only benefits the future employee but it also subsidizes firms by using public money to train their workforce. Post-secondary education must also fulfill the Dewey criteria of fostering fully functioning citizens, capable of contributing to a democracy. In addition to these student-focused roles, which post-secondary education holds in common with K-12 schooling, universities also play a crucial role in research. As in teaching, where there is a tension between whether the citizen-fostering role or the labor-market preparation should dominate, there is a tension surrounding the goals of university research. On one hand, universities should conduct genuinely independent and, therefore, trusted research. On the other, it subsidizes the private sector by conducting research that often has commercial applications from which firms can benefit (O'Connor, 1973).

The state of post-secondary education

The US has one of the highest levels of post-secondary achievement in the world. In 2016, 45.7 percent of 25-to-64-year-olds completed post-secondary (tertiary) education. This ranked the US seventh out of 45 countries, just behind the UK and well above the OECD average of 35.7 percent (OECD, 2016). However, if one were looking for a note of caution in this admirable achievement it might be that other nations appear to be catching up to the US. Among the younger, 25-to-34-year-old population, the percent of the US population with a tertiary education is still 47.5 percent, but this ranks only twelfth out of the 45 nations, not far above the OECD average of 43.1 percent. This reflects the fact that the percentage of the population graduating from post-secondary institutions has increased more quickly in other nations that it has in the US. In 2000, the share of 25-to-34-year-olds with a tertiary education increased by 17 percentage points on average in the OECD and by a more modest 9 percentage points in the US. In part, this reflects the already high level of educational attainment in the US, but it does demonstrate that the educational gap in post-secondary attainment enjoyed by the US over other nations is shrinking (OECD, 2017, p. 3). The high overall level of US tertiary education also hides a substantial difference between states. Only 29 percent of West Virginia's population graduated from tertiary education in 2016, well below the OECD average (OECD, 2017, p. 3). Finally, the fact that adults in the US have more modest rankings in literacy, numeracy, and science compared to other nations may suggest that the level of education at some of the tertiary institutions is not always particularly high.

Spending on post-secondary education in the US is also relatively high compared to other countries. Of the 38 nations in a 2014 OECD sample, the US ranked second ($29,300) in spending per student in public and private institutions. Of this considerable spending per student, the US relies more on private financing than most nations. Private financing made up 65 percent of post-secondary spending, behind only Korea, Japan, and the U.K. At the other end of the spectrum, private finance accounted for only 3.5 percent of tertiary funding in 2014 in Finland and Norway. While some of this private spending comes in the form of donations from the private sector, 46 percent of total tertiary spending comes from the pockets of students and their parents in the US. By way of comparison, in Denmark and Finland, household spending makes up zero percent of the total (OECD, 2014).

Post-secondary education delivery is split between different ownership models. Of the post-secondary institutions eligible for Title IV (federal student aid) financing, 34 percent were public, 35 percent private non-profit and 31 percent private for-profit in 2012. The number of for-profit institutions has expanded dramatically, from 791 in 2002 to 1451 in 2012. However, the growth in for-profit institutions has not reflected a change in student enrollment. The vast majority of undergraduates attended public institutions in 2012 (about 76 percent), about the same percentage as in 1970. During this period, the share of students in non-profits fell from 23 to 15 percent while the share in for-profit increased from 1 to 9 percent (Cahalan & Perna, 2015).

Neoliberalism in post-secondary education

Neoliberalism in post-secondary education has manifested itself in several important ways, some of which are familiar from the K-12 discussion, but some of which are unique to education beyond high school, especially at colleges and universities. Post-secondary education has been impacted by the neoliberal trend to cut taxes and, therefore, the spending capacity of the public sector. Both the cutbacks in public funding and the neoliberal conception of education as a private, market benefit to be translated into future income gains has resulted in growing tuition payments for students and their families. The labor market in the university also increasingly follows the neoliberal policies of flexibility and accountability. The key difference between the university and K-12 on the accountability front is that in K-12 the standardized accountability metrics are imposed on the students and delivered by the teachers. In universities, it is the professors that are increasingly subject to the pinching and weighing of standardized metrics. The decline in public funding has also meant that universities have increasingly sought out corporate partnerships of which the Berkeley–BP deal is only one, particularly large, example. This increasing corporate presence has crucial implications for the autonomy of the university, both for the student experience, in terms of the courses taught and programs offered, and for the independence of what are supposed to be the foremost research institutions in the nation (Canaan, 2008; Lave et al., 2010; Clawson, 2013; Giroux, 2014).

As was the case in K-12, the purpose of post-secondary education is subject to the Dewey–Mann debate about whether universities and colleges should be turning out future workers with job-ready skills or more broadly trained people ready to act as democratic citizens. This debate around the role of educating the next generation is mirrored in the appropriate role of research at universities. On one hand, universities provide research that often, directly or indirectly, subsidizes the private sector. On the other, the university is a center of independent learning and research that benefits society as a whole. While these two roles are not always at cross-purposes, a focus on the second priority would lead to more research that often has little direct commercial application or could, in some cases, actually harm the interests of business. If one looks beyond the student experience in post-secondary education, the Dewey–Mann division can be recast as a tension between its roles in supporting the profitability of business and as a center of critical thought and independent research. It should come as little surprise that the impact of neoliberalism on the university has resulted in a tilt towards the former and away from the latter.

Funding post-secondary education: the Mann principle of equality of access

Mann's crusade for free, public education failed to make it to post-secondary education. While, to varying degrees, the government in the US does contribute to funding universities, defraying some of the cost to the student, the largely accepted policy is that (with the exception of the 2017 move by New York) students should pay for some portion of their post-secondary education. However, Mann's entreaty that education should be accessible to all rings as true in post-secondary education as it does in K-12.

The most telling transformation of post-secondary education funding has been the decline in state money and the rise in dependence on tuition revenue. In 1977, state and local governments contributed 57 percent of higher-education revenues and personal spending accounted for 33 percent. By 2012, state and local governments were contributing only 39 percent, while personal spending increased to 49 percent (the federal government's contribution remained relatively unchanged at 12 percent during this period) (Cahalan & Perna, 2015, p. 26). This has frequently been portrayed as universities being forced to increase tuition in order to replace the revenue decline from the government, but the timing does not quite work for this explanation. As University of California-Santa Barbara professor Christopher Newfield explained in *The Great Mistake*, universities and colleges started raising tuition fees well before the cuts in funding from state governments. During the 1980s, they increased tuition fees by about 50 percent (in constant dollars). In the 1990s real tuition fees went up by 38 percent. Yet, during these two decades, real state funding increased, if only slightly (Newfield, 2016, p. 42). Newfield argues that the ability of universities to generate tuition revenue allowed the states to reduce their financial contribution. It was after 2000 that the funding cuts really kicked in. Between 2000 and 2016, state funding per student in public universities declined by 25 percent (Daniels, 2016). Returning to the Berkeley example, in 2000, around 50 percent of its revenues came from the state, but by 2016 that number had fallen to 13 percent (Daniels, 2016).

Recently, part of the increases in tuition fees have been compensated for by increases in federal spending, most prominently from Pell Grants, a need-based program of financial aid. Between 2000 and 2012, revenue per student from federal sources going to post-secondary institutions (public, non-profit, and for-profit) grew by 32 percent after inflation (Pew Charitable Trusts, 2015). Despite the shift from state budget spending to federal aid for tuition, the out-of-pocket expenses for students have grown dramatically since the late 1970s. While the maximum Pell Grant has increased from $4690 in 1974 to $5550 in 2012 (in constant 2012 dollars), the average cost of college (which includes tuition, fees, room, and board) went up from $8858 in 1974 to $20,234 in 2012. It is also worth noting that most students do not get this full maximum Pell amount. The average student grant was $3579 in 2012 (Cahalan & Perna, 2015, p. 19).

Of course, the average cost of university masks a tremendous difference between educational institutions. The cost of attending a two-year community college is vastly different from paying a full ride at Harvard. Tuition at the grand old private universities does create a certain sticker shock among those of modest means. In 2015, tuition at Harvard was over $45,000, 17 times more than in 1971. If Harvard's yearly fees had increased at the rate of inflation, the 2015 tuition would be a more affordable $15,000 (Schoen, 2015). Despite the fact that poor families are more likely to attend cheaper post-secondary institutions, with its implications for educational quality and earnings after graduation, college is increasingly unaffordable for lower-income families. The net price of university (the cost of college plus transportation minus grant aid), even outside the elite circles of Harvard and its ilk, has increased for rich and poor alike. Between 1990 and 2012 the average net price of college for students from families in the bottom quintile (below $34,000) of incomes increased from $10,881 to $13,699 after inflation. For students from the top quintile of incomes (over $108,650) it increased from $18,123 to $26,580 (Cahalan & Perna, 2015, p. 20). As a percentage of average family income, the average net price of university for those in the top quartile increased from 10 percent in 1990 to 15 percent in 2012. However, for those in the bottom quartile the average net price of college increased from 45 to 84 percent of average family income (Cahalan & Perna, 2015, p. 27).

While the gap between low- and high-income post-secondary attendance has shrunk, as a result of these increased costs the gap between high- and low-income university graduation rates has grown. In 1970, 74 percent of the top quartile attended post-secondary compared to 28 percent of lowest quartile (a gap of 46 percentage points). By 2012 the gap between top and bottom quartiles had closed to 37 percentage points (82 to 45 percent). However, this closing gap is not reflected in university graduation rates. The gap between high and low incomes getting a bachelor's degree by age 24 has grown. In 1970, 6 percent of those in the bottom quartile earned a bachelor's by 24 compared to 40 percent from the top. By 2013, the percent from the bottom quartile had increased only to 9 percent while 77 percent of those from the top quartile received a bachelor's degree (Cahalan & Perna, 2015, p. 30). Thomas Kane, from Harvard, found that states with the highest increases in tuition had the largest increase in enrollment gaps between high- and low-income students (Kane, 1995). A review of the empirical work on the connection between tuition and enrollment in the US concluded that, in general, increases in tuition fees lead to declines in enrollment and that "lower income students are more sensitive to changes in tuition and aid than are students from middle and upper income families" (Heller, 1997, p. 650). It should hardly come as a surprise that increasing tuition fees creates a larger deterrent for those with lower incomes.[2]

For those who do complete university, debt is becoming as much a part of the college experience as lectures and drinking. The percentage of those with a bachelor's degree who borrowed to help finance their education was 49 percent in 1992 and 71 percent in 2012. Not only are more students borrowing but they are also borrowing more. For those borrowing during their bachelor's degree, the average amount almost doubled in constant dollars from $16,500 in 1993 to $29,400 in 2013 (Cahalan & Perna, 2015).

The shift in cost of university education from governments (and taxpayers) to students and their families has compromised the Mann principle of accessible education. University education has become far more a privilege determined by parental income that compromises social mobility, than a ladder to higher incomes available to all with the ability and desire to learn. Even those who do cough up the higher fees of today's university are worse off after graduation than previous generations because of the debt that increasingly accompanies their educational experience.

Neoliberalism inside the university

The administrative structure at most universities has historically been much more democratic than most workplaces. While most companies, and even most places in the public service, have a top-down command chain, where those at higher levels dictate to those below them, employees at the university have considerable say in running their institutions. In the American Association of University Professors (AAUP) shared governance model, professors traditionally had, and in many places still have, considerable control over their work lives through the tradition of collegial governance. They could determine course content, the structure of degrees, and what they chose to research. They often even had a say in who their administrative "superiors," such as Deans and department heads, would be. Indeed, the administrative apparatus of the university was originally conceived as a structure to facilitate the policies and programs desired by the professoriate. Further, many of the administrators were drawn from the academic ranks, and often returned to their professorial roles after a stint in the upper offices.

Academics also enjoy considerably more job security that is the case in other workplaces. After a probationary "tenure-track" period in which universities get to evaluate their new hire, the academic applies for tenure. If granted, it provides some guarantees against being let go for having and expressing unpopular opinions. This is the crucial concept of academic freedom, which permits professors, and the universities in which they work, to be a genuine source of innovative, critical, and even controversial ideas. This protection became the norm on campuses only after professors across the country fought back after many of their colleagues had been released from their positions for the temerity of publicly expressing and researching unpopular opinions (Schrecker, 1986). Prior to 1915, professors could be fired without recourse if they in any way offended their administrative pay masters. It was in this year that the AAUP produced its first statement on academic freedom, a code that was elaborated on and extended to include the process of tenure by 1940. It is worth noting that the widespread acceptance of these principles was largely a voluntary agreement between academics and their universities in the sense that the AAUP had no real mechanism to enforce the principles that it had laid down (Lee, 2015).

The structure of tenure, academic freedom, and collegial governance ensured that the university, far more than other workplaces, was a place in which the employees had considerable say in what they did and how their institution was run. Of course, from the standpoint of many university administrators, this created a lack of flexibility and control over their labor force. As Richard Chait, professor of higher education at Harvard University explains, according to many university administrators, the system of tenure "limits management's capacity to replace marginal performers with demonstrably or potentially better performers" (Chait, 2002, pp. 13–14). In insisting on a more flexible labor supply and the growing use of accountability metrics we again see the hallmarks of neoliberalism.

The world of academic labor has been transformed from a secure job, with a salary that reasonably compensated for the lengthy PhD quest required for tenure-track employment, into a precarious and poorly paid world of contingent employment. In the US between 1976 and 2011, a period in which enrollments were increasing dramatically, part-time faculty increased by 286 percent and full-time non-tenure-track faculty by 259 percent, but tenured and tenure-track faculty grew by only 23 percent (AAUP—American Association of University Professors, 2014; Baker, 2014). As a result, the composition of academic workers has undergone a dramatic transformation since the mid-1970s (Table 5.2). Tenure or tenure-track faculty made up 45 percent of academic labor force in 1975. By 2014 that number had dropped to 29 percent. On the other hand, unsecure labor (either non-tenure-track or part-time), increased from 34 to 58 percent.

For faculty working on course by course contracts, wages are poor and precarious. A study of part-time sociology instructors found that the median pay for a course in the fall 2010 term was $2235 at two-year colleges and $3400 at four-year doctoral or research universities (American Sociological Association, 2017, p. 11). At the two-year college rate, a grinding load of four courses a term, over three terms would bring in $26,820. Even that salary depends on the instructor being able to cobble together a full load of courses every term, which is far from guaranteed. Contingent faculty members have no guarantees of continued employment

Table 5.2 Composition of US academic labor force (%)

	1975	2014
Full-time tenured	29	21
Full-time tenure track	16	8
Full-time non-tenure track	10	17
Part-time employees	24	41
Graduate student employees	21	13

Source: AAUP—American Association of University Professors, 2016, p. 13

and have to hope that courses are available for them to teach. It is no wonder that one-quarter of college faculty on part-time appointments are forced to draw on some form of public assistance (Jacobs et al., 2015, p. 3). In addition, because they rely on a steady renewal of teaching contracts, non-tenured faculty do not benefit from the same academic freedom protections as their tenured colleagues, reducing their freedom to teach and research more controversial subjects.

At the same time, academics' control over their own institutions has been eroded. While the number of tenured faculty increased only marginally (23 percent) between 1976 and 2011, the number of full-time non-faculty professional positions (buyers and purchasing agents; human-resources, training, and labor-relations specialists; management analysts; loan counselors; lawyers; and other non-academic workers) shot up by 369 percent (AAUP—American Association of University Professors, 2014). The growing administrative overhead is engaged in a wide variety of activities, from student assistance to fund raising, but an important part of it is dedicated to increasing control over the faculty. Colleges and universities have replaced the collegial, or shared, governance model with more traditional workplace structures and management techniques (Schultz, 2005; Ginsberg, 2011). In addition to reducing faculty input into hiring, course content, and program structure, faculty are increasingly subject to Taylorist methods of weighing, measuring, and judging their academic performance.

Just as the use of test results to reward and punish teachers created unwanted and undesirable effects, the use of these kinds of metrics in universities has resulted in problematic changes. First, one of the most popular metrics, citations counts (the number of times a journal article is cited by other researchers), reward controversy as much as they reward quality. A nice example of this is the article "The Case for Colonialism" by Bruce Gilley which appeared in *Third World Quarterly*. Gilley argues that colonies were actually profoundly beneficial to the colonized and that the world might be improved by recolonizing some areas. It has been roundly criticized as an obvious distortion of the historical record (Robinson, 2014). However, it has also been wildly successful by citation metrics, achieving the highest Altmetric Attention Score of any article in *Third World Quarterly* (Roelofs & Gallien, 2017). Second, it is difficult to conceive of any system of metrics that could not be successfully gamed by clever academics. One easy example of this is for academics to cite each other's work in order to inflate citation counts. The result would be that these kinds of metrics would be a better measure of ability to collude than any genuine scholarly impact. Third, using metrics like citation counts has also been shown to create a bias against female and racialized faculty members (Lariviere et al., 2013). Finally, just as teachers altered their in-class time to ensure success in testing at the expense of other learning, professors will change their activities, doing less of the work that is not rewarded and more of the work that ticks the evaluation boxes. In one example of this, because attracting funding scores nicely on university metrics, faculty in sociology have moved from more theoretical work to obtaining grants from private or government funding agencies. This has the effect of narrowing and directing research in the discipline (Seybold, 2014). In a job that has diverse and impossible-to-quantify tasks from student advising to career advice, to graduate supervision, rewarding the quantifiable will result in a decrease in the unquantifiable. Because so many of the unquantifiable elements of an academic's job involve time with students, the educational experience at the university is destined to suffer.

The influence of corporate funding: research

Two neoliberal trends have combined to undermine one of the most crucial roles of the university. On one hand, increasingly entrepreneurial universities have been more actively searching for sources of money beyond their traditional revenue streams of government and students (Bok, 2003). On the other, corporations have become increasingly aware of the benefits of using the supposedly independent research produced in the ivory tower to more closely reflect corporate interests (Schrecker, 2010). The Berkeley–BP deal is only one example of a growing trend towards corporate funding influencing research at universities. Only the most naive commentator would claim that, in some golden age of the past, research done at universities reflected the academic utopia of an unbiased search for the truth. Obviously, research across all disciplines reflected a variety of economic dependencies. Government funding during the Cold War influenced not only the direction of scientific research at universities but also the evolution of the discipline of economics, whose mathematical, game theoretic approaches were deemed useful by the Rand Corporation and the Department of Defense (Bernstein,

2003). However, there can be little question that university research has become increasingly influenced by the growing corporate funding of their institutions.

The very credibility of university research is being jeopardized by corporate funding. As David Michaels has shown, seeding the scientific world with misleading information, pioneered by the tobacco industry's clouding of the scientific record on smoking and lung cancer, is now standard practice for US business (Michaels, 2008). The techniques include funding studies that contradict any inconvenient scientific findings and hiring experts to cast doubt on the methods employed by the offending study. These techniques have a long history. In the 1960s when Irving Selikoff established the link between asbestos and cancer, the asbestos industry attempted to discredit it by claiming Selikoff's conclusions were "based on limited reports relating to a relatively small group of workers who install and/or remove a variety of insulation materials, including some which contain asbestos" (Bohme et al., 2005, p. 335). The industry also hired lawyers to write to Selikoff warning against "unwise" use of his research in public discussions, and claimed falsely after his death that Selikoff was a fraud because he had never obtained a medical degree (Bohme et al., 2005, p. 342).

Most obviously problematically, researchers at universities, under pressure to improve their academic metrics, have been approached to put their names on papers written by firms that contain research results that support their products (Lave, Mirowski, & Randalls, 2010). A particularly audacious example involved industry ghost-writing a paper published in the *Journal of Occupational and Environmental Medicine* that attempted to downplay the health risks associated with chromium (VI) when OSHA and the state of California were trying to set new regulatory standards. The article was eventually exposed and retracted (Pearce, 2008).

According to a review of the state of research in pharmacoepidemiology and occupational epidemiology, there is far more industry-funded research that artificially downplays the dangers of products than there is independent research. Problematically, the sources of funding are frequently not disclosed (Pearce, 2008). The connections between the medical industry and university research are also too close for comfort (Fisher, 2009). In one notorious example, studies by Dr. Joseph L. Biederman, professor of psychiatry at Harvard Medical School and chief of pediatric psychopharmacology at Harvard's Massachusetts General Hospital, found that bipolar disorder in young children could be treated with prescription drugs. A 2009 Senate investigation found that Biederman had received $1.6 million in speaking and consulting fees from a variety of drug companies, some of which made the drugs that he was advocating as treatments for bipolar disorder. The intimate relationship between researchers and industry is more common practice than isolated malfeasance. In the alarming words of Harvard Medical School's Marcia Angell, "It is simply no longer possible to believe much of the clinical research that is published, or to rely on the judgment of trusted physicians or authoritative medical guidelines. I take no pleasure in this conclusion, which I reached slowly and reluctantly over my two decades as an editor of *The New England Journal of Medicine*" (Angell, 2009).

It is not only in the harder sciences that the direction of inquiry is being influenced by corporations looking for more control over how their donation dollars are spent. Although the social sciences appear, at first glance, to offer less immediate reward for firms than innovations in medicine, engineering, and science, they too have been the recipient of the golden straitjacket of strings-attached funding. In the social sciences, especially economics, the funding is driven more by a desire to change the broader policy environment in which firms operate than it is the immediate benefits of direct commercial gain. The infamous Koch brothers were heavily involved in this kind of directed donation. The free-market Mercatus Center received a $30 million donation from the Koch family to move to George Mason University in the 1980s (Johnson, 2017). The Charles Koch Foundation spent $140 million in the decade after 2005 funding over fifty research centers at colleges and universities. A veritable cottage industry of free enterprise, free market, and just plain freedom institutes has developed in response to the influx of corporate money. At West Virginia University, Ken Kendrick, the owner of the Arizona Diamondbacks, and the Koch Foundation each donated $2.5 million to launch The Center for Free Enterprise. Universities in Arizona appear to be especially keen. With the help of Koch Foundation funding, the department of philosophy at the University of Arizona opened the Center for the Philosophy of Freedom, dedicated, unsurprisingly, to all aspects of freedom. One of its faculty members, Matt Zwolinski, published "Sweatshops, Choice, and Exploitation," arguing that because sweatshop laborers agree to the terms of their employment, this creates a "moral claim against interference in the conditions of sweatshop labor by third parties such as governments," to improve their conditions (Zwolinski, 2007). Not to be outdone by its state rivals, in 2014 Arizona State's Center for Political Thought and Leadership, which received $1.3 million from the Koch Foundation, insisted that a new job be filled by a candidate with expertise on "the relations between free-market institutions and political liberty in modern history" (Hiltzik, 2016).

The ideal of impartial, independent university research in the quest for the public good may never have been. However, there can be little question that the twin imperatives of corporate interest in research and universities' desperation for funds has created a Faustian bargain. The direction of research, its conclusions, and the uses to which those conclusions are put are increasingly being influenced by corporate funding with strings very much attached. In this environment, the very information on which society depends to make both its day to day decisions as consumers and its overarching decisions on the extent of government intervention is less the result of independent scientific inquiry and more the result of big money guns for hire. "In selling its services to specific businesses, the corporate university undermines its legitimacy" (Schultz, 2005).

The funding of research centers and faculty appointments at universities by corporate interests has also impacted the student experience. While the trends in tuition compromise the Mann criteria of accessibility, the changing priorities of university have compromised the Dewey principle of fostering citizens. Increasingly cash-strapped universities have had to narrow their course offerings. In this belt-tightening context, both government and corporate funders have encouraged universities to prioritize labor-market-ready education at the expense of other, supposedly less marketable, course offerings (Nussbaum, 2010). In the words of the governor of North Carolina, Pat McCrory, "If you want to take gender studies, that's fine, go to a private school and take it. But I don't want to subsidize that if that's not going to get someone a job" (Cole, 2016).

Even the faculties that are geared towards educating citizens have been influenced by corporate funding. In one example, the bank BB&T provided grants that averaged around $1 million to over sixty colleges and universities to promote the "moral foundations of capitalism." In order to receive the grant, institutions had to include a course in which Ayn Rand's ode to libertarianism *Atlas Shrugged* was a crucial component. The BB&T deal also requires chaired faculty positions, something called designated capitalism centers, and complimentary student copies of *Atlas Shrugged* (Beets, 2015). Similarly, the Koch Foundation was among the donors who gave $6.6 million to create a "Program for the Study of Political Economy and Free Enterprise" within the Florida State University economics department's Gus A. Stavros Center for the Advancement of Free Enterprise and Economic Education. The Stavros Center promotes the free-market text *Common Sense Economics* and runs courses and seminars on its use in the classroom (Hiltzik, 2016). Other groups in society could fund academic institutions with different ideological stipulations. Unions could fund labor studies departments and environmental groups could provide funding for courses in ecology. However, these efforts would fall afoul of two problems: it's an arena in which corporations have a considerable advantage and it compromises the intellectual role of free inquiry that university should play in society.

Not only has the student experience been diminished in terms of access but the students who are able to attend have had their choices narrowed as courses deemed less immediately applicable to the labor market are cut and the content of those courses influenced by corporate funding. Universities are forsaking their role in producing citizens in favor of producing workers. Further, even those students who are choosing a more citizen-oriented education are receiving instruction that is increasingly dictated by the desires of funders.

Conclusion

When neoliberalism is applied to education it exacerbates rather than alleviates the inequalities that exist in society. In K-12 education the emphasis on reducing taxing and spending has negatively impacted some locations far more than others. Predictably, it has had a relatively more harmful effect in poor districts than in those that are richer. Neoliberalism has also opened up education to the profit motive and its accompanying mantra of choice, accountability, and labor-market flexibility. The results have not been particularly positive. Accountability has taken the problematic form of student standardized testing as a measure of teacher and school quality, with predictable transformations in the emphasis on learning (and cheating) in the classroom. While the growth in charter schools has successfully reduced the unionization of teachers, its record of improving student outcomes has been much more mixed, with some notable disasters in places like Louisiana.

Government funding of American public universities has plummeted as a result of fiscal constraints created by neoliberal policy in the areas of taxation and spending. Public universities in the US have come to rely more and more on corporate donations and rising tuition fees where, critics argue, profits, not the public good are served and where student access is determined more by privilege than merit. This has manifested itself in three important areas. First, although the university as a truly independent and unbiased bastion of research was more the ideal than reality, in the neoliberal period corporate financing has undermined both the independence and the objectivity of university research. The subject of inquiry has become increasingly shaped by the demands of funding and even the results of those investigations have been biased towards the interests of their paymasters. Second, the content and structure of what is taught at the university has been altered by the demands of both corporate funding and the demand that post-secondary education should train workers rather than create citizens. Finally, in the postwar period, tuition at public universities was subsidized to make university access less dependent on the income of students or their families. As universities have increased tuition fees, post-secondary education is increasingly the realm of the affluent, compromising its role facilitating social mobility between generations.

Education should enable individuals to lead "meaningful lives" (Nussbaum, 2010, p. 23). At a bare minimum this should mean a system that ensures that students have an equal opportunity to develop the skills and abilities that would enable them to make the best out of the unequal economic system into which they will be thrust once they step into the "real world." This would involve a drastic restructuring of the K-12 system to equalize educational conditions and ensuring that all students were admitted to post-secondary education based on merit rather than family income. The reason that this would be considered merely a minimum is that it might also imply a narrow, job-training focus and the role of education should be so much more. To help students lead fulfilling lives means more than merely finding an acceptable place on the food chain, it also means developing the capacity to understand and influence the broader world around them, including the policy environment in which they live. Educational institutions are one, although far from the only, place where this has historically happened. For this role to continue, students need to be offered a wide range of courses beyond those which narrowly train them for the job market.

It also requires that university faculty remain free to research topics they deem important and publish their conclusions without influence from funders. These two issues are not unrelated. As universities are restricted to offering job skills that narrowly benefit the recipient by moving them up the societal job ladder, and abandon (or are pressured to abandon) their role in fostering citizenship, the less justification the universities can claim for state support, leaving them more beholden to corporate funding for revenue (Lave et al., 2010). This is especially important in the context of growing mistrust of "facts". Paradoxically, many of the facts under dispute, like climate change, are actually true, while the suspect research, influenced and driven by corporations, goes unquestioned. However, the ability of research to be bought and paid for by any interest, and it is increasingly commercial interests that are doing this, helps undermine the role of research in uncovering facts and increasing our knowledge of the world around us.

Education has often been characterized as a bridge to the right side of the tracks, providing people from all backgrounds a path to a more fulfilling life. Those from more privileged backgrounds may start out on the "right" side, but anyone who applied themselves and studied hard could cross over. Under neoliberalism, this bridge has been steadily dismantled. Further, what is left of the education system is increasingly focused on having desperate people make an increasingly unlikely race across the shaky bridge before it collapses rather than providing people with an understanding that it needs to be fixed.

Notes

1 No Excuses is an educational trend whose practices include more instructional time, greater community engagement, a strict curriculum, and a rigid disciplinary code. Discussion of the merits of this package is beyond the scope of this chapter, but, tellingly in the framework of the debate of the role of education, one study of No Excuses concluded that they "develop worker-learners—children who monitor themselves, hold back their opinions, and defer to authority—rather than lifelong learners" (Golann, 2015).
2 Similar results were found in other countries. In Canada, for example tuition fee increases had a much larger negative effect on enrollment of low-income youth than those from higher incomes (Coelli, 2009).

References

AAUP—American Association of University Professors. (2014). Losing Focus: The Annual Report on the Economic Status of the Profession, 2013–14. *Academe*, 100(2), 4–38.

AAUP—American Association of University Professors. (2016). Higher Education at a Crossroads: The Annual Report on the Economic Status of the Profession, 2015–16. *Academe*, 102(2), 9–22.

American Sociological Association. (2017). *ASA Task Force on Contingent Faculty Interim Report*. Washington, DC: American Sociological Association.

Angell, M. (2009). Drug Companies & Doctors: A Story of Corruption, January 15. *New York Review of Books*.

Angrist, J., Cohodes, S., Dynarski, S., Pathak, P., & Walters, C. (2016). Stand and Deliver: Effects of Boston's Charter High Schools on College Preparation, Entry, and Choice. *Journal of Labor Economics*, 34(2), 275–318.

Angrist, J., Pathak, P., & Walters, C. (2013). Explaining Charter School Effectiveness. *American Economic Journal: Applied Economics*, 5(4), 1–27.

Au, W. (2009). *Unequal by Design: High-Stakes Testing and the Stanardization of Inequality*. New York: Routledge.

Baker, B. (2014). The End of the Academy? *BioScience*, 64(8), 647–652.

Baldwin, R., & Wawrzynski, M. (2011). Contingent Faculty as Teachers: What We Know; What We Need to Know. *American Behavioral Scientist*, 55(11), 1485–1509.

Beets, D. (2015). BB&T, Atlas Shrugged, and the Ethics of Corporation Influence on College Curricula. *Journal of Academic Ethics*, 13(4), 311–344.

Behr, T., Christofides, C., & Neelakantan, P. (2004). *The Effects of State Public K-12 Expenditures on Income Distribution*. Washington, DC: National Education Association.

Bernstein, M. (2003). Rethinking Economics in Twentieth Century America. In E. Fullbrook (ed.), *The Crisis in Economics* (pp. 154–159). New York: Routledge.

Biddle, B. (1997). Foolishness, Dangerous Nonsense, and Real Correlates of State Differences in Achievement. *Phi Delta Kappan*, 79(1), 8–13.

Biddle, B., & Berliner, D. (2002). A Research Synthesis / Unequal School Funding in the United States. *Educational Leadership*, 59(8), 48–59.

Bloom, H., & Unterman, R. (2012). *Sustained Positive Effects on Graduation Rates Produced By New York City's Small Public High Schools of Choice.* New York: mdrc.

Bohme, S., Zorabedian, J., & Egilman, D. (2005). Maximizing Profit and Endangering Health: Corporate Strategies to Avoid Litigation and Regulation. *International Journal of Occupational and Environmental Health,* 11(4), 338–348.

Bok, D. (2003). *Universities in the Marketplace: The Commercialization of Higher Education.* Princeton: Princeton University Press.

Booher-Jennings, J. (2005). Below the Bubble: Educational Triage and the Texas Accountability System. *American Educational Research Journal,* 42(2), 231–268.

Brathwaite, J. (2017). Neoliberal Education Reform and the Perpetuation of Inequality. *Crtical Sociology,* 43(3), 429–448.

Brown, D. (2011). *Why We're Seeing Corruption in American Classrooms: Comparing the US to Finland and Singapore,* October 26. Retrieved October 30, 2017, from Center for Teaching Quality: www.teachingquality.org/content/blogs/dan-brown/why-we-re-seeing-corruption-american-classrooms-comparing-u-s-finland-and-singapore.

Brown, M. (2017). Beyond Privatization in US Higher Education. In W. Halffman and H. Radder (eds), *International Responses to the Academic Manifesto: Reports from 14 Countries.* Retrieved on November 28, 2018, from https://socialepistemologydotcom.files.wordpress.com/2017/07/manifesto_reports_from_14_countries1.pdf, 9–14.

Bruce, M. (2010). *Duncan: Katrina Was the "Best Thing" for New Orleans School System,* January 29. Retrieved October 30, 2017, from ABCNews.com: http://blogs.abcnews.com/politicalpunch/2010/01/duncan-katrina-was-the-best-thing-for-new-orleans-schools.html.

Bruckmeier, K., & Wigger, B. (2014). The Effects of Tuition Fees on Transition from High School to University in Germany. *Economics of Education Review,* 41, 14–23.

Bureau of Labor Statistics (BLS). (2014). *Teacher Staffing and Pay Differences: Public and Private Schools.* Retrieved October 30, 2017, from Monthly Labor Review: www.bls.gov/opub/mlr/2014/article/teacher-staffing-and-pay-differences-5.htm.

Cahalan, M., & Perna, L. (2015). *Indicators of Higher Education Equity in the US.* Washington, DC: The Pell Institute.

Callender, C., & Jackson, J. (200). Does the Fear of Debt Constrain Choice of University and Subject of Study? *Studies in Higher Education,* 33(4), 405–429.

Canaan, J. (2008). *Structure and Agency in the Neoliberal University.* London: Taylor and Francis.

Carey, K. (2017). Dismal Voucher Results Surprise Researchers as DeVos Era Begins, February 24. *New York Times,* p. A20.

Chait, R. (2002). *The Question of Tenure.* Cambridge, MA: Harvard University Press.

Chapman, C., Laird, J., Ilfill, N., & KewalRamani, A. (2011). *Trends in High School Dropout and Completion Rates in the United States: 1972–2009.* Washington, DC: National Center for Education Statistics.

Chomsky, N. (2011). *Public Education under Massive Corporate Assault – What's Next?,* August 5. Retrieved October 3, 2017, from AlterNet: www.alternet.org/story/151921/chomsky%3A_public_education_under_massive_corporate_assault_%E2%80%94_what%27s_next.

Clawson, D. (2013). Faculty Unions at the Crossroads: Why Playing Defense Is a Losing Strategy. *New Labor Forum*, 22(1), 29–35.

Clotfelter, C., Ladd, H., & Vigdor, J. (2010). Teacher Credentials and Student Achievement in High School: A Cross-Subject Analysis with Student Fixed Effects. *The Journal of Human Resources*, 45(3), 656–681.

Coelli, M. (2009). Tuition Rees and Equality of University Enrolment. *Canadian Journal of Economics / Revue canadienne d'économique*, 42, 1072–1099.

Cole, J. (2016). The Pillaging of America's State Universities. *The Atlantic*, April 10.

Coulson, A. (2014). *State Education Trends Academic Performance and Spending over the Past 40 Years*. Washington, DC: Cato Institute.

Condron, D., & Roscigno, V. (2003). Disparities within: Unequal Spending and Achievement in an Urban School District. *Sociology of Education*, 76(1), 18–36.

Cremin, L. (1957). *The Republic and the School: Horace Mann on the Education of Free Men*. New York: Columbia University Press.

Daniels, R. (2016). Free the Public Universities, May 5. *The Chronicle of Higher Education*.

Darling-Hammond, L. (2004). Standards, Accountability, and School Reform. *Teachers College Record*, 106(6), 1047–1085.

de Vise, D. (2011). UC-Berkeley and other "public Ivies" in fiscal peril, December 26. *The Washington Post*.

Dee, T., Dobbie, W., Jacob, B., & Rockoff, J. (2016). *The Causes and Consequences of Test Score Manipulation: Evidence from the New York Regents Examinations*. NBER Working Paper No. 22165. Cambridge, MA: National Bureau of Economic Research.

Denny, K. (2014). The Effect of Abolishing University Tuition Costs: Evidence from Ireland. *Labour Economics*, 26, 26–33.

Dewey, J. (1916). *Democracy and education*. New York: Macmillan.

Elliott, M. (1998). School Finance and Opportunity to Learn: Does Money Well Spent Enhance Students' Achievement? *Sociology of Education*, 71(3), 223–245.

Elton, L. (2004). Goodhart's Law and Performance Indicators in Higher Education. *Evaluation & Research in Education*, 18(1–2), 120–128.

Evans, J. (2010). Industry Collaboration, Scientific Sharing and the Dissemination of Knowledge. *Social Studies of Science*, 40(5), 757–791.

Figlio, D., & Karbownik, K. (2016). *Evaluation of Ohio's EdChoice Scholarship Program: Selection, Competition, and Performance Effects*. Columbus, OH: Thomas B. Fordham Institute.

Fisher, J. (2009). *Medical Research for Hire: The Political Economy of Pharmaceutical Clinical Trials*. New Brunswick: Rutgers University Press.

Friedman, M. (1955). The Role of Government in Education. In R. Solow, *Economics and the Public Interest*. New Brunswick: Rutgers University Press.

Gilley, B. (2017). The Case for Colonialism. *Third World Quarterly*, 38, September. Reprinted in *Academic Questions*, Summer 2018, 167–185.

Ginsberg, B. (2011). *The Fall of the Faculty*. New York: Oxford University Press.

Giroux, H. (2014). *Neoliberalism's War on Higher Education*. Toronto: Between the Lines.

Golann, J. (2015). The Paradox of Success at a No-Excuses School. *Sociology of Education*, 88(2), 103–119.

Greenberg, D. (2007). *Science for Sale*. Chicago: University of Chicago Press.

Han, E. (2016). *The Myth of Unions' Overprotection of Bad Teachers: Evidence from District-Teacher Matched Panel Data on Teacher Turnover*. Working paper series, Labor and Worklife Program at Harvard Law School. Retrieved November 28, 2018, from http://haveyouheardblog.com/wp-content/uploads/2016/07/Han_Teacher_dismissal_Feb_16.pdf.

Haney, W. (2000). The Myth of the Texas Miracle in Education. *Education Analysis Policy Archives*, 8(41). Retrieved on November 28, 2018, from https://epaa.asu.edu/ojs/article/view/432/828.

Hanushek, E. (1997). Assessing the Effects of School Resources on Student Performance: An Update. *Educational Evaluation and Policy Analysis*, 19(2), 141–164.

Hanushek, E., and Lindseth, A. (2009). *Schoolhouses, Courthouses, and Statehouses Solving the Funding-Achievement Puzzle in America's Public Schools*. Princeton: Princeton University Press.

Harris, E. (2017). 10% of New York City Public School Students Were Homeless Last Year, October 10. *New York Times*.

Harter, E. (1999). How Educational Expenditures Relate to Student Achievement: Insights from Texas Elementary Schools. *Journal of Education Finance*, 24(3), 281–302.

Heller, D. (1997). Student Price Response in Higher Education: An Update to Leslie and Brinkman. *The Journal of Higher Education*, 68(6), 624–659.

Hiltzik, M. (2016). When Universities Try to Behave Like Businesses, Education Suffers, June 3. *Los Angeles Times*.

Hout, M. (2012). Social and Economic Returns to College Education in the United States. *Annual Review of Sociology*, 38(1), 379–400.

Hu, S., & McMahon, W. (2010). Higher Learning, Greater Good: The Private and Social Benefits of Higher Education. *Higher Education*, 60(1), 123–125.

Hübner, M. (2012). Do Tuition Fees Affect Enrollment Behavior? Evidence from a "Natural Experiment" in Germany. *Economics of Education Review*, 31(6), 949–960.

Hursh, D. (2007). Assessing No Child Left Behind and the Rise of Neoliberal Education Policies. *American Educational Research Journal*, 44(3), 493–518.

Jackson, C., Johnson, R., & Persico, C. (2016). The Effects of School Spending on Educational and Economic Outcomes: Evidence from School Finance Reforms. *Quarterly Journal of Economics*, 131(1), 157–218.

Jacobs, K., Perry, I., & MacGillvary, J. (2015). *The High Public Cost of Low Wages*. Berkeley, CA: UC Berkeley Center for Labor Research and Education.

Johnson, D. (2017). Academe on the Auction Block. *The Baffler*, 36. Retrieved on November 28, 2018, from https://thebaffler.com/salvos/academe-on-the-auction-block-johnson.

Kane, T. (1995). *Rising Public College Tuition and College Entry: How Well Do Public Subsidies Promote Access to College?* Cambridge, MA: National Bureau of Economic Research.

Katz, M. (2010). Public Education as Welfare. *Dissent*, Summer. Retrieved November 28, 2018, from www.dissentmagazine.org/article/public-education-as-welfare.

Kelderman, E. (2016). Confronting a "New Normal," Berkeley Considers Cuts, February 11. *Chronicle of Higher Education*.

Koretz, D. (2009). *Measuring Up: What Educational Testing Really Tells Us.* Cambridge, MA: Harvard University Press.

Larivière, V., Ni, C., Gingras, Y., Cronin, B., and Sugimoto, C. (2013). Bibliometrics: Global Gender Disparities in Science. *Nature*, 504(7479), 211–213.

Lave, R., Mirowski, P., & Randalls, S. (2010). Introduction: STS and Neoliberal Science. *Social Studies of Science*, 40(5), 659–675.

Leachman, M., Albares, N., Masterson, K., & Wallace, M. (2016). *Most States Have Cut School Funding, and Some Continue Cutting.* Washington, DC: Center of Budget and Policy Priorities.

Lederman, D. (2005). *Graduated But Not Literate*, December 16. Retrieved October 10, 2017, from Inside Higher Ed: www.insidehighered.com/news/2005/12/16/literacy.

Lee, P. (2015). *Academic Freedom at American Universities.* Lanham, MD: Lexington Books.

Lipman, P. (2011). *The New Political Economy of Urban Education: Neoliberalism, Race, and the Right to the City.* New York: Routledge.

Macpherson, C. (1977). *Democratic Theory: Essays in Retrieval.* Oxford: Oxford University Press.

Mandrioli, D., Kearns, C., & Bero, L. (2016). Relationship between Research Outcomes and Risk of Bias, Study Sponsorship, and Author Financial Conflicts of Interest in Reviews of the Effects of Artificially Sweetened Beverages on Weight Outcomes: A Systematic Review of Reviews. *Plos One*, 11(9), e016219. Retrieved on November 28, 2018, from https://journals.plos.org/plosone/article?id=10.1371/journal.pone.0162198.

Marcucci, P. (2013). The Politics of Student Funding Policies. In D. Heller & C. Callender (eds), *Student Financing of Higher Education: A Comparative Perspective* (pp. 9–31). New York: Routledge.

McCoy, S., & Smyth, E. (2011). Higher Education Expansion and Differentiation in the Republic of Ireland. *Higher Education*, 61(3), 243–260.

Merrow, J. (2017). *Addicted to Reform.* New York: The New Press.

Michaels, D. (2008). *Doubt Is Their Product: How Industry's Assault on Science Threatens Your Health.* Oxford: Oxford University Press.

Mills, J., Egalite, A., & Wolf, P. (2016). *How Has the Louisiana Scholarship Program Affected Students?* New Orleans: Education Research Alliance for New Orleans, Tulane University.

Mirowski, P. (2010). *ScienceMartTM.* Cambridge, MA: Harvard University Press.

Nathanson, L., Corcoran, S., & Baker-Smith, C. (2013). *High School Choice in New York City.* New York: Institute for Education and Social Policy, NYU.

National Center for Education Statistics. (2005). *A First Look at the Literacy of America's Adults in the 21st Century.* Washington, DC: US Department of Education.

National Center for Education Statistics. (2015a). *Private Elementary and Secondary Enrollment, Number of Schools, and Average Tuition, by School Level, Orientation, and Tuition: Selected Years, 1999–2000 through 2011–12.* Retrieved October 11, 2017, from National Center for Education Statistics: https://nces.ed.gov/programs/digest/d15/tables/dt15_205.50.asp?current=yes.

National Center for Education Statistics. (2015b). *Private Elementary and Secondary School Enrollment and Private Enrollment as a Percentage of Total*

Enrollment in Public and Private Schools, by Region and Grade Level: Selected Years, Fall 1995 through Fall 2013. Retrieved October 10, 2017, from National Center for Education Statistics: https://nces.ed.gov/programs/digest/d15/tables/dt15_205.10.asp?current=yes.

National Center for Education Statistics. (2016). *Program for International Student Assessment (PISA).* Retrieved October 11, 2017, from National Center for Education Statistics: https://nces.ed.gov/surveys/pisa/pisa2015/pisa2015highlights_6a_2.asp.

National Center for Education Statistics. (2016). *Total and Current Expenditures per Pupil in Fall Enrollment in Public Elementary and Secondary Schools, by Function and Subfunction: Selected Years, 1990–91 through 2013–14.* Retrieved October 11, 2017, from National Center for Education Statistics: https://nces.ed.gov/programs/digest/d16/tables/dt16_236.60.asp?current=yes.

Neumann, E. (2015). *Not So Fast: At UC Berkeley, Biofuel Research Takes Hit as BP Oil Company Backs Away,* February 20. Retrieved November 8, 2017, from California Magazine: https://alumni.berkeley.edu/california-magazine/just-in/2015–02–20/not-so-fast-uc-berkeley-biofuel-research-takes-hit-bp-oil.

Newfield, C. (2016). *The Great Mistake: How We Wrecked Public Universities and How We Can Fix Them.* Baltimore, MD: Johns Hopkins University Press.

Nichols, S., & Berliner, D. (2005). *The Inevitable Corruption of Indicators and Educators Through High-Stakes Testing.* Tempe, AZ: Education Policy Research Unit (EPRU), Arizona State University.

Nussbaum, M. (2010). *Not for Profit: Why Democracy Needs the Humanities.* Princeton: Princeton University Press.

O'Connor, J. (1973). *Fiscal Crisis of the State.* New York: St. Martin's Press.

OECD. (2013). *OECD Skills Outlook 2013: First Results from the Survey of Adult Skills.* Paris: OECD.

OECD. (2014). *Spending on Tertiary Education.* Retrieved November 12, 2017, from OECD Data: https://data.oecd.org/eduresource/spending-on-tertiary-education.htm#indicator-chart.

OECD. (2016). *Adult Education Level.* Retrieved November 13, 2017, from OECD Data: https://data.oecd.org/eduatt/adult-education-level.htm#indicator-chart.

OECD. (2017). *Education at a Glance 2017: United States.* Paris: OECD.

Payne, K., & Biddle, B. (1999). Poor School Funding, Child Poverty, and Mathematics Achievement. *Educational Researcher,* 28(6), 4–13.

Pearce, N. (2008). Corporate Influences on Epidemiology. *International Journal of Epidemiology,* 37(1), 46–53.

Pew Charitable Trusts. (2015). *Federal and State Funding of Higher Education.* Philadelphia, PA: The Pew Charitable Trusts.

Portnoi, L. (2016). *Policy Borrowing and Reform in Education.* New York: Palgrave Macmillan.

Rastrollo, M., Schulze, M., Ruiz-Canela, M., & Martinez-Gonzalez, M. (2013). Financial Conflicts of Interest and Reporting Bias Regarding the Association between Sugar-Sweetened Beverages and Weight Gain: A Systematic Review of Systematic Reviews. *Plos Medicine,* 10(12), e1001578. Retrieved on November 28, 2018, from https://journals.plos.org/plosmedicine/article?id=10.1371/journal.pmed.1001578.

Ravitch, D. (2010a). *The Death and Life of the Great American School System: How Testing and Choice Are Undermining Education*. New York: Basic Books.

Ravitch, D. (2010b). *Leading Education Scholar Diane Ravitch: No Child Left Behind Has Left US Schools with Legacy of "Institutionalized Fraud"*, March 5. Retrieved November 6 2017, from Democracy Now: www.democracynow.org/2010/3/5/protests.

Rebarber, T., & Zgainer, A. (2014). *Survey of America's Charter Schools 2014*. Washington, DC: The Center for Education Reform.

Robinson, N. (2014). A Quick Reminder of Why Colonialism Was Bad, September 14. *Current Affairs*.

Roelofs, P., & Gallien, M. (2017). *Clickbait and Impact: How Academia Has Been Hacked*, September 19. Retrieved October 2, 2017, from LSE Impact Blog: http://blogs.lse.ac.uk/impactofsocialsciences/2017/09/19/clickbait-and-impact-how-academia-has-been-hacked/.

Sanders, R. (2007). *BP selects UC Berkeley to Lead $500 Million Energy Research Consortium with Partners Lawrence Berkeley National Lab, University of Illinois*, February 1. Retrieved November 8, 2017, from UC BerkeleyNews Press Release: www.berkeley.edu/news/media/releases/2007/02/01_ebi.shtml.

Schillinger, D., Tran, J., Mangurian, C., & Kearns, C. (2016). Do Sugar-Sweetened Beverages Cause Obesity and Diabetes? Industry and the Manufacture of Scientific Controversy. *Annals of Internal Medicine*, 165(12), 895–897.

Schoen, J. (2015). Why Does a College Degree Cost So Much?, June 16. *CNBC*.

Schrecker, E. (1986). *No Ivory Tower: McCarthyism and the Universities*. New York: Oxford University Press.

Schrecker, E. (2010). *The Lost Soul of Higher Education: Corporatization, the Assault on Academic Freedom, and the End of the American University*. New York: The New Press.

Schultz, D. (2005). The Corporate University in American Society. *Logos*, 4(4). Retrieved on November 28, 2018, from www.logosjournal.com/issue_4.4/schultz.htm.

Seybold, P. (2014). *Servants of Power: Higher Education in an Era of Corporate Control*, June 22. Retrieved December 11, 2017, from Truthout: www.truthout.org/news/item/24305-servants-of-power-higher-education-in-an-era-of-corporate-control.

Sowell, T. (1993). *Inside American Education*. New York: The Free Press.

Strauss, V. (2015). How and Why Convicted Atlanta Teachers Cheated on Standardized Tests, April 1. *The Washington Post*.

Tabb, W. (2002). *Unequal Partners: A Primer on Globalization*. New York: The New Press.

Taylor, A. (2012). *Why Finland's Unorthodox Education System Is the Best in the World*, November 27. Retrieved October 30, 2017, from Business Insider: www.businessinsider.com/finlands-education-system-best-in-world-2012–11.

Thomas, P., Date, J., Sandell, C., & Cook, T. (2008). Living in the Shadows: Illiteracy in America, February 25. *ABC News*.

Turner, C. (2016). *Can More Money Fix America's Schools?*, April 26. Retrieved October 11, 2017, from NPR: www.npr.org/sections/ed/2016/04/25/468157856/can-more-money-fix-americas-schools.

Turner, C., McCorry, K., Worf, L., Gonzalez, S., Carapezza, K., and McInerny, C. (2016). Can More Money Fix America's Schools? nprEd, April 25. Retrieved November 28, 2018, from www.npr.org/sections/ed/2016/04/25/468157856/can-more-money-fix-americas-schools.

US Department of Education. (2016). *High School Graduation Rates by State.* Retrieved October 11, 2017, from Governing the States and Localities: www.governing.com/gov-data/high-school-graduation-rates-by-state.html.

US Census Bureau. (2015). *Per Pupil Spending Varies Heavily Across the United States.* Washington, DC: US Census Bureau.

Washburn, J. (2005). *University, Inc.: The Corporate Corruption of Higher Education.* New York: Basic Books.

Washburn, J. (2007). Big Oil buys Berkeley, March 24. *Los Angeles Times.*

Wenglinsky, H. (1997). How Money Matters: The Effect of School District Spending on Academic Achievement. *Sociology of Education,* 70(3), 221–237.

Wenglinsky, H. (1998). Models of the Relationship Between Education Spending and the Social Distribution of Achievement. *ETS Research Report Series,* 2, 1–44.

Zaleski, A. (2017). *New York Is Offering Free College — California May Be Next,* July 11. Retrieved December 20, 2017, from CNBC: www.cnbc.com/2017/07/11/free-college-in-new-york-california-may-be-next.html.

Zwolinski, M. (2007). Sweatshops, Choice, and Exploitation. *Business Ethics Quarterly,* 17(4), 689–727.

6

Politics: a threadbare democracy

Writing in the mid-1950s, the American sociologist C. Wright Mills opened his account of the "power elite" by illuminating a divide within US society, between those with the capacity to shape the world, and those for whom it is shaped. Mills's account, told at a time well before neoliberalism and during an expansion of working-class economic fortunes, makes for grim reading. "The very framework of modern society," says Mills, "confines [the masses] to projects not their own, but from every side, such changes now press upon the men and women of the mass society, who accordingly feel that they are without purpose in an epoch in which they are without power." Mills goes on to detail how a small group of individuals occupying the "command centers" of the military, political offices, and corporations form an inner circle with the power to make decisions that "mightily affect the everyday worlds of men and women" (Mills, 2000 [1956], p. 3).

Much has changed since the mid-1950s, and the intent of this chapter is to chronicle the ways in which the political life of people living under neoliberalism has been even further diminished. Politics—the collective struggles in which we engage to define, shape, challenge, and reproduce our social reality—is an essential aspect of living a full, flourishing life. In defining the major capabilities which found good living and whose distribution can be used to assess the goodness of a polity, for example, Aristotle underlines the importance of the opportunity for participation in judicial and deliberative functions (Nussbaum, 1987, p. 24). Without entering into an extended debate on the value of the capabilities approach in political philosophy, we agree with Aristotle (and Amartya Sen, and others who pursue this approach; see e.g. Sen (1999)) that a life well-lived involves the opportunity for taking an active role in shaping the institutions which in turn condition our day to day practices and relationships. While Plato elevated the work of the *polis* (the public sphere) above that of the *oikos* (the household), seeing the latter as mere repetitive labor and denigrating those who engaged in it (slaves and some women), one needn't engage in such elitism in order to recognize the importance of political agency for human well-being. Marx retained in his work the importance of political action as crucial for a full life (in contrast to "mere life" as the struggle to put food on the table), but held out a vision for its universality. It is only beyond the struggle for bare existence, with a material basis allowing for intellectual and political pursuits, that Marx suggested lay the "true realm of freedom" (quoted in Brown (2015), p. 43). Rather than being the realm of a small elite, Marx argued that everybody must have the chance to exercise this freedom. Put as simply as possible then, our view is that human life is badly stunted under the conditions that Mills describes above, in which people feel "without purpose in an epoch in which they are without power." The fullest possible extent of political participation, we believe, is a fundamental part of human flourishing, and the conditions for such participation should be broadly distributed.

Democracy may be a crucial element of human flourishing, offering people participation in decisions that affect the context in which they live, but it can also be deeply damaging to those who may be negatively impacted by those democratic processes. The outcome of democracy is a set of rules by which people agree (or are coerced) to abide. These rules will often impinge on activities that some actors in society would dearly love to undertake. This creates a conflict in society over the outcomes of democratic decisions. One of the most important of these conflicting interests is between firms and citizens. Conceivably, in a democracy, a citizenry outraged over the debilitating impacts of the actions of firms could pass wide-ranging policies that firms would very much like to avoid. This means that democratic structures are both a venue for human fulfillment and a site of crucial conflict with enormous stakes. This conflict can take the more obvious form of applying influence of various kinds to tilt democratic decisions in favor of one group or another using the existing rules of the democratic game. However, because the rules of the democratic game, like who can vote or how much money can be donated, also have an impact on the likely outcome, they too become the subject of conflict.

In the first chapter, we documented the transformation in the US business community from a reluctant acceptance of what Kotz described as the three pillars of postwar Keynesianism (collective bargaining with unions, Keynesian full employment macro policy, and welfare state) to active support of neoliberal policies. In doing so, the business community very deliberately set out to use the existing rules of the political game to increase its influence and to change the rules of the political process in its favor.

How, then, has neoliberal life affected this? To what extent are people under neoliberal conditions provided with the opportunities to pursue a political life—to take an active role in the creation of their world? In the US, we argue, politics is yet another sphere of increasing exclusion in which these capacities are heavily skewed to the top end of the wealth distribution, in which the horizon of the possible becomes ever shorter, and in which the range of aspects of life available to democratic controls becomes ever more narrow. In this chapter, we lay out the ways in which a neoliberalizing US political system deprives people of political power, discuss how this has been an aspect of class warfare from the top, and outline how we see the US working class having responded to neoliberalism as a political project.

The subversion of electoral power

Political struggles have been amazingly successful over the past century at extending democratic rights to those formerly excluded. As Göran Therborn (2013) relates, there has been an uneven but progressive move-ment towards the spreading of democratic rights globally—a process that took two hundred years to formally complete in the United States. From constitutionally empowered states restricting voting to property-owning or tax-paying white men in 1789, the US finally managed to enable people regardless of race, property, tax payment, or gender to vote by 1965. However, Therborn cautions that while "within nations, social movements, collective associations and wide franchised elections— democratization, in short—have brought about a major equalization of political resources ... as with economic resources, political equalization has been stopped or reversed recently" (2013, p. 99).

Elections and the policy process

Research beginning to emerge after 2010 was particularly alarming on this front, suggesting that a resurgent economic form of exclusion from democracy was being laid over the widely acknowledged racial line. Equally troublingly, the latter is reasserting itself. With the 2013 Supreme Court decision to ditch the so-called "preclearance provision" of the Voting Rights Act, Southern states were again free to alter their elections laws without federal approval. Texas and North Carolina immediately did so, ushering in what the *Guardian* described as "stunningly restrictive new voting laws that have since been denounced in federal court as openly discriminatory and in violation of Voting Rights Act provisions that are still in force" (Gumbel, 2017). Voter ID laws, at-large voting requirements, and redistricting are all on the table or the horizon as Republican strategists work to disenfranchise Democratic party-leaning minority groups. A twenty-year narrowing of the voter turnout gap between non-Hispanic whites and blacks in the US was reversed in 2016, as black voter turnout declined by a distressing 7 percent (Krogstad & Lopez, 2017). So, states— and the Republican Party in particular—continue to work to limit opportunities to vote, most aggressively for African Americans, and for the poor, who are most heavily affected by photo ID requirements.

These overt and serious civil rights issues are just one example of a broader trend of rising political inequality—referred to by Hacker and Pierson (2010) as "Winner-Take-All politics." By this they aren't referring to a first-past-the-post system (which has its own problems), but to a system in which political power is skewing ever more heavily towards the very top of the income distribution, in which elections are increasingly money-driven, and in which electoral outcomes weigh less heavily than the resource-intensive ability to engage in the policy process. Their analysis is perhaps even harder reading for democrats than Mills, since it essentially eviscerates any remaining hope one might have clung to that the demo- cratic openings of the past century might move forward under liberal capitalist structures.

Liberalism, as Domenico Losurdo (2014) shows, has always grappled with a contradiction at its heart: that, in a regime that privileges the right of private property above all others, the liberal freedoms and responsibili- ties enjoyed by some rest on the unfreedoms of some Other. Since its inception, liberalism has carefully drawn lines between those deserving of and suited for liberal subjectivity, and those who are not. These have been drawn most visibly on the basis of geography and nationhood, gender, race, and property-ownership. This conflict at the heart of liberalism was for a long time muted in the US, due to an unprecedented expansionary period that enabled political and social conflict to be submerged beneath a broadly rising prosperity. As that rising prosperity began to fizzle in the late 1970s, neoliberalism has offered a conservative response to this conflict: restrict the community of the free once again—pulling politics back into the grip of the wealthy and excluding the rest from any genuine freedom to shape the world. Both cause and effect of the tipping of class forces decisively in the favor of business, the line between liberal subjects and the governed is drawn increasingly between the rich and the rest, which of course intersects with historical racial and gender inequalities.

This seems paradoxical in a time when the legal right to vote is widely shared. The expansion of the franchise does open a door to the possibility of political transformation by and on behalf of working-class people—a possibility that the founding fathers were both aware of and very nervous about. This possibility, however, has been made increasingly unlikely through the neoliberal period. What recent research (Hacker and Pierson, 2010; Gilens and Page, 2014; Bartels, 2010) suggests is not dissimilar to what sociologists like William Domhoff (2002) (who follows in the tradition of Mills) have been warning us about for some time: empirically, votes and elections do matter in that they provide a means for rival power groups to resolve disputes without bloodshed, allow "everyday citizens" to help determine which rival group will lead, allow some influence over economic and social policy through electoral coalitions, or enable policy innovation during times of crisis (Domhoff, 2002, pp. 123–124). But the normal business of governing in the US is largely untroubled by the preferences and desires of anybody but the wealthy (Gilens, 2012), and the views of elites carry even more weight during periods of "exception" (like the financial crisis of 2007 or in the aftermath of terrorist attacks).

There are several trends that serve to detach the potentially powerful act of voting from what is supposed to be the real prerogative of liberal subjectivity—having an effect on laws, regulations, and institutions: the rising influence of money in political campaigns, the complexity and opaqueness of the policy process, and the increasing disparity of the ability of capital to organize relative to labour.

Perhaps the most obvious form of political power wielded by the wealthy in the US is through the financing of political campaigns. The role of money in US politics is central, and although spending more is not a guarantee of victory (Clinton outspent Trump, for example, by a considerable margin in 2016), inability to raise the millions required to mount a campaign effectively bars you from competing. The amounts raised by successful presidential primaries campaigns, for example, rose from $94 million in 1980 (both candidates) to over $700 million in 2004. By 2016, the Clinton campaign alone spent about $800 million, and the successful Trump campaign spent a little more than half of that. Money matters mostly in order to weed out candidates unacceptable to those wealthy enough to make and coordinate large donations. What this means, in practice, is that the candidates available to choose from in the vast majority of presidential, Senate, and House races have already been vetted by the business class. There are exceptions, and small donations can add up, as the unexpected strength of the Sanders primary campaign in 2016 demonstrated, and, indeed, the unexpected success of the Trump primary campaign, in which he was far from the favored pick of the Republican donor base. Nonetheless, one campaign strategist in 2012 estimated that you need about $500 million to run viably for President (Bai, 2012).

The "Citizens United" decision of the Supreme Court has likely contributed to the entrenchment of corporate financing of elections, though corporations and wealthy individuals have for many years found avenues to translate money into political voice and effect. "Soft money" (unlimited contributions from rich individuals, corporations, or unions) was the usual means prior to 2002. Following the passage of the Bipartisan Campaign Reform Act, which banned such donations, the wealthy channeled their money primarily through so-called "527s"—formally "social welfare groups" unaffiliated with a particular party or candidate but which could spend whatever they liked on thinly veiled attack ads. The most famous of these was probably the Swift Boat Veterans for Truth that did such damage to the Kerry campaign. Others include the anti-tax Club for Growth, the Koch-funded Americans for Prosperity, and Karl Rove's Crossroads GPS (Bai, 2012). In 2010, 527s as a vehicle for finance became more-or-less obsolete, when the Supreme Court ruled that corporations, as persons, had a constitutional right to free speech, which was violated by limits on campaign donations. A follow-up 2012 ruling confirmed that this applied at the state, as well as the federal level. Citizens United made the fictions of the 527 (the primary one being that they were essentially doing "issue advocacy" rather than "electioneering") unnecessary, and opened the door to Super PACs, which can electioneer to their hearts' content with money from the wealthy and from corporations, but which (unlike 527s) do have to disclose their donors.

Whether Citizens United is the cause or not, US elections have seen an amazing expansion of funding from corporate and wealthy donors. Looking just at presidential election years, 2008 saw an infusion of $338.4 million in "outside spending" (which includes any spending outside of official party committees), rising to just over $1 billion in 2012, and to $1.4 billion in 2016. It is widely recognized, and then shrugged off, that money is the beating heart of US politics. What this suggests is that, under neoliberal conditions, people have come to accept as legitimate that wealth should produce political power. There are occasional expressions of concern about "crony capitalism" and suggestions to reduce the role of money in politics, including from within the business class (Committee for Economic Development, 2015). Nonetheless, the trend has been to increase, rather than to limit, the scope for translating cash into power, and the "voice" available to the vast majority of US citizens within electoral politics is massively drowned out by the megaphonic blare of the moneyed. As more and more of the nation's wealth and income accrues to a tiny fraction of the population, their degree of political power continues to expand. There are two important points here. One is that US politics are increasingly subject to the logic of the market, in which income has weight. Simply holding citizenship is no guarantor of equal voice or participation in politics. The other is that the rules structuring political participation are themselves a target of class struggle. Rather than gauging political wins and losses strictly by observing the outcomes of elections, or even policy battles, we need to broaden our focus to the conflict over the rules of the game. It is in this latter arena that the most lasting and significant bruises are dealt out to the working class. If you hope to be an effective participant in democracy in 2018, you'd better be a multi-millionaire.

Beyond the fairly visible influence of campaign financing, money has been put to use very effectively in shaping the horizon of acceptable political alternatives, and in directly writing or shaping specific policy. We discussed the roots of this movement in Chapter 1, in outlining the rise of conservative foundations and think tanks, which collectively function as a network advancing what would have once, not so long ago, been considered a radical conservative political program. Both Jane Mayer (2016) of the *New Yorker* and historian Nancy Maclean (2017) have recently published revelatory books on the influence of this network on American politics, both of which suggest that neoliberal ideas, far from having a resonant connection to the lived experience of a broad swath of the American public, were from the get-go understood as democratically non-viable. They were simply unacceptable to working- and middle-class voters. Nonetheless, they were advanced through massive expenditures, cloaking, and misdirection, all as part of a successful effort at dominating the process of policy formation. The public unpalatability of capital's ambitions, as reflected in the policies advanced through this network, was plainly acknowledged internally, and blamed largely on the fact that people actually benefited from—and knew that they benefited from—publicly provided goods and services. James Buchanan argued as much in his transparently titled *The Limits of Liberty* (1975). "Democracy," Buchanan writes, "may become its own Leviathan, unless constitutional limits are imposed and enforced" (p. 205). In Buchanan's view, as Maclean convincingly shows, universal voting rights and the protection of property rights are incompatible. The former will relentlessly work to undermine the latter, through taxation, transfers, and the provision of public goods. There was no democratic way to create what in Buchanan's view was most important: a society that constitutionally prioritized private property rights, and immunized the wealthy from the threat of redistributive taxation. After all, "what poor man in his right mind would ever consent to rules that would keep him poor?" (p. 151). We will return to this question, posed rhetorically by Buchanan and in considerable despair. The Mont Pelerin Society (MPS) of which Buchanan was a member, contemplated this conundrum as well in 1978. Maclean's account of one invitation-only meeting at which this occurred is worth quoting. A question posed by University of Chicago economist and MPS President George Stigler began as follows:

> "If in fact we seek what many do not wish, will we not be more successful if we take this into account and seek political institutions and policies that allow us to pursue our goals?" He did not equivocate, adding that this might mean "non-democratic" institutions and policies. One "possible route," Stigler suggested for achieving the desired future was "the restriction of the franchise to property owners, educated classes, employed persons, or some such group." (Maclean, 2017, p. 152)

While their dreams of keeping working-class democratic power caged by limiting the franchise have yet to bear fruit, other avenues have served to amplify their own power, and to limit the power of those who might be casting a questioning eye at the wealthy's sports car collections, private jets, and tax-dodging offshore accounts. Central among these was to engage much more intimately and closely in the policy-formation process, and in defining the limits of the possible. The endless stream of messaging from state-based and national think tanks, rhetorically deploying the virtues of the market and a mythical narrative of individual self-sufficiency and hard work as the ticket to success in America, has done much to accomplish the latter of these goals. Combined with the justification of an amorphous "globalization" that put strict limits on the manoeuverability of governments, neoliberals effectively enforced the idea that there is no alternative. The former—influencing the policy process, rather than just elections—relied on less public, but more intensive, organizational work.

As Hacker and Pierson suggest, the process of actually making policy is opaque and complex, requiring significant resources to effectively engage with. Agenda setting, identifying opportunities through regulatory reform, proposing low-visibility but high-impact exemptions and loopholes, influencing agency funding, and working to forestall disadvantageous legislative or regulatory changes (ensuring and capitalizing on what Hacker and Pierson call "policy drift," a process whereby government fails to make necessary and appropriate changes to law in response to new or changing economic circumstances)—all of these require enormous organizational resources, the foremost of which is money. Money is used to pay lobbyists, lawyers, and experts to engage in keeping abreast of policy formation, identifying relevant areas, and intervening with elected politicians and staff. Sometimes, as in the case of ALEC, it goes to pay people to actually write proposed legislation. Lobbying expenses for Congress and federal agencies nearly tripled between 1998 and 2008, from $1.45 billion to $3.31 billion. They peaked in 2010 at just over $3.5 billion. Add in the state level, and things balloon yet further. In 2016, in the 20 states with data available through the National Institute on Money in State Politics, lobbyists spent another $1.4 billion.

Much of this lobbying is on narrow issues, and much of it is equally narrowly self-interested. However, it also carries with it a broadly neoliberal policy program that favors corporations, shareholders, and the wealthy at the expense of working-class Americans. Launched famously from the point of the 1971 Powell memo, the conservative organizational offensive involved a fivefold increase in the number of corporations with Washington, DC-based public-affairs offices within a decade. As Hacker and Pierson detail,

> In 1971, only 175 firms had registered lobbyists in Washington, but by 1982, 2,445 did. The number of corporate PACs increased from under 300 in 1976 to over 1200 by the middle of 1980 … The Chamber of Commerce…doubled in membership between 1974 and 1980. Its budget

tripled. The National Federation of Independent Business doubled its membership between 1970 and 1979. The Business Roundtable, designed to mobilize high-level CEOs for the advancement of shared interests, formed in 1972. (Hacker & Pierson, 2010, p. 176)

Corporate money poured both into direct lobbying on specific, narrow issues, and into the foundations, think tanks, policy-formation groups, media outlets, and university institutes that promoted a broader neoliberal agenda. This organizational push has been incredibly successful, choking off access to policy formation by everyday citizens. The union representatives of workers in this process (who are themselves often too-willing or forced to speak in the terms dictated by neoliberal hegemony), while often listed among the major players in campaign finance and lobbying, are actually two-bit. While the health lobby alone has habitually spent around a half-billion dollars in recent years, labor spends about one-tenth of that amount on lobbying for workers across all sectors of the US economy.

Of course, spending isn't the only means of influence that unions have historically held. They also have a wide variety of other measures available to any social movement, from mobilizing members to vote, to rallies, and other forms of public pressure. Evidence suggests that unions do influence their members' opinions on policy. For example, a study of union members' opinions on the merits of trade liberalization (which unions have generally opposed) found that unions can alter policy preferences by providing information to their members. Union members were more likely to oppose trade liberalization than other workers. Further, workers belonging to unions with more active communications efforts had a stronger effect on member opinions than did unions with more meagre information campaigns (Kim & Margalit, 2017). This supports the conclusion of another study that found that workers in a union with a particularly strong information campaign can persuade their members to oppose policies that are in their own interest but harmful to workers as a broader group (Ahlquist et al., 2014, p. 40).

In addition to these levers unions also had the power of strikes. While often understood as a tactic in industrial conflicts over wages, benefits, and conditions in specific workplaces, collectively strikes have a much broader impact on the balance of power between workers and bosses politically. As two of us have reported elsewhere, in the 1930s to the 1950s, workers in the US won substantial changes to the structure of the labor market. As we pointed out in Chapter 2, the percentage of the workforce that was unionized increased steadily, as did the ability and willingness of workers to strike for higher wages and better working conditions. In 1934, a strike by west coast longshoremen from Seattle to San Diego paralyzed shipping for 83 days. It inspired strikes throughout the country that protested businesses' use of the Great Depression to attack wages and working conditions. The year 1946 was one of the most militant in the history of US labor unions, with general strikes in cities from coast to coast. In spite of anti-union government sentiment in the Truman period, strike activity continued unabated in the 1950s. From the mid-1930s into the 1950s, pressure from labor also created the context for government legislation that promoted rising wages and social programs, which in turn created an economically and politically important social wage. During this period, the Wagner Act (1935) safeguarding unions' right to organize was passed. In 1933, Frances Perkins was named Secretary of Labor (the first woman named to a cabinet position) with a pro-labor agenda calling for minimum wage laws, unemployment insurance, old-age pensions, and the abolition of child labor. That agenda was translated into policy with the Fair Labor Standards Act of 1938 (Chernomas & Hudson, 2014, p. 251). Unfortunately, the rise of business unionism in the US, a long history of violent repression of radical union elements, and a committed crackdown on even moderate union power beginning with Ronald Reagan's breaking of the air traffic controllers' union (PATCO) in 1981 and continuing today with legal challenges aiming to end the legality of the agency fees, in which non-union workers in unionized workplaces pay the union a fee for its collective bargaining efforts (Paarlberg, 2018), have raised the perceived costs of using strikes as a political tool. By 2003 the number of strikes had fallen to 14. It rose to 21 in 2007 and had fallen to just seven in 2017—the second-lowest since data were collected (Paarlberg, 2018).

Beyond the important role that unions play transmitting information and pressuring for labor interests in and outside the political system, they also provide a valuable venue for appreciating and practicing democratic skills. Union members actively engage in democratic activities in running and organizing their union. Participating in union activities contributes to people's understanding of the complex and collective decisions that must be made in a democratic process (Bowles, 1991). The authors of a recent study on the role of unions in a broader democracy, put this very nicely: "in between elections, unions also help develop political interest and skills among workers who might not otherwise devote much time to thinking about politics. And, on a deeper level, unions shape how working-class Americans perceive their political and economic interests" (Feigenbaum et al., 2018a).

As a result, the decline in unionization should create a thinner democracy in which people are less willing and able to participate. It should also tilt information provision further in employers' favor as the countervailing voice of union advocacy for labor issues becomes increasingly silent. In comparing adjoining counties with and without right-to-work laws, which compromise union revenues from its members, both of these trends can be seen. First, voter turnout is about two points lower in right-to-work states than others. Second, results tilt towards Republicans at the ballot. Democrat candidates fared two to five points worse in right-to-work counties. Even more tellingly, prior to the implementation of right-to-work laws the counties had almost identical voting patterns (Feigenbaum et al., 2018b).

US politics has been monetized under neoliberalism, and the organizational clout of its beneficiaries has grown accordingly. Meanwhile, the organizational power of the working class has plummeted. The tale of the tape in the fight over crucial aspects of policy for American workers, and for the very wealthy, yields terrible odds against the former, with little change from the record since the late 1980s. The very wealthy remain the overwhelming favourites. Summarizing the results of their impressive research on preferences and outcomes across 1779 policy issues in the US, Gilens and Page (2014) bluntly report that "economic elites and organized groups representing business interests have substantial independent impacts on U.S. government policy, while mass-based interest groups and average citizens have little or no independent influence." That's not to say that the latter never get what they want. They do. But only when the rich and business interests happen to want the same thing.

Money has thus created a skewed structure of opportunity to influence elections and policy, with the very wealthy being heavily advantaged. Democratic power, though, relies on other material bases for its exercise. We have discussed at some length the deterioration of education—one important basis for democratic action—under neoliberalism. Perhaps equally important in terms of the erosion of democratic capacity have been neoliberalization's effects on the quality and content of the news media.

Private media and the demise of journalism

Media—including entertainment and advertising—have a huge influence on the formation of subjectivity and on what people understand as appropriate and inappropriate conduct, acceptable limits on discourse, and the formation of social and political norms. Couldry (2010, pp. 71–82) for example argues convincingly that reality TV amplifies and models neoliberal rationality by setting the stage for displays of ideal neoliberal work norms and social norms, and by offering a form of "distorted recognition" through the commodification of humans and their relationships. However, our concern here is more narrowly on the news media, since the "free press" is assumed to be a central pillar of democracy, and indeed, is something of a prerequisite for informed and effective political action.

A "free" press is often considered to be a press that is free from government interference and censorship. The "free" press in countries like the US can then be favorably compared with the propaganda engines that make up the media landscape in dictatorships like North Korea. However, free from overt government intervention does not mean free from bias. Indeed, in a privately owned media landscape, bias is as inevitable as it was when Pravda was reporting Stalin's every whim in the old Soviet Union, although it is of a different and more subtle kind. As A.J. Liebling wrote in 1960, "freedom of the press is guaranteed only to those who own one" (Liebling, 1960, p. 105). Bias in privately owned media can come from two sources. It can reflect the individual bias of particular owners, all of whom, by definition, are owners of businesses. For example, the "anti-liberal" bias of News Corporation has been explained through the ideological leanings of its CEO Rupert Murdoch (McNight, 2010). Alternatively, bias can be created by the search for profits. If media firms are profit-maximizing entities, they will be unlikely to provide information or run stories that compromise their own corporate profitability. Most obviously this means that the media are unlikely to run stories that criticize their own corporation. Media outlets are often part of a much larger corporate empire: Fox is part of the 21st Century Fox Inc. empire, NBC is part of Comcast, and ABC is owned by Disney. This means that news outlets have a much larger group of companies within their corporate umbrella that individual news outlets will be reluctant to sully. It also means that they are unlikely to be particularly critical of the institution of private ownership in general.

For-profit media may also be constrained by their need to generate advertising revenue. While this is particularly true of media content that is provided free to viewers, such as radio and television, even newspapers, which earn income from direct sales to their audience, earn most of their revenue from advertising. This influences the type of information that will be provided by media outlets in two ways. First, advertisers prefer content that is complementary to their marketing message and that places potential consumers in a purchasing mood. Style and home sections in newspapers are prime examples of where news can very nicely lead in to advertising messages. Second, firms may be reluctant to advertise in outlets that portray a particular corporation, or corporations in general, in a negative light. For example, Exxon might not be overjoyed to find its advertisement across the page from an article on the environmental damage done by burning fossil fuels. These two factors should create an incentive for the media, in general, to emphasize less hard news, especially news that criticizes advertisers (Herman & Chomsky, 2002; McChesney, 2004). As a result of business people owning the media, and revenue that depends on other business people, for-profit media are likely to have a pro-business bias. While this logic precedes the neoliberal period, trends during the neoliberal period have exacerbated this problem.

An important problem with for-profit information provision is that information will be provided only if it is profitable. As Natalie Fenton argues in the UK context (and her research highlights many of the deleteri-ous trends also outlined in the US by McChesney (2015)), public interest journalism—once the occupation dedicated to providing politically relevant information—is in crisis.

As platforms and spaces for news have expanded enormously, Fenton argues that the commercial model of news production, through which journalism was funded by ad revenue and subscriptions (a problematic enough model in its own time because of its inherent pro-business bias—see Chernomas & Hudson, 2011) has been fatally undermined. The response to this crisis has been to protect shareholder profit by closing papers, eliminating journalistic staff in favor of generating cheaper (or—even better—free) content, and investing in online platforms. Predicting our own argument about nature outlined in Chapter 3, Fenton argues that "In a neoliberal free market economy, news has no right to exist if it cannot pay its way. But news is not an 'ordinary' commodity—it has a special status by dint of its relationship to democratic life" (Fenton, 2011, p. 66). Far from being the product of technological change alone, the decline of journalism predates the explosion of on-line blogs and news sources, though it accelerates afterwards. Rather, the pressures of profit-ability have, over time, eaten away at the quality of the journalism upon which most of us once relied to guide political action. Through more than two years of interviewing participants in the news business, Fenton finds that journalists are

> being thrust into news production more akin to creative cannibalization than the craft of journalism—there may be fewer of them but they need to fill more space and to work at greater speed while also having improved access to stories and sources online. Consequently, they talk less to their sources and find themselves captured in desk-bound, cut-and-paste admin-istrative journalism … In a commercial environment, news organizations foreground rationalization (cutting journalists' jobs) and marketization (commodifying all available space) at the expense of ideal democratic objectives in a way that has led to the homogenization of content. (Fennton, 2011, p. 64)

Further, the cost-cutting required by media to remain profitable reinforced the pro-business bias of the private media. For increasingly cost-constrained media outlets desperate for content, the free material provided by corporate public relations departments became irresistible. Increasingly, content from either the public relations departments of corporations or government press releases was merely reprinted uncritically as news, rather than investigated or critiqued. One measure of the transformation of the media is the decline in paid journalists relative to public relations agents. In 1960 there were more journalists than public relations specialists in the

US. In 2012, there were four times as many public relations agents as journalists. The change in the ratio was due both to the increase in public relations employment and the sharp drop in the number of working journalists (McChesney, 2012, p. 686). Communications between corporations and those whom they want to influence through the media is increasingly uncritically published as fact under the guise of independent journalism rather than mediated by professional journalists.

The promised (or at least optimistically predicted) rise of an Internet-based media democracy keeping the politicians and the corporations accountable and ensuring we stay informed of local and global goings-on has not come to pass. It has certainly not made up for the death of journalism resulting from the inability of advertising to pay for journalism. In an age in which advertisers no longer need to support journalism in order to access eyeballs (always an uneasy alliance, but the one that enabled privately produced news) nothing has arisen to replace "old media" in this role. McChesney argues that "As a replacement for professional journalism, the Internet has largely been a flop" (2015, p. li).

There has been a longstanding tension between providing information to the public through the market logic of for-profit media and the acknowledgement that information is a crucial part of a functional democracy. Historically in the US, government intervention attempted to correct for the dearth of information that is a chronic problem in the for-profit media model. In the late 1700s Congress decided that an informed voting public was too important to leave to the vagaries of the market and opted to subsidize newspapers by allowing them to be mailed at well below cost (McChesney & Nichols, 2011). In the early days of radio, US lawmakers were also unwilling to give the privately owned media a completely free hand to do as they chose. The 1934 Communications Act granted private broadcasters rights to a specific part of the radio spectrum, but these licenses would be renewed only if these trustees of the airwaves served the public interest. Further, to ensure that one voice did not dominate local markets, regulations were put in place that prohibited industry concentration and expansion by one firm into other forms of media. In radio, for example at the beginning of the 1990s there were over ten thousand radio stations in the US. No single firm owned more than 12. No one company owned more than two stations in any local market. In addition, radio and television stations had to set aside time slots for public service and educational content (McChesney, 2015).

The idea that government should intervene in the media, especially in ways that reduced corporate profitability, such as the restrictions on concentration and expansion, ran counter to the emphasis of neoliberal policy. Since the 1980s, these restrictions have been removed. For example, the Telecommunications Act passed in 1996 deregulated many of the restrictions imposed by the 1934 Communications Act and resulted in a series of mergers within and across different types of media, dramatically limiting the number of outlets from which people could choose to get their information (McChesney, 2015). Again, we see an important distinction between the neoliberal emphasis on corporate profitability as opposed to the classical liberal desire for competition. The state was aggressively used to dismantle the rules that had previously constrained profits and encouraged competition by limiting the amount and type of holdings that individual media companies were allowed to own.

The decline of information in the US is not an inevitable consequence of shifting technology. Other countries have followed a less neoliberal path with their media. Countries like Denmark, Finland, and the UK have invested far more in public broadcasting than is the case in the US. This reduces the pro-business bias created by ownership and advertising in the media. It also decommodifies the provision of information, buffering it from the calculus of profitability. They also subsidize different media forms in a variety of ways to ensure that more private providers will enter the information industry. At least in broad measures, this has resulted in a more informed citizenry than exists in the US. A mid-2000s survey of people's knowledge about domestic and international issues found that citizens of Denmark, Finland, and the UK were more informed than those in the US. Further, the gap between the US and these other nations was much greater for those with low levels of education (high school or less) than for those with university degrees, suggesting a greater importance of media information for those with less formal education (McChesney & Nichols, 2011, p. 267). This suggests that the decline of information and a pro-business media bias are not technological inevitabilities. Rather, they are symptomatic of a nation that has, since 1980, dismantled protective regulation of the "old" media, while refusing to intervene to correct for the problems created by the "new" media forms.

Remaking states and citizens

Neoliberalism's effects on political life come in layers. The impact of neoliberalism's economic inequality on elections, on the realm of policy, and on journalism, form the topmost—meaning they are the most visible and have huge implications for the distribution of power. However, at a deeper level, neoliberalism is affecting a more insidious change, drastically narrowing the scope of politics, and conducting a campaign to reinvent the state and the citizen as economic, rather than political, entities. This has been expressed in different tones by a number of political and social theorists (e.g. Foucault, 2008; Wolin, 2008; Dardot & Laval, 2014; Galbraith, 2017). Wendy Brown (2015), for example, diagnoses the damage done as part of the neoliberal project of constructing humans[1] in the image of *homo economicus*—a transformation beyond Smith's famous formulation of the self-interested trader. In Brown's view, it involves the propagation and internalization of the view that we are (or should be) entrepreneurs of the self—cultivators of a basket of assets (knowledge, skills, networks) constituting our "human capital," and that each human's worth will be (and should be) determined by the value realized through such cultivation. In other words, we are each a tiny firm (or investment portfolio) in competition with other tiny firms. Rather than the default of equality on the basis of shared humanity, we have a default of market-justified inequality. As part of this, she points out some devastating implications which we argue are actually among the intended ends of neoliberal politics—intensified insecurity and the end of collective or solidaristic categories like the "working class," for example. Key among these for our argument are that, first, our capacity to think in terms of public goods or even a common interest (a concept that neoliberal commentators and politicians have insisted is meaningless as anything other than an aggregate of individual interests) is eroded; and, second, market rationality colonizes politics to the extent that governments are judged almost exclusively on their capacity to facilitate growth, and to provide the conditions for market (rather than human) flourishing.

The first of these, Brown argues, explains much of the widely disparaged character of contemporary politics. While there is no shortage of tut-tutting at the shameful conduct of modern politicians, few people bother to understand it as an inevitable consequence of the denigration and destruction of public life more broadly. "As neoliberalism wages war on public goods and the very idea of a public," Brown argues,

> it dramatically thins public life without killing politics. ... This persistence of politics amid the destruction of public life ... combined with the marketization of the political sphere is part of what makes contemporary politics peculiarly unappealing and toxic—full of ranting and posturing, emptied of intellectual seriousness, pandering to an uneducated and manipulable electorate, and a celebrity-and-scandal-hungry corporate media. (Brown, 2015, p. 39)

And this was before the Trump phenomenon. Note here that Brown implies that the uneducated and manipulable electorate is a *product* of politics itself, and not the result of some essential characteristic of the masses. Democracy, it is proposed, requires not just legal rights but institutions to support an effective democratic public—including education, access to reliable and relevant information through media, practiced deliberation, and, perhaps above all, a conception of what would constitute a "good life" apart from the shoddy version represented by the stock ticker. Without these very material bases, the idea of rule by the people is at best only notional and performative. The absence or deterioration of these material bases for democratic practice is not an oversight but a solution to the problem, perceived by those in power, of a potentially effective demos (Wolin, 2008).

The second item, whereby "the legitimacy and task of the state becomes bound exclusively to economic growth, global competitiveness, and the maintenance of a strong credit rating" (Brown, 2015, p. 40), represents a further thinning of the possibilities of political life. It is, in fact, part and parcel of changing the state from a potentially democratic vehicle of liberation to what James Galbraith (and his father before him) have described as the "predator state": a state which actively governs to enrich a small number of people, while either impoverishing or "passing along— perhaps—a diluted benefit" to the vast majority (Galbraith, 2017). Brown's account of the erasure of the "modest ethical gap" between democratic liberalism and market rationality (one holding out an aspirational inherent equality between subjects, and the tolerance of moral or ethical rationality, the other assuming always a fundamental inequality, and a narrow economistic calculus as the basis of all action) suggests that it cannot be an inevitable consequence of the functioning of the economic system. We agree, but argue that it *is* the *political expression* of businesses' restless need to overcome the constraints placed on them by democratic decisions. It is the product, in our view, of an organized and effective class-based political movement to transform the state and the citizenry not into some kind of stateless, Smithian competitive marketplace but into a tool for redistributing wealth and power upwards. Brown also, by foregrounding the Foucauldian emphasis on the reconstitution of political subjects into entrepreneurs, discounts the extent to which a shift of accountability occurs in a globalizing, financialized capitalism, from citizens to capital, providing another means through which citizens are severed from political power.

Brown (2003) argues that the remaking of the state in a neoliberal mold involves, first, the state, in all of its operations (fiscal and monetary policy, welfare state provision, policing, etc. …), openly responding to the needs of the market; second, market rationality of cost-benefit calculation and the quest for (narrow) efficiencies coming to dominate within the state's decision making; and third, the legitimacy of the state becoming bound exclusively to its success in supporting the market, as indicated by measures of economic growth. The last is not quite accurate. While the language of jobs and investment is certainly a key tool of legitimation, we shouldn't mistake growth for the actual goal, since this would involve a policy set very different from those adopted under neoliberalism. Actually striving for economic growth would not involve defunding public schools for example. The neoliberal objective is primarily an upward redistribution, rather than growth. However, Brown's second point is important. The language of policy increasingly reflects the subservience of what were previously considered to be public goals and public interest to the supremacy to the private market. Wolin (2008), for example, discusses how a mythos of democracy, a kind of celebration of an increasingly empty idea, plays an important role in the creation of a disempowered and demobilized electorate. They have largely adopted the rationality that government should be run on business principles of efficiency and customer satisfaction. There has been an erosion of the broad social solidarity that once accompanied citizenship (problematic as that was for those excluded from such citizenship). There is widespread acceptance of the state's ultimate accountability to credit-rating and bond-rating agencies, and, through them, to financial markets (this is a concession, but one rooted in an economic reality). And they have accepted a transformation of the state through which its legitimacy as a producer has been hamstrung, in favor of outright privatization or arrangements like Public–Private Partnerships and Social Impact Bonds for the provision of once-social goods and services.

All of these radically narrow the possibilities of democratic power, by placing economic policy (and that is a very broad category indeed) in an ideologically and structurally locked box. This quarantining of democratic control (even as expressed through allegedly sovereign public powers like the state) is institutionalized at the transnational level through treaties, trade agreements, and investment protection deals that, in Galbraith's (2017) words, "place absolute and strict limits on the margin of maneuver of any political forces or national polities that attempted to propose an independent course or, thwarted in that effort, engaged in rebellion" (13).[2] Economist John Weeks has also pointed to the connection between de-democratization and neoliberalism, wherein the state is understood to have been both actively constrained from limiting capital mobility, and recruited to enforce "free markets." Rather than government being democratically enlisted to ameliorate the social strains resulting from capitalism, as it was in the New Deal, for example, or in postwar social democratic Europe, Weeks argues that it is now capital that regulates the state, ushering in an era of authoritarian capitalism (Weeks, 2018).

So, political life has been dramatically thinned, the possibilities of the state—even were it under the control of its citizens—have been grossly narrowed, the material bases of effective political action, such as free and independent media to hold politicians accountable, have been whittled away, and the waves of cash and organizational power swamping both the electoral and the policy-making processes have significantly detached the power of the vote from the determination of law, regulation, and policy. Nonetheless, periodically, a fragmented, demobilized, disempowered electorate is called upon to participate in a moneyed spectacle through which they deliver up to the lobbyists their preferred set of candidates from among a pre-screened and pre-approved stable of suits and skirts.

These choices do have some impact, creating variation within a fairly tight band of oscillation. As such, it remains to explain how this electorate is conscripted into selecting its own oppressors—many of whom openly advertise that they will adopt policies that further restrict public power and privilege the rich.

The impact on working-class politics: Republican LEWS

> A public union employee, a tea party activist, and a CEO are sitting at a table with a plate of a dozen cookies in the middle of it. The CEO takes II of the cookies, turns to the tea partier and says "watch out for that union guy. He wants a piece of your cookie."

The thinning of democracy by subjecting it to the principles of neoliberalism compromises people's ability to actively participate in the public sphere on which so many of their living conditions depend. If this were all it did, we would have cause enough for complaint. However, the impact of these changes, many of which are on the rules of the game for campaign finance, or constitute the underpinnings on which a solid democracy are built, actually tilt the political playing field in favor of further neoliberal policies. As a result we do not have a simple cause-and-effect relationship between the changes to democratic structures as a result of neoliberalism and the changes in political outcomes. Instead, we have more of a vicious cycle, where the thinning of democracy biases electoral outcomes towards neoliberal policies. Those very neoliberal policies then make it more likely that democracy will be further thinned.

Unionization in the US provides one example of this. The thinning of democracy that occurred when firms used their financial and lobbying clout through organizations like ALEC to pass right-to-work legislation made it more difficult to form unions and unions less politically powerful. The decreasing number of union members and their more limited political reach meant that unions' role as a countercurrent of information about worker interests dwindled. As a result of fewer voices opposing the predominant neoliberal messages, neoliberal parties and policies are more likely to win electoral support.

The degree of cooperation or complicity of the working class in effecting this change is hotly debated. After all, it would be possible for the majority of the population, who have been diminished steadily under neoliberalism, to use electoral politics to reverse many of these trends. And yet, depending on the extent of your optimism surrounding the Bernie Sanders run at the Democratic nomination, even an electoral threat to neoliberal policies has yet to really emerge in the US. This raises the question: why do large sections of the American electorate vote for and support policies that favor the very business class that has profited from their economic decline? We have thus far devoted a great deal of energy to explaining the efforts of businesses in the US to transform the political landscape in their favor. What we have spent much less time explaining is why these attempts so successfully took root among certain segments of the US population. As Konings (2015) argued, in order to properly explain what he termed "neoliberal populism," one must move beyond insisting that it is something completely imposed on populations from above and attempt to formulate an explanation of why so many people have embraced it as their own.

It is, first, very important to acknowledge that this is hardly a new question. In fact, it is one of the most vexatious issues with which any proponent of working-class politics must wrestle. If there are so many workers and so few owners, why is it that democratic decisions generally favor owners? One of the most famous, and much derided, explanations is that of "false consciousness." This Marxist concept refers to the systematic misrepresentation of dominant social relations in the consciousness of subordinate classes. Members of a subordinate class (workers, peasants, serfs) suffer from false consciousness in that their mental representations of the social relations around them systematically conceal or obscure the realities of subordination, exploitation, and domination those relations embody. Giddens defines ideology as "shared ideas or beliefs which serve to justify the interests of dominant groups" (Giddens, 1997, p. 583). Its relationship to power is that it legitimizes the differential power that groups hold and as such it distorts the real situation that people find themselves in. Different people have grappled with how it is that people's actions, and even beliefs, can run counter to their own interests. The 1914 novel *The Ragged Trousered Philanthropists* was essentially a series of harangues about false consciousness by the enlightened and class-conscious main character against what he considered to be the "philanthropy" of his fellow workers who eagerly threw themselves, body and soul, into the work of making profit for their masters at their own expense (Tressell, 1914). Antonio Gramsci explained this tendency using the idea of the cultural hegemony enjoyed by the dominant class (Gramsci, 1971). The trends mentioned in the preceding section on the dwindling of the political sphere are merely recent incarnations of a more long-term truth—that at any time there is a conflict between dominant ideas that support the current societal structures and those that are "deviant" that oppose them. These ideas do not have equal weight. Writing about the UK in the 1960s, sociologist Frank Parkin argued that, in a capitalist economic system, the dominant ideas (those that supported a free rein for firms and received a largely favorable airing in the institutions in charge of communicating information in society) largely accorded with the policies of the Conservative Party, while the Labour Party's more socialist policies were deviant. As a result, the extent to which Labour could be successful in attracting votes, even from those whose interests it represented, depended on the extent to which people were exposed to these deviant ideas. Since they were not, generally, part of the dominant discourse, exposure to deviant ideas depended on where people worked, the extent to which they were unionized, the people with whom they associated, and the communities in which they lived (Parkin, 1967). The general idea in this longstanding discussion is that people do not inherently or inevitably perceive their own interests. People's understanding of the world around them, and what constitutes desirable economic policy, is influenced by the ideas to which they are exposed. In any society, ideas do not have equal purchase. Those that support the current system will have dominance over those that argue for a transformation. In this context, it should scarcely be a surprise that some members of the working class should vote against their economic interests. Nor should it be a surprise that in the context of dwindling democracy generally, and labor institutions particularly, the deviant voice countering the interests of firms should be more muted than even Parkin perceived in the 1960s UK.

Having said this, a debate has emerged about the extent to which a specific subsection of US voters has switched political allegiances to their own detriment. Specifically, the debate is whether members of the "white working class" have changed their political loyalty from Democratic to Republican and, more generally, from "Left" to "Right" across the spectrum of social and economic issues. The focus on party affiliation implies that whether Democrats or Republicans are in office matters. This is not obvious, particularly since both Democrats and Republican governments have presided over the neoliberal shift since the late 1970s, beginning not with Nixon but with Carter in the White House, and Democrat-controlled House and Senate. In discussing whether Americans benefited from the policies of different parties, Hacker and Pierson argue that "Republicans wore black hats, Democrats grey" (Hacker & Pierson, 2010, p. 239). That is, the Republicans were the zealots and could claim primary authorship for tax cuts and other measures that increased inequality while the Democrats could only be charged with allowing "drift." In the words of Republican President George W. Bush, surveying the guests at the $800 per plate dinner in New York, "This is an impressive crowd—the haves and the have-mores. Some people call you the elite; I call you my base" (CNN, 2000).

While the very rich do very well indeed under both Democrat and Republican administrations (as Chapter 2 demonstrated), it does seem to be the case that the bottom 20 percent tend to do less badly under Democrats than under Republicans. Bartels surveyed the economic landscape from President Truman to President George W. Bush. "Under Democratic presidents," he writes, "poor families did slightly better than richer families (at least in proportional terms), producing a modest net decrease in income inequality; under Republican presidents, rich families did vastly better than poorer families, producing a considerable net increase in income inequality" (Bartels, 2008, p. 34). He concludes that the income gap increased under Republican Presidents Eisenhower, Nixon, Ford, Reagan, and both Bushes, while it declined under four of the five Democratic presidents who have served during this period—all except Jimmy Carter. That pattern, he asserts, "seems hard to attribute to a mere coincidence in the timing of Democratic and Republican administrations" (Bartels, 2008, p. 34). Rather, Democratic and Republican presidents have pursued different economic policies, with Democrats generally focused more on raising employment and output growth, which disproportionately benefit poor and middle-class families. On tax policy, Republican presidents, especially since Reagan, have pushed tax cuts that have disproportionately helped the wealthiest Americans.

A second way to investigate the extent to which partisanship matters in the distribution of income gains is to look at the fraction of gains (and losses) captured by the top 1 percent under different partisan arrangements. Emmanuel Saez has done just such an analysis, beginning with the Clinton years, as shown in Table 6.1.

The table shows that, under Clinton, the working class fared better during the expansion, with the bottom 99 percent capturing 55 percent of the gains. Under Bush, however, the shares flip, and the bottom 99 percent manage to capture only 35 percent of the gains. Throwing a bit of a wrench into Bartels's partisanship analysis is the period of three

Table 6.1 Income gains, 1993–2012 (%)

	Average income real growth	Top 1% income real growth	Bottom 99% income real growth	Fraction of total growth (or loss) captured by top 1%
Full Period	17.9	86.1	6.6	68.0
Clinton expansion (1993–2000)	31.5	98.7	20.3	45.0
2001–2002 recession	−11.7	−30.8	−6.5	57.0
Bush expansion 2002–2007	16.1	61.8	6.8	65.0
2007–2009 recession	17.4	−36.3	−11.6	49.0
Obama recovery 2009–12	6.0	31.4	0.4	95.0

Source: Saez, *Income and Wealth Inequality: Evidence and Policy Implications*, available at https://eml.berkeley.edu/~saez/lecture_saez_chicago14.pdf, table 1

years following the financial crisis, during which Obama oversaw the capture by the top 1 percent of an astounding 95 percent of the (overall small) gains. Income gains by the bottom 99 percent in the first three years of the Obama "recovery" came in at an underwhelming 0.4 percent.

Before we get into the debate about the voting behavior of the working class itself, it is worth pointing out that much of the debate turns on the definition of the white working class and that the only real lesson that can be gleaned from the different participants' use of this term is that none of them is really capturing anything that could be reasonably described as the actual working class. Most commentators rely on some cut-off for educational attainment or income, neither of which provides a great definition of the working class. Lack of data availability makes the use of more meaningful indicators of class, such as wealth, ownership, or whether one is "managed" very difficult. While we do think that there is something to the idea that a subsection of the working class has shifted its political stance, defining that group as the white working class requires some careful qualifications, all of which have been identified by others (see especially Roediger, 2017). First, it is far from monolithic in its views, preferences, and attitudes. Second, the qualifier "white" is really, really important. More and more of the US working class is not white, and non-whites vote overwhelmingly Democratic when they are not barred from doing so by lack of documentation, by transience, or by felony records. Third, a massive proportion of the white working class does not vote at all, presumably since, for many years, neither party has offered them more than crumbs. Fourth, the use of "class" in the formulation denotes only what E.P. Thompson would have called a class-in-itself, and not a class-for-itself (Thompson, 1963). W. E. B. DuBois, back in 1935, used a much better term when he spoke of "the White Worker," a subject who by choosing whiteness as an identity became unable to act out his or her class interests, who "alternates between individualism and a willingness to mobilize collectively around narrow racial fears" (Roediger, 2017). There is no "white working class" as a self-aware political subject. There are white workers.

Attempts at finding a measurable proxy for the working class have created considerable controversy. Bartels (2005) used the bottom third of the income distribution, those with incomes below $35,000. However, one-third of Bartels's "working class" are retirees and a further 8 percent disabled. If this were labelled more accurately it would simply be called what it is: "the poor," some of whom, but by no means all, are working class. In her explanation of growing working-class resentment against professionals, Joan Williams (2016) employs a definition of the working class in which median income is $75,000, which includes, for example, restaurant owners, but manages to exclude restaurant employees (too poor to be working class) (Roediger, 2017). Thomas Frank opts to operationalize the white working class as all whites without a college degree. Again, this is obviously problematic as it includes those who own businesses without a college degree as working class, when they are not. It also excludes all those with college degrees who are clearly members of the working class in the sense that they work for, or are managed by, others. This, too, should be more correctly termed what it actually is, less educated whites (LEWs).

It turns out that the differing Frank and Bartels definitions are important since, as a group, the poor have not generally moved to the right (Bartels 2005; Bartels 2010), while the LEWs have. This shift started a long time ago. Between the 1960–64 and 1968–72 election cycles, the LEW (lack of college education) support for the Democratic candidate dropped from 55 percent to 35 percent (Abramowitz & Teixeira, 2009, p. 400). In the 1980 and 1984 elections, Reagan averaged 61 percent support among the LEWS compared to 35% for Carter and Mondale (Abramowitz & Teixeira, 2009, p. 400). Over the course of one generation, the LEWs' (here "less educated" is less than 12 years of education) support for the Democratic Party (as opposed to just their voting during elections) dropped by about 20 percentage points by 2004 (Kenworthy, 2007). In the 2004 Presidential race, LEWs (without college) favored George W. Bush over John Kerry by 24 points (Abramowitz & Teixeira, 2009, p. 401). This result holds true at different income levels. For example, among poorer LEWs (without college) with household incomes between $30,000 and $50,000, Bush (62 percent) beat Kerry (38 percent) by 24 points. However, in the same income group, whites with college split evenly (49 each) between Bush and Kerry. Moving up to the $50,000 to $75,000 household income group, a massive 70 percent of the LEWs voted for Bush with only 29 percent opting for Kerry, a gap of 41 points. For college-educated whites Bush's lead on Kerry was only 5 points (52 to 47) (Abramowitz & Teixeira, 2009, p. 401). In the 2012 election, Romney beat Obama 48 percent to 35 percent among the LEWs (without college), while among college educated whites the vote was split almost evenly (Landsberg, 2012).

It is important to point out that affluent whites can more reliably be counted on to vote Republican—and often for good reason. This is the traditional Republican constituency, and their economic interests more often align with Republican economic policies. What needs explaining is not their continued allegiance, but the tipping of a portion of the LEWs, who are undeniably harmed by the pursuit of aggressive neoliberalism, towards hard neoliberal candidates in sufficient numbers to make an electoral difference.

So, there has been a shift, and we know that, because of the structure of US elections, even very small shifts in particular states can swing elections. Although the percent of LEWs in the total population is dwindling, they still make up about 50 percent of the electorate nationally (Abramowitz & Teixeira, 2009, p. 411). But we still have no clear answer as to why the LEWs vote for Republicans. Why aren't they voting for Democrats and pulling them further to the left as they did in earlier decades, which would be the rational course for poor people looking to improve their economic lot? Better yet, why not grab a pitchfork and head for the next gated mansion demanding progressive tax and labor-market policies for all?

One answer to the increasing Republican leanings of the LEWs is that the Democratic Party has ceased to represent their interests. It is certainly true that, despite the different income growth going to different groups highlighted above, the Democrats are a different party than they were in the past. According to Abramowitz and Teixeira, between the 1930s and 1960s the LEWS supported a Democrat platform based on the expansion of the welfare state and government infrastructure spending on "roads, science, schools, and whatever else seemed necessary to build up the country" (Abramowitz & Teixeira, 2009, p. 397). Broadly speaking, the Democrats were backed by an organized working class due to their policies that helped lower-skilled workers attain middle-income lifestyles in a policy package in which cultural issues were peripheral. As the voting data mentioned previously demonstrate, by the early 1970s this arrange-ment was crumbling.

It was crumbling, in part, because Democratic policies offered little to the LEWs. As Noam Chomsky pointed out, in terms of economic policy, "in many respects Nixon was the last liberal president" (Conetta, 2014). His initiatives included the Occupational Safety and Health Administration (OSHA), the Environmental Protection Agency (EPA), the Earned Income Tax Credit and significantly raising the minimum wage. No president since Nixon (including Democrats Carter, Clinton, and Obama) has introduced such progressive initiatives. It is here that we begin to see actual policy shift in a neoliberal direction, and Jodi Dean voices a common complaint about US politics when she claims that both Republicans and Democrats are parties of the elite, beholden to corporate interests and perfectly willing to erode working-class protec-tions (Dean, 2011, p. 649). According to Frank's book *Listen Liberal* (2016), Democrat policies pandered to the corporate interests of Silicon Valley and Wall Street and the highbrow concerns of the Ivy League professional class. The economic policies that followed from this alliance of the elites at best ignored, and at worst harmed, the Democrats' traditional working-class base.

However, as Abramowitz and Teixieira argue, this was not simply a one-way street in which a Democratic Party increasingly came to represent the neoliberal policies that offered so little to the LEWS, or so many other Americans. During the 1960s and 1970s the Democrats broadened their reach to include people and issues that had so far been largely ignored by the two dominant parties. Perhaps most importantly this included supporting the demands of black America for equality and economic progress but the party also attempted to expand its constituency by backing equality of gender and sexuality along with an admittedly perfunctory tip of the hat to the anti-war and environmental movements (Abramowitz & Teixeira, 2009, p. 398). In the eyes of many of the LEWs, the Democratic Party liberalism of the New Deal had degenerated into a "liberal fundamentalism," associated with high taxation, welfare dependence, tolerance of crime, and antipathy towards traditional cultural values. Generally, the LEWs felt they were displaced by this grab bag of interests, a phenomenon that Texieira and Abramowitz term "white backlash" (Abramowitz & Teixeira, 2009, p. 400).

It was only after the Democrats under Lyndon Johnson pursued a progressive agenda to expand their constituency that the LEWs shifted to the Republicans, resulting in the heavy McGovern defeat by Nixon in the 1972 election. It is then that the nascent Democratic Leadership Council proposed a reconfiguration of the Democratic approach that included fiscal conservatism, mandatory sentences, welfare reform, and, among other things, support for capital punishment (Abramowitz & Teixeira, 2009, pp. 400–401).

Yet, again, the fact that LEWs rejected this broader Democratic platform needs to be explained. Barack Obama offered a common explanation for this, famously opining that in response to economic hardship "They [the working class] get bitter, they cling to guns or religion or antipathy to people who aren't like them or anti-immigrant sentiment or anti-trade sentiment as a way to explain their frustrations" (Pilkington, 2008). That is to say, one explanation is a turn to what we can broadly label as a *culturally* conservative politics. Obama's cultural argument is mirrored by Frank with one important caveat. Frank would concur with Obama's claim that many poor white voters make their political decisions on primarily cultural issues, such as liberal bias in the news, bible banning, flag burning, gay marriage, guns, and school prayer. He further points out that these cultural votes deliver economic policy that helps those with high incomes at the expense of the rest of the population. In his engaging style, he claims that this cultural rebellion against what are perceived as elite values results in a populist uprising that benefits only the people it is supposed to be targeting. "They are massing at the gates of Mission Hills, hoisting the black flag, and while the millionaires tremble in their mansions, they are bellowing out their terrifying demands. 'We are here,' they scream, 'to cut your taxes'" (Frank, 2004, p. 109). Frank's crucial caveat to Obama's claim is that, to a large extent, the cultural shift is a response to the fact that the Democratic Party offers so little to poorer and less educated white workers. According to Frank, given that there is so little difference between the Democratic and Republican economic approach, culture becomes the only real dividing line.

A subset of the cultural theory pinpoints a specific issue: racism, and its associated geographical distribution. Only 28 percent of Southern LEWs (no college degree) identify themselves as Democratic, compared with 40 percent of non-South LEWs. Among the LEWs who said blacks are lazy, 20 percent were Democrats and 60 percent were Republicans and, driven by racial stereotypes about blacks, they are "dramatically more conservative on services and spending" (McElwee, 2015). However, as Teixeira (2018) argues, and as we point to above, lumping the LEWs together and identifying them as monolithically "racist and reactionary" is to ignore that they are in fact a "vast and variegated" group. Their opinions diverge enormously by age, for example, and by gender. Racism is there—perhaps even pervasively. It motivates some LEW voters to ally with Republicans, so that less of their money ends up being redistributed to undeserving, lazy, and/or criminal blacks and "illegal" Latinos. However, this does not sum up the LEWs.

To the extent that the Democrats have branded themselves as the party of inclusion—of different races, genders, ethnicities and sexualities—while the Republican Party has, to put it politely, placed more emphasis on more traditional values, it is unsurprising, if not still disappointing, that the Republican message would gain traction with LEWs, whose color premium has been in decline. In a number of important ways, not the least of which is economic, white males have historically enjoyed considerable privileges over a wide range of "others," but that hierarchy, while still present, is not now what it once was. Between 1996 and 2014, the real mean wage and salary of LEWs (with only high school) fell by 9 percent, while college-educated whites enjoyed wage increases of 23 percent (Coder & Green, 2016, p. 6). The gap between white wages and those of African Americans has also been declining. In 1960 an African American male without a high-school degree earned 36 percent less than a white male with the same education. By 2014, this gap was only 4 percent. For those with only a high-school degree the trend was similar but less pronounced. Between 1960 and 2014 the income gap between African American and white males with only high school fell from 35 percent to 29 percent (Rose, 2016, p. 20). Similar trends reveal themselves in poverty data. In the 1970s, about 30 percent of African Americans lived below the poverty line, compared to about 8 percent of whites. By 2014, the poverty rates of African Americans declined slightly (to 26 percent), while those of whites increased to 10 percent (Pew Research Center, 2016, p. 23). Recall from Chapter 4 that it is this group whose mortality rates have been increasing due to a combination of deaths by "despair" and worsening economic determinants of health (Case & Deaton, 2017). The optimism of white Americans about their future economic prospects was at a 25-year low in the mid-2010s (Narayan, 2017, p. 2490). So, those who argue that whites are still privileged members of the labor force are correct, but the premium of that privilege has been dwindling.

The idea that a section of the working class would enjoy a position of relative affluence compared to (or perhaps built on) their less well positioned compatriots has a long history. In the US context, this was described as the "wages of whiteness" (Roediger, 2007). Although the incomes of LEWs have been pushed towards those from other, less well compensated, racial groups, this has not resulted in growing solidarity with other workers who share increasingly similar material conditions. The very understandable discontent of LEWs, who correctly perceive that they are not doing as well either as they did prior to the 1980s or relative to other groups, has been expressed as opposition to programs, such as affirmative action, quotas, and social assistance, which they feel are helping "line cutters" from other groups at their expense (Newton, 2002; Abramowitz & Teixeira, 2009, p. 400; Narayan, 2017, p. 2490). This channeling of legitimate discontent among the LEWs against those gaining on them was both tapped into, and deliberately fostered by, the Republican Party. As early as the late 1970s, Ronald Reagan was peddling the myth of the "Welfare Queen," a racialized story of black women living a luxury lifestyle by manipulating the lenient and overly generous welfare system (Black & Sprague, 2016). To the extent to which there has been a rightward shift in LEWs' political preferences, it should not be interpreted as exogenous. How the LEWs interpret the causes of their economic malaise, and, therefore, the policy solutions that they seek to arrest their slide, are not determined exclusively outside the political system. Rather, they are conditioned by all the forces that we have discussed above, from the transformation of the media to the growing influence of finance.

Conclusion

As Mills pointed out, the golden age of a democratic utopia, in which all people (or at least adults) enjoyed meaningful input on political outcomes, has never really existed. Yet, a case could be made that, for a while, at least there was a trend towards a more inclusive and meaningful democracy. At the very least the franchise was gradually extended beyond white men of property. This is no small accomplishment. At every turn, this growing participation had to be fought for against the opposition of those who worried that expanded franchise would spell disaster, as the interests of the established elite would be overwhelmed by those of the great unwashed, that the liberty of the affluent would be destroyed by the tyranny of democracy. The principle of one person, one vote is profoundly egalitarian and sits awkwardly alongside an economic system in which inequality is the norm. They had some reason to fear, as after World War II it did appear as though the franchise was used to transfer economic power away from the minority of the wealthy towards the less affluent many. If this trend were to be reversed, the very institutions of democracy must also be altered. And so they were.

This chapter warned of the reversal of these democratic gains across a wide variety of fronts. Rules were changed to allow finance to have a much larger role in electoral outcomes allowing those with larger incomes much more access to policies that they prefer. The information on which the public depends to make an informed democratic decision has been degraded, so that opinion is considered by many to be fact and fact considered to be opinion. Indeed the very goals of politics have been restricted to those activities that are argued to support and enhance the economy, although in practice they have the effect of redistributing income upward. This thinning of democracy is of concern in and of itself. Living a good life includes having some control over the system in which you live. It is also concerning because the thinning of democracy has not been policy-neutral. It has resulted in some gaining far more access to favorable political outcomes, while disempowering others. As a result, neoliberal policies are much more likely to be implemented, and, in a vicious circle, the more neoliberal policies are implemented, the more the political system is tilted so that neoliberal policies are the increasingly likely outcome.

The LEWs have aided and abetted this transformation through their political activities. While they are not really the primary Republican base, they are the most perplexing portion of Republican support in that they are voting so obviously against their economic interests. The LEWs' understandable discontent about their dwindling economic prospects, and their less gracious resentment about their declining privilege, has been actively channeled by the Republican Party, and those who have a financial stake in its election, into resentment against the interventionist, redistributive government from which other groups are seen to dispro-portionately benefit. Divisions in the working class along racial, ethnic, and gender lines are not new. Nor is the desperate attempt by a labor aristocracy to maintain its slim advantages over other workers. While it may not be new, or particularly surprising, it has deeply problematic consequences not only for the "others" ahead of which the LEWs are attempting to remain, but also the LEWs themselves.

Notes

1 While Brown does not do so, we would add specifically *working-class* humans, since one important aspect of neoliberalism as a fundamentally conservative

restoration is about creating two different kinds of people—those bound to abide by a strictly economic rationality, and those who can operate beyond it.

2 Galbraith's assessment is in the context of discussing Greece's attempt to ameliorate the brutal austerity policies imposed, on behalf of finance capital, by the International Monetary Fund, the European Central Bank, and the European Commission. Borrowing from comments by then-Greek Finance Minister Yanis Varoufakis, Galbraith refers to the "poisoned chalice"—a "political condition in which economic structures that have very obviously failed ... can be locked into place by a complex web of prior commitments and power structures that are designed to prevent both innovation and exit" (14).

References

Abramowitz, A., & Teixeira, R. (2009). The Decline of the White Working Class and the Rise of a Mass Upper-Middle Class. *Political Science Quarterly*, 124(3), 391–422.

Ahlquist, J., Clayton, A., & Levi, M. (2014). Provoking Preferences: Unionization, Workers' Attitudes toward International Trade, and the ILWU Puzzle. *International Organization*, 68(1), 33–75.

Bai, M. (2012). How Much Has Citizens United Changed the Political Game?, July 17. *New York Times Magazine*. Retrieved January 11, 2017, from www.nytimes.com/2012/07/22/magazine/how-much-has-citizens-united-changed-the-political-game.html.

Bartels, L. (2005). Homer Gets a Tax Cut: Inequality and Public Policy in the American Mind. *Perspectives on Politics*, 3(1) (March), 15–31.

Bartels, L. (2008). *Unequal Democracy: The Political Economy of the New Gilded Age.* Princeton: Princeton University Press.

Bartels, L. M. (2010). *Unequal Democracy: The Political Economy of the New Gilded Age.* Princeton: Princeton University Press.

Black, R., & Sprague, A. (2016). The "Welfare Queen" Is a Lie, September 28. *The Atlantic*. Retrieved April 10, 2018, from www.theatlantic.com/business/archive/2016/09/welfare-queen-myth/501470/.

Bowles, S. (1991). What Markets Can and Cannot Do. *Challenge*, 34(4), 11–16.

Brown, W. (2003). Neo-liberalism and the End of Liberal Democracy. *Theory and Event*. Retrieved December 4, 2018, from http://muse.jhu.edu/journals/theory_&_event/.

Brown, W. (2015). *Undoing the Demos: Neoliberalism's Stealth Revolution.* New York: Verso.

Buchanan, J. (1975). *The Limits of Liberty: Between Anarchy and Leviathan.* Chicago: University of Chicago Press.

Case, A., & Deaton, A. (2017). *Mortality and Morbidity in the 21st century.* Washington, DC: Brookings Institution.

Chernomas, R., & Hudson, I. (2011). *The Gatekeeper: 60 Years of Economics According to the New York Times.* New York: Routledge.

Chernomas, R., & Hudson, I. (2014). On Thomas Pikettty's Capital in the Twenty-First Century. *Canadian Journal of History*, 49(2), 247–253.

CNN. (2000). *Campaign 2000: Whose Tax Plan is Best for You?*, October 23. Retrieved April 30, 2018, from CNN.Transcripts: www.cnn.com/TRANSCRIPTS/0010/23/tl.00.html.

Coder, J., & Green, G. (2016). *Comparing Earnings of White Males for Selected Age Cohorts*. N.P.: Sentier Research.

Committee for Economic Development. (2015). *Crony Capitalism: Unhealthy Relations Between Business and Government*. Arlington, VA: Committee on Economic Development of the Conference Board.

Conetta, C. (2014). *Noam Chomsky: Richard Nixon Was "Last Liberal President"*, February 21. Retrieved February 26, 2014, from www.huffingtonpost.ca/entry/noam-chomsky-richard-nixon_n_4832847.

Couldry, N. (2010). *Why Voice Matters: Culture and Politics after Neoliberalism*. London: Sage Publications.

Dardot, P., & Laval, C. (2013). *The New Way of the World: On Neoliberal Society*. Trans G. Elliot. New York: Verso.

Dean, J. (2011). Class Politics, American-Style: A Discussion of Winner-Take-All Politics: How Washington Made the Rich Richer—And Turned Its Back on the Middle Class. *Perspectives on Politics*, 9(3), 648–651.

Domhoff, W. G. (2002). *Who Rules America? Power and Politics*. 4th edn. Boston: McGraw Hill.

Feigenbaum, J., Hertel-Fernandez, A., & Williamson, V. (2018a). Right-to-Work Laws Have Devastated Unions—and Democrats, March 8. *New York Times*. Retrieved March 22, 2018, from www.nytimes.com/2018/03/08/opinion/conor-lamb-unions-pennsylvania.html.

Feigenbaum, J., Hertel-Fernandez, A., & Williamson, V. (2018b). *From the Bargaining Table to the Ballot Box: Political Effects of Right to Work Laws*. Cambridge, MA: NBER Working Paper No. 24259.

Fenton, N. (2011). Deregulation or Democracy? New Media, News, Neoliberalism, and the Public Interest. *Continuum: Journal of Media and Cultural Studies*, 25(1), 63–72.

Foucault, M. (2008). *The Birth of Biopolitics: Lectures at the College de France 1978–79*. Ed. M. Senellart & trans. G. Burchell. Basingstoke: Palgrave Macmillan.

Frank, T. (2004). *What's the Matter with Kansas? How Conservatives Won the Heart of America*. New York: Henry Holt and Co.

Frank, T. (2016). *Listen Liberal: Or, What Ever Happened to the Party of the People?* New York: Metropolitan Books.

Galbraith, J. (2017). The Predator State. *Catalyst*, 1(3), 11–19.

Giddens, A. (1997). *Sociology*. Third Edition. Cambridge: Polity Press.

Gilens, M. (2012). *Affluence and Influence: Economic Inequality and Political Power in America*. Princeton: Princeton University Press.

Gilens, M., and Page, B. (2014). Testing Theories of American Politics: Elites, Interest Groups, and Average Citizens. *Perspectives on Politics*, 12(3), 564–581.

Gramsci, A. (1971). *Selections from the Prison Notebooks of Antonio Gramsci*. London: Lawrence & Wishart.

Gumbel, A. (2017). America's Shameful History of Voter Suppression. *The Guardian*, September 13. Retrieved September 14, 2017, from www.theguardian.com/us-news/2017/sep/13/america-history-voter-suppression-donald-trump-election-fraud.

Hacker, J., & Pierson, P. (2010). Winner-Take-All-Politics: Public Policy, Political Organization, and the Precipitous Rise of Top Incomes in the United States. *Politics & Society*, 38(2), 152–204.

Herman, E., & Chomsky, N. (2002). *Manufacturing Consent: The Political Economy of the Mass Media*. New York: Pantheon.

Kenworthy, L. (2007). *How Democrats Lost Their Class*, December 17. Retrieved January 9, 2018, from https://lanekenworthy.net/2007/12/17/how-the-democrats-lost-their-class/.

Kim, S., & Margalit, Y. (2017). Informed Preferences? The Impact of Unions on Workers' Policy Views. *American Journal of Political Science*, 61(3), 728–743.

Konings, M. (2015). *The Emotional Logic of Capitalism: What Progressives Have Missed*. Redwood City: Stanford University Press.

Krogstad, J. M., & Lopez, M. H. (2017). *Black Voter Turnout Fell in 2016 Even as Record Number of Americans Cast Ballots*, May 12. Retrieved January 11, 2018, from Pew Research Center Fact Tank: www.pewresearch.org/fact-tank/2017/05/12/black-voter-turnout-fell-in-2016-even-as-a-record-number-of-americans-cast-ballots//

Landsberg, M. (2012). *White Working Class: Clinging to Guns, Religion and Romney*, September 12. Retrieved September 25, 2017, from Los Angeles Times: http://articles.latimes.com/2012/sep/21/news/la-pn-white-working-class-guns-religion-20120920.

Liebling, A. (1960). The Wayward Press: Do You Belong in Journalism?, May 14. *New Yorker*.

Losurdo, D. (2014). *Liberalism: A Counter-History*. New York: Verso.

MacLean, N. (2017). *Democracy in Chains: The Deep History of the Radical Right's Stealth Plan for America*. New York: Viking.

Mayer, J. (2016). *Dark Money: The Hidden History of the Billionaires Behind the Rise of the Radical Right*. New York: Doubleday.

McChesney, R. (2004). *The Problem of the Media*. New York: Monthly Review Press.

McChesney, R. (2012). Farewell to Journalism? *Journalism Studies*, 13(5–6), 682–694.

McChesney, R. (2015). *Rich Media, Poor Democracy: Communication Politics in Dubious Times*. New York: New Press.

McChesney, R., & Nichols, J. (2011). *The Death and Life of American Journalism*. Philadelphia: Nation Books.

McElwee, S. (2015). The Truth about the White Working Class: Why It's Really Allergic to Voting for Democrats, November 29. *Salon*. Retrieved April 4, 2018, from www.salon.com/2015/11/29/the_truth_about_the_white_working_class_why_its_really_allergic_to_voting_for_democrats/.

McNight, D. (2010). Rupert Murdoch's News Corporation: A Media Institution with a Mission. *Historical Journal of Film, Radio and Television*, 30(3), 303–316.

Mills, C.W. (2000 [1956]). *The Power Elite*. New York: Oxford University Press.

Narayan, J. (2017). The Wages of Whiteness in the Absence of Wages: Racial Capitalism, Reactionary Intercommunalism and the Rise of Trumpism. *Third World Quarterly*, 38(11), 2482–2500.

Newton, H. (2002). *The Huey P. Newton Reader*. New York: Seven Stories Press.

Nussbaum, M. (1987). *Nature, Function, and Capability: Aristotle on Political Distribution*. Helsinki: World Institute for Development Economics Research of the United Nations University.

Paarlberg, M. (2018). The Future of American Unions Hangs in the Balance, February 26. *The Guardian*. Retrieved April 29, 2018, from www.theguardian.com/commentisfree/2018/feb/26/janus-afscme-supreme-court-case-labor-unions-impact.

Parkin, F. (1967). Working-Class Conservatives: A Theory of Political Deviance. *The British Journal of Sociology*, 18, 278–290.

Pew Research Center. (2016). *On Views of Race and Inequality Blacks and Whites Are Worlds Apart*. Washington, DC: Pew Research Center.

Pilkington, E. (2008). Obama Angers Midwest Voters with Guns and Religion Remark, April 14. Retrieved from The Guardian: www.theguardian.com/world/2008/apr/14/barackobama.uselections2008.

Roediger, D. (2007). *The Wages of Whiteness: Race and the Making of the American Working Class*. London: Verso.

Roediger, D. (2017). Who's Afraid of the White Working Class?: On Joan C. Williams's "White Working Class: Overcoming Class Cluelessness in America", May 17. *Los Angeles Review of Books*. Retrieved January 10, 2018, from https://lareviewofbooks.org/article/whos-afraid-of-the-white-working-class-on-joan-c-williamss-white-working-class-overcoming-class-cluelessness-in-america/#!

Rose, S. (2016). *White Working-Class Men in a Changing American Workforce*. Third Way. Retrieved April 10, 2018, from https://thirdway.imgix.net/downloads/white-working-class-men-in-a-changing-american-workforce/NEXT_White_Working-Class_Men_in_a_Changing_American_Workforce.pdf.

Sen, A. (1999). *Development as Freedom*. New York: Knopf.

Teixeira, R. (2018). *The Math Is Clear: Democrats Need to Win More Working-Class White Votes*, January 29. Retrieved January 30, 2018, from Vox.com: www.vox.com/the-big-idea/2018/1/29/16945106/democrats-white-working-class-demographics-alabama-clinton-obama-base.

Therborn, G. (2013). *The Killing Fields of Inequality*. Cambridge: Polity.

Thompson, E. (1963). *The Making of the English Working Class*. New York: Vintage Books.

Tressell, R. (1914). *The Ragged Trousered Philanthropists*. Manchester: Northern Grove Publishing Project.

Weeks, J. (2018). Free Markets and the Decline of Democracy. *American Economics Association*. Philadelphia: primeconomics.org. Retrieved February 10, 2018, from www.primeeconomics.org/articles/free-markets-the-decline-of-democracy.

Williams, J. C. (2016). What So Many People Don't Get About the U.S. Working Class, November 10. *Harvard Business Review*. Retrieved May 3, 2018, from https://hbr.org/2016/11/what-so-many-people-dont-get-about-the-u-s-working-class.

Wolin, S. (2008). *Democracy, Inc.: Managed Democracy and the Specter of Inverted Totalitarianism*. Princeton: Princeton University Press.

7

President Trump: the end of neoliberalism?

If neoliberalism were a cat it would have used up two of its nine lives. The first reports of its death came after the crushing economic crisis of 2008. The origins of the crisis were correctly traced to increased finan-cialization of the housing market and the growing indebtedness of US households as they attempted to maintain their consumption levels in the face of stagnant real wages. These problems were also, again correctly, laid at the feet of deregulation and labor-market policy that created more power for employers, both of which were cornerstones of neoliberalism. There were calls for a return of regulation, especially in finance, measures to improve the income of middle-class America, and a massive increase in government spending to stimulate the economy. All of these would strike, to varying degrees, at some of the policies that had become associ-ated with neoliberalism. Of these options, the federal government restricted itself to the third, with a massive surge in spending, most of which went to save the financial industry from its own speculative folly.

This was far more a minor wound than a fatal injury. While it is true that small government was one of the policies that was associated with neoliberalism, equating small government with neoliberalism is to mistake the means for the ends. The means of small government, in the form of reduced regulation and some forms of spending (such as social assistance), did fit nicely in the neoliberal policy package because it contributed to the neoliberal goal of enhancing profits, at least in the short term. When the crisis hit, the deficit-creating response to the crisis reflected a sacrifice of one element of the stated policy package of neoliberalism in the service of its overarching goal. It is also telling that stimulus spending was the only real change in policy. There were no real changes to labor-market policy to shift power to employees, nor were the meagre final provisions of the Dodd–Frank act, meant to re-regulate the financial industry, a genuine renewal of government oversight. The ability of neoliberalism to rise from the dead despite its obvious contribution to the economic crisis led John Quiggin to term it "Zombie Economics" (Quiggin, 2012).

The election of Donald Trump ushered in a second round of obituaries for neoliberalism, based on his campaign rhetoric vilifying some of the elements of globalization, such as immigration and free trade, which were longstanding elements of neoliberal policy. Writing in *The Guardian*, Cornell West declared that the "neoliberal era in the United States ended with a neofascist bang" (West, 2016). In *Jacobin*, Nicole Aschoff predicted that the election was the end of neoliberalism's heyday (Aschoff, 2017) (see also Peters, 2018). While it is undoubtedly true that President Trump's "America First" slogan did not square easily with the neoliberal idea of globalization, the extent to which his administration, once in office, would usher in a broad restructuring of policy away from neoliberalism was a more open question. In order to evaluate the Trump election and its aftermath, we will first examine whether the voting patterns that brought Trump to power marked a continuation of, or a deviation from, previous elections during the neoliberal period discussed in Chapter 6. We will then proceed to evaluate the early policy changes implemented by the Trump administration in the areas that have been discussed in previous chapters. At the time of writing his administration had been in power for over a year and, although definitive conclusions about policies may be a little premature, it is possible to examine what it has attempted to do and what it has succeeded in doing thus far to form a reasonable, although admittedly preliminary, determination of whether it is time to begin sizing neoliberalism's coffin.

The sound and the fury: voting for Trump

> I could stand in the middle of 5th Avenue and shoot somebody and I wouldn't lose voters. (Donald Trump)

Donald Trump campaigned against business as usual in Washington. There was no question that, at least in style, his calls of "lock her up," angry diatribes, flirtations with racism, locker-room talk, and tolerance of violence were a radical departure from the conventions of politics that may have garnered him some support, if voters' claims to appreciate his supposed straight talk could be believed. In terms of actual policy, he ran on a broad message of system change that should have had superficial appeal to a population that, as the previous chapters have attempted to persuade you, has fared very poorly over the last four decades or so. In this he was a sharp break with his Republican predecessors, like Mitt Romney, who were staunch defenders of a status quo that had functioned so well for the elite from which they were drawn. While Candidate Trump tapped into a legitimate source of anger and frustration over the failings of the status quo, making him a much more attractive candidate to those left behind by the current economic policies than others like Jeb Bush on the Republican ticket, when it came time to actually spelling out the economic policies behind the "drain the swamp" rhetoric, there were some important departures from the policies that had been associated with neoliberalism, but these were in the minority.

Trump is often referred to as a populist, which usually means an appeal to average citizens based on the idea that there is a group of elites that stand in their way. However, there are very different kinds of populism depending on how the elites are defined. In some ways, Bernie Sanders was also a populist, but his elites were accurately identified as big businesses and the top 1% of income-earners who own and control them. Trump's elite were primarily the government. It was the government that had allowed jobs to move away by signing "bad" free-trade deals. It was the government that killed jobs by regulating corporations. It was the government that allowed unskilled immigrants to flood into the country and steal American jobs. Many of the campaign promises that sprang from this diagnosis of the ills facing America were cures long prescribed by neoliberal advocates: lower taxation (particularly for the rich and corporations), across-the-board reductions in cost-increasing regulations, and the famous "repeal and replace" of Obamacare. Other planks in the policy platform were fairly radical departures from the neoliberal playbook. His promise of job creation for American workers rested, in large part, on shielding them from competition from foreign workers through renegotiating free-trade deals and restricting immigration. Free trade, especially as it has been operationalized by organizations like the WTO, has been particularly advantageous for business in the US. Candidate Trump's departures from neoliberalism were largely on the globalization front where he rejected the international in favor of the national.

Perhaps the most obvious voting trend that tilted the election in President Trump's favor was his overwhelming support among the white non-college-educated population. As we pointed out in Chapter 6, the trend of less-educated whites (LEWs) voting Republican is a long-term trend, but it was further strengthened in the 2016 election. While whites as a group preferred Trump—with white non-Hispanic men being particularly enthusiastic (Hong, 2017), and affluent white males even more so (Carnes & Lupu, 2017)—as education increased, support for Trump fell. College-educated whites preferred Romney to Obama by 14 percentage points in 2012. They supported Trump over Clinton only by four points. However, Trump's advantage over Clinton among non-college-educated whites was nearly 40 points. One study of this trend concluded that this "was possibly the single most uniquely important divide documented in 2016" (Schaffner et al., 2017).

Evidence of whether the LEWs supporting Trump were economically disadvantaged was mixed. On one hand, Trump supporters are
less likely to be unemployed or work part-time. Household income for
those who favored Trump was slightly higher than those who did not
(Rothwell & Diego-Rosell, 2016, p. 13). On the other hand, Trump's
support was strongest in counties with the highest levels of "economic
distress," and correspondingly high levels of high drug, alcohol, and
suicide rates (Monnat, 2016). Trump voters were more likely to work
in traditional blue-collar occupations (albeit in higher-paying ones like
construction) and were less likely to be professionals. To the extent that
the LEW component of Trump support suffered from absolute economic
distress or whether, as we pointed out last chapter, they experienced a
decline in their previously privileged status, Trump's message to them
was that it was not the economic system that was to blame, but rather
it was "external elements," like immigration, that were the culprits
(Samuels, 2016).

The question, then, is why the legitimate discontent of the American
public, particularly that of LEWs, was channeled away from anger at the
neoliberal policies that have so favored business at their expense, towards
animosity for foreigners, whether of the immigrating or job-luring variety.
One explanation for this hinges on the connection between these economic
explanations for the decline of America and Trump's broader message
of animosity towards groups that were not Christian, white and male
(despite Trump only really personifying two of those three traits). In
non-economic characteristics, Christians (though not Mormons), het-
erosexuals, those over 40, males, and non-Hispanic whites were more
likely to vote Trump (Rothwell & Diego-Rosell, 2016, p. 13). According
to Robert Samuels, Trump appealed to the LEW population's "nationalistic
hatred for people of color, Muslims and immigrants." In this, Trump's
coarse language plays an important role because his supporters would
"also like to speak their minds and feel free to attack every social group
that is not like them. In a sense, they are voting for the right to hate
other people in an open and unchallenged way" (Samuels, 2016). Similarly,
another attempt to explain the propensity of less-educated whites to vote
for their race but against their class noted that racist and sexist appeals
increased Trump's support among "whites with less education" and
concluded that this was a determining factor in the election result (Schaffner et al., 2017). While much of the US population had ample justification
for being disgruntled about the neoliberal regime, less-educated whites
most strongly identified the source of that discontent in a state that sided
with "others" (whether this meant minorities, women, or foreigners) at
their expense. The fact that the economic privilege (the social and cultural
dominance was more concrete) of a less-educated, white American could
have been considered a privilege only when compared to the even more

marginal circumstances endured by the less-educated members of the African American population or recent (especially undocumented) migrants perhaps meant that advantage over so few needed to be protected all the more fiercely.

The power and the glory: President Trump

President Trump came to power on the promise of ending business as usual in Washington. If business as usual meant at least a tangential connection with fact, some commitment to tolerance, and multisyllabic words, he has kept his promise. On the other hand, if business as usual is the continuation of almost four decades of neoliberal policies that have favored business at the expense of the US population, the record of transformation is considerably more mixed. At the time of writing the Trump administration has just marked its first year in office. Although definitive conclusions may be somewhat premature, certain trends are emerging.

One of the first tasks of any incoming administration is to staff the major branches of the federal government. The people who are chosen for positions at the top of the bureaucracy provide an important indication of the policy direction of the government. The Trump administration's appointments for top positions are a combination of the very rich and the personally connected. The ex-CEO of ExxonMobil Rex Tillerson was appointed the Secretary of State. James Mattis, who was on the board of military contractor General Dynamics, was nominated as Defense Secretary. Secretary of the Treasury, in charge of the federal budget, went to former Goldman Sachs hedge-fund manager Steven Mnuchin. The Secretary of Energy went to Rick Perry, the former Governor of Texas, and a climate change skeptic who in 2011 proposed eliminating the department that he was appointed to head. Scott Pruitt, the former Oklahoma Attorney General, who, like Perry, does not believe in human-caused climate change and claimed that the EPA was "unlawful and overreaching", was Trump's choice for Administrator of the EPA. Billionaire investor Wilbur Ross, who helped Trump maintain control of his financially troubled Taj Mahal casino in the 1990s, was given the Secretary of Commerce job. Secretary of Transportation went to Elaine Chao, who is the daughter of a shipping magnate and earned more than a million dollars in 2015 on the boards of NewsCorp, Wells Fargo, Ingersoll Rand, and Vulcan Materials. Linda McMahon, professional wrestling magnate and husband of Vince, was made the Administrator of the Small Business Administration (McCarthy, 2017). According to NBC news, Trump's cabinet appointments had an estimated combined wealth of $14.5 billion (Popken, 2016). Naomi Klein summarized his appointments as a combination of "billionaires and multimillionaires" and a few career politicians selected "either because they do not believe in the agency's core mission, or do not think the agency should exist at all" (Klein, 2017). If President Trump's goal was to end the corruption he argued was endemic in Washington, he has done so by placing the corrupters directly in positions of power. You could argue that at least he cut out the intermediary. In addition to populating the top levels of government with corporate executives and their long-time political supporters, the Trump administration has passed, or attempted to pass, a number of important changes in the areas that we have investigated in the previous chapters.

Trump and income distribution

> If the tax cut passes, it will constitute the largest heist in human history. This is daylight robbery by the super-rich against the rest of society. (Jeffrey Sachs, 2017)

The signature success of the first year in office of the Trump Presidency was the passage of the tax bill, which he described as a wonderful Christmas present to the American people when it was passed in late 2017. The bill includes cutting the corporate tax rate from 35 to 21 percent, decreasing the personal income tax rate for most tax brackets including reducing the highest income rate from 39.6 to 37 percent, doubling the exemption amount for the Estate tax, lowering the inflation rate of the Consumer Price Index, eroding the Earned Income Tax Credit that rewards work, and a repeal of the individual mandate of the Affordable Care Act (Joint Committee on Taxation, 2017). Many of the provisions that benefit those in lower-income groups are scheduled to end after 2025, so those with incomes below $75,000 would actually see their taxes increase after 2027 (Walsh et al., 2017).

Despite President Trump's claims that the tax reform will cost him a lot of money personally, it will actually benefit him and those in his country-club income bracket handsomely. According to the Tax Policy Center at the Brookings Institution, by 2027 the top 0.1 percent will receive 60 percent of the tax cuts. The top 1 percent gets 83 percent (Tax Policy Center, 2017a). As a result of the tax changes, those with income over $3.4 million, the top 0.1 percent of households, will receive an average tax break of $193,000 in 2018 (Tax Policy Center, 2017b). The Center for Budget and Policy Priorities commented that the tax bill provided a "bonanza to the most well-off Americans and profitable corporations" (Greenstein, 2017). A *New York Times* editorial referred to it as "A Historic Tax Heist" that amounted to "looting the public purse by corporations and the wealthy" (Editorial Board, 2017). The top-heavy distributional consequences of the tax cuts have elicited the ire not only of economist Jeffrey Sachs, whose quote leads off this section, but also of those who have historically supported much of the neoliberal platform. Economic advisor to Presidents Clinton and Obama, former Vice President of the World Bank, former President of Harvard, and self-described "pro-business" economist, Lawrence Summers described the Trump administration's claims of wide-ranging benefits from the tax cut as "disgraceful," and the analysis in support of the tax cuts by the Business Roundtable as "fake fact" (Summers, 2017).

The impact of the tax cut will be exacerbated by the distributional impacts of the budget cuts that will almost certainly follow. While the Business Roundtable attempted to justify the tax changes based on their ability to stimulate investment and create jobs, no serious analyst thinks that the very uncertain increase in economic activity will boost revenue enough to compensate for the reductions caused by the tax cuts. In fact, reputable estimates suggest that the hole in the budget caused by the tax cuts is certain to be massive. The Joint Committee on Taxation estimated that it would create a $1 trillion increase in the federal debt between 2018 and 2027 (Joint Committee on Taxation, 2017). The Committee for a Responsible Federal Budget placed the revenue lost over a decade at somewhere between $3 and $7 trillion (Committee for a Responsible Federal Budget, 2017).

It is possible that the debt could simply be left to accumulate, but immediately after the tax cuts were passed both President Trump and senior Republicans claimed that cuts to social assistance were needed to reduce the deficit. According to Senator Mark Rubio, "the driver of our debt is the structure of Social Security and Medicare." Republican Senate Finance Committee Chairman Orrin Hatch argued that the US was "spending itself into bankruptcy" because of wasteful programs for the poor (Stein, 2017). President Trump's 2018 budget proposed cutting the Supplemental Nutrition Assistance Program, which used to be called food stamps and provides food aid to around 42 million people, by $140 billion over ten years. The 2018 presidential budget also called for a reduction in spending on the Supplemental Security Income program, which supplements the income of poor seniors and people with disabilities (Greenstein, 2017). If implemented, these changes will inevitably increase inequality and the depth and breadth of poverty. These are the kind of incentives to work reminiscent of the poor laws in a Dickensian era.

Trump's legislative changes also represent a continuation of the neoliberal trend to cut back the labor-market rules that protect workers. He has repealed legislation that prevented companies from receiving federal contracts if they had previously violated labor laws around safety, workplace harassment, or wage theft. The Trump administration filed a brief supporting the Supreme Court case, financed primarily by the Bradley Foundation, which struck down the practice of non-union members of a workplace paying an "agency fee" to the union to cover the costs that the union incurs negotiating a collective agreement. The "Janus decision," as this came to be called, has essentially made contributions to unions purely voluntary, and will dramatically reduce union revenue and compromise their power in the negotiating process. The decision, according to close observers, "will likely have the most significant impact on workers' freedom to organize and bargain collectively in 70 years" (McNicholas et al., 2018). In addition to these moves there are plans to change legislation to allow 16- and 17-year-olds to work in the logging sector under the supervision of an adult (The Future Logging Careers Act) and end legislation that requires national park contractors to pay $10.10 an hour along with overtime and sick pay (The Outdoor Recreation Enhancement Act) (Rushe, 2018).

Free trade has placed downward pressure on the earnings of many American workers. This issue is the most important, possibly the only, point on which President Trump opposes what had previously been considered fundamental neoliberal policy. His "it disadvantages the U.S." opposition to the TransPacific Partnership was supported by Bernie Sanders and a more reluctant Hillary Clinton (Bremmer, 2017). President Trump has opened up the North American Free Trade Agreement (NAFTA) between Canada, the US, and Mexico, but the extent to which this involves a rethinking of free-trade policy remains to be seen. Some of the US demands during the renegotiation involve eliminating the protectionist policies of other nations. For example it wants to pry open the Canadian supply-managed agriculture industry that currently impedes imports from the US. Other demands appear to more directly violate the principle of free trade. For example, the Trump administration has negotiated a deal with Mexico that would see 40 to 45 percent of automobiles be produced by workers earning over $16 an hour. The extent to which these are genuine demands, political posturing, or a negotiating tactic is not yet clear. Finally, in keeping with the campaign rhetoric around dealing with the US trade deficit with China, there have only been escalating protectionist measures implemented by the President, most prominently tariffs on aluminum and steel but also on less flashy goods such as washing machines and solar panels (Gillespie, 2017). The same questions about whether this is posturing, tactics, or a determined effort to remake the international trading regime apply here. According to the *Financial Times*, the Trump administration's plans to levy tariffs on steel imports faced considerable resistance "from the broader business community and Republicans in Congress" (Donnan, 2018). However, if they do stand as official policy it would mark a sharp break with the previous neoliberal policy of free movement of goods and services between nations.

Environment

> I believe in clean air. I believe in crystal-clear, beautiful ... I believe in just having good cleanliness in all. Now, with that being said, if somebody said go back into the Paris accord, it would have to be a completely different deal because we had a horrible deal. (President Donald Trump)

President Trump's disregard for our need for a liveable planet is well-known. He campaigned on a pledge to pull out of the Paris Agreement, and famously called climate change a hoax perpetrated by the Chinese. We have already mentioned the problematic initial appointment of Scott Pruitt as head of the EPA, and, prior to his resignation, Mr. Pruitt's actions in office were the subject of no fewer than 11 federal inquiries (Griggs & Yourish, 2018). These, and his testimony before Congress, related primarily to his spending practices, penchant for flying first-class, or using military and private planes, his establishment of a full-time 20-person security detail, and the installation of a $43,000 sound-proof phone booth in his office. He was also renting, for the cut-rate price of $50.00 per night, a Washington, DC townhome which was owned by the wife of an energy lobbyist, and has allegedly been firing staff who disagree with him. Less publicized were his efforts, in tandem with Interior Secretary Ryan Zinke, and now being carried on by his successor, to enable businesses to (more) freely loot and despoil the nation's land, air, water, and minerals, without regard for human- and non-human health and well-being.

Since taking office, Trump and his appointees have instigated so many attacks on environmental protection, on behalf of such a wide variety of industries, that a full accounting here would be impossible. The onslaught is so relentless that *National Geographic* has begun an on-line running tally of environmentally relevant policy, regulatory, and legislative changes, beginning with the scrubbing of references to climate change on federal government websites and the greenlighting of the Keystone XL and Dakota Access pipelines in January, 2017. Harvard's Environment and Energy Law Program also has an extensive and detailed database on environmental de- and re-regulation under Trump, which the *New York Times* drew on to document "67 Environmental Rules on the Way Out Under Trump" (Popovich et al., 2018). The list is long and disheartening. Here, we focus on just a few of the major environmental policy changes that are illustrative of Trump's approach to nature. The latter is, in some ways, a move away from the form that neoliberalism has been taking in much of the rest of the world: an effort to treat nature as a form of capital, to create markets for it via the enforcement of scarcity, and the justification of conservation and environmental protection on the basis of economic benefit. Trump's approach is a decisive shift back to Reagan-era policies of deregulation and loosening restrictions on access to public lands and resources. From a regime in which nature was being brought visibly into the circuit of capital via the attribution of prices, there is a move towards a regime of free appropriation. This is a more naked form of neoliberal restoration, in which the influence of scientists and environmental organizations is undercut, and the power of businesses and industrial associations rises.

On climate change, surely the highest-profile environmental issue, and the one that has become most divided on partisan lines in the US, Trump was clear from the outset. At a strategically located speech in Bismarck, North Dakota, heart of the US shale boom, Trump made it clear that he was throwing in with the fossil fuel industry, and he has done so. He has followed through on his promises to pull out of the Paris Agreement, signaling the US's intention to withdraw from the Agreement by 2020 (there is a built-in four-year time period before a signatory can withdraw). This, along with approval of the Keystone XL pipeline, opening up more land and sea for oil and gas development, and ending what he termed a "war on coal" (though no such war was being waged; coal was suffering mostly from low natural gas prices, rather than from the oppressive hand of the state), were all promises laid out as part of his nomination campaign. Since taking office, Trump and his appointees have attacked the entire edifice of greenhouse gas regulation that Obama attempted to put in place. Two key aspects of this edifice were the Clean Power Plan (CPP), which was an attempt to authorize the EPA to regulate greenhouse gas emissions from power generators, but which Trump characterized as a "crushing attack on American industry" (quoted in Dillon et al., 2018) and more stringent standards for fuel efficiency imposed on the nation's auto makers. Trump's attacks on these measures are at the behest of industry groups. The auto industry had been heavily critical of the 54.5 mpg average standard that would be enforced by 2025, despite the standard being less demanding than the EU's enacted 2021 target in terms of carbon dioxide emitted per kilometer (Tietge et al., 2017). The CPP, and the more general principle of the EPA's duty to regulate greenhouse gases, had been fought by industry giants like Peabody Energy, Southern Company, and ExxonMobil, backed by their industry associations and allies like the American Coalition for Clean Coal Electricity, ALEC, and the US Chamber of Commerce (Union of Concerned Scientists, 2016). These groups enthusiastically lauded Pruitt's October, 2017 repeal of the CPP and his signaled intention to replace it with something designed by fossil fuel and utility companies. It does need to be noted that the

CPP was detested particularly by this fraction of the US capitalist class, and not universally. The Supreme Court's consideration of the CPP resulted in briefs being filed in support of the CPP by economic giants like Microsoft, Google, Amazon, and Apple. Pushed by climate activists to address their carbon footprint, these companies were looking for a more level playing field and the development of more renewable energy options to meet their massive electricity demand (Semuels, 2017). So, Pruitt's decision to repeal the CPP responds more to the concerns of traditional fossil-fuel-based capital than to the giants of Silicon Valley, reflecting a more specific process of regulatory capture—in which the regulated industries specifically come to dominate the agency (Dillon et al., 2018).

Trump's policies here aren't exceptional in opening up rifts within the US ruling elite, evidence of which was plentiful during his campaign for the Republican nomination, and which did not mend entirely even once he won. These splits can be seen internally within the state, as well. One climate-relevant example is the gap between how climate change is treated in the National Security Strategy, and in the National Defense Authorization Act for 2018. The National Security Strategy (NSS) is a high-level expression of presidential priorities on defense and security, providing an assessment of how the White House sees the landscape of threat. In 2015, Obama's second NSS put climate change prominently forward as a major threat to US interests. According to the 2015 NSS,

> Climate change is an urgent and growing threat to our national security, contributing to increased natural disasters, refugee flows, and conflicts over basic resources like food and water. The present day effects of climate change are being felt from the Arctic to the Midwest. Increased sea levels and storm surges threaten coastal regions, infrastructure, and property. In turn, the global economy suffers, compounding the growing costs of preparing and restoring infrastructure. (President of the United States, 2015, p. 12)

Under Trump, climate change is dropped entirely in the NSS, and the only reference to anything remotely related to fossil fuels is the claim that

> Climate policies will continue to shape the global system. U.S. leadership is indispensable to countering an anti-growth energy agenda that is detrimental to U.S. economic and energy security interests. Given future global energy demand, much of the developing world will require fossil fuels, as well as other forms of energy, to power their economies and lift their people out of poverty. The United States will continue to advance an approach that balances energy security, economic development, and environmental protection. The United States will remain a global leader in reducing traditional pollution, as well as greenhouse gases, while expanding

our economy. This achievement, which can serve as a model to other countries, flows from innovation, technology breakthroughs, and energy efficiency gains, not from onerous regulation. (President of the United States, 2017)

This reflects a fairly substantial departure, reflective of Trump's desire to scrub any and all reference to climate change from the federal government's public-facing materials. However, the 2018 National Defense Authorization Act, signed by Trump, but unlikely to get much public readership, still contains a section on threats from climate change, including projected damage to military infrastructure at home and abroad, increased likelihood of failed states arising from climate disasters and associated violence and extremism, increased migration likely to outstrip resources to handle it, and geopolitical instability. The Act also mandates a report on the defense implications of climate change going forward twenty years. Clearly, those charged with planning for the nation's defense continue to see climate change as very real.

Climate change is just one of the areas in which Trump's desire to liberate business from the threat of regulation comes to light. EPA enforcement of environmental regulation has plummeted, accelerating a trend initiated under Obama (Baker Hostetler LLP, 2018); it has suspended pending prohibitions on the use of certain hazardous chemicals—some of which are known to the EPA to be highly dangerous and still used in common household products like paint strippers. One EPA advisor active during the decision to suspend the ban, who was also initially nominated by Trump to head up its chemical safety wing, was a former lobbyist for the Halogenated Solvents Industry Alliance (Kaplan, 2017); it has also rolled back the "once in always in" rule which locked in reductions of hazardous air pollutant emissions (Environmental Protection Agency, 2018). The Department of the Interior, meanwhile, repealed its Stream Protection Rule, which was finalized shortly before President Obama left office, and which placed stricter restrictions on dumping mining waste into surrounding waterways (Henry, 2017). The Office of Surface Mining Reclamation and Enforcement's budget has all but vanished, and mining inspections are disappearing along with it (Olalde, 2018). Where "foreseeable but accidental" deaths of migratory birds (say, those that resulted from birds landing in an unprotected, oil-covered evaporation pond) were once prosecutable, they are no longer. On public lands, Trump's EPA and Department of the Interior (DOI) are bending over backwards to enable more leases and development, rescinding species and habitat protections (such as for the Greater Sage Grouse) that restricted such leases in the past, and shrinking two national monuments (Bears Ears and Grand Escalante) by 85 percent and 50 percent respectively. DOI has proposed auctioning off oil and gas leases for 77 million acres of federal waters within the Gulf of Mexico—the largest lease auction of its kind ever announced—and it is "streamlining" the leasing process on public lands. It issued a memo in January, 2018, which directs its field offices "to simplify and streamline the leasing process" so that federal leases to the oil and gas industry can be expedited "to ensure quarterly oil and gas lease sales are consistently held." According to the memo, doing so will ease such "impediments and burdens" as months-long environmental reviews that assess the impacts of drilling and potential spills on land and wildlife (US Department of the Interior, Bureau of Land Management, 2018). DOI has also ended the use of Master Lease Plans that gave hunters, anglers, and cultural preservation or heritage groups a voice in how leased lands are managed.

Finally, Trump is following the well-worn strategy of starving the beast that was pursued under Reagan initially, and then mimicked by every neoliberal administration since. Interior and Environment funding from Congress for 2018 was $824 million below 2017, but about $4 billion more than Trump recommended in his budget. The President's budget for 2019 proposes a 23 percent cut to $6.1 billion for the EPA, along with a full-time equivalent reduction from about 15,000 to 12,000 employed.

So, Trump and his DOI and EPA appointees are following a broadly tried and true neoliberal agenda aimed at ensuring that nature is available as a source of profit. It is not the neoliberalism of "natural capital." Rather, it works to more aggressively remove obstacles to the free appropriation of nature in a way that Anne Gorsuch and James Watt attempted in the 1980s. So far, however, the assault has been more successful. Whether it founders on the rocks of public opposition to its rapacity remains to be seen. Certainly environmental groups and public land defenders in the US have been vocally resistant to the Trump agenda, and Pruitt has come in for special scrutiny by Congress. However, industry forces are on the offensive, and the damage done to water, soil, air, and species, even within a four-year Trump administration, will be long-lasting if not irreversible.

Health

After the first year of the Trump administration, repealing and replacing Obamacare has proved a more difficult task than was made out on the campaign trail. Despite the lack of success in implementing an alternative to Obamacare, it is worth examining the proposals that have been put forward. Although different Republican proposals had different specifics, they all had in common the desire to eliminate the government subsidies for health insurance and a reduction of the number of poor who would be eligible for government insurance under Medicaid. The changes proposed by the American Healthcare Act (AHCA or Trumpcare) in 2017 would have saved the federal government $377 billion between 2017 and 2026 but increased the number of uninsured by 24 million. Further, it would have reduced premiums by eliminating regulation that required insurance companies to offer coverage to those with pre-existing conditions (Congressional Budget Office, 2017). Using previous estimates of the effect of changing insurance coverage on mortality, one study estimated that the reduction in the number of insured under the AHCA would cause "217,000 additional deaths over the next decade" and as many as 27,700 in 2026 alone (Crawford-Roberts et al., 2017). Obamacare may have been quite neoliberal in the sense that it was a particularly profit-enhancing (at least for insurance companies) method of extending health insurance, but the replacements that have been proposed during the first year of the Trump administration would have reversed the benefits of expanded insurance coverage.

The Trump administration's commitment to reducing the regulatory burden of the state will also negatively impact the economic determinants of health. The author of a study that found that Trump's share of the vote was higher in counties with lower increases in life expectancy between 1980 and 2014 expressed skepticism that health conditions would improve in these areas. In addition to the plans to cut insurance for the poor, President Trump's proposals to cut "social programs, health research, and environmental and worker protections" are likely to increase the health gaps between rich and poor (Bor, 2017). Similar concerns were raised about President Trump's plans to pare back health and safety regulations below their 1960 level, a time when "hazardous working conditions killed an average of 14,000 workers annually," triple the current rate (Negin, 2017).

Education

Chapter 5 provided the case against the neoliberal trends towards for-profit education, charter schools, and the voucher system. Trump's Education Secretary, Betsy Devos, is a billionaire Republican fundraiser, donor, and advocate for vouchers, for-profit education, and market-oriented reform of the education system. While she has yet to implement any wide-scale reforms, she has been hiring executives, like Julian Schmoke Jr. and Robert Eitel from dubious for-profit colleges. The colleges at which both men were employed prior to their work with DeVos were forced to pay damages for deceiving students. That might explain why the Department of Education delayed legislation that would have forgiven the loans of students who were defrauded by for-profit colleges and eliminate funding for colleges that failed to provide students with the skills necessary for the job market while increasing their debt (Collins, 2017).

President Trump's proposed 2018 budget called for a 13.5 percent federal spending cut to K-12 and aid to higher education, including cuts to financial assistance for low-income students. This would put substantial pressure on state education budgets and make education more unaffordable for poorer students (Mann, 2017). Also included in the 2018 budget was a $10.6 billion reduction in funding for programs such as college work-study and public-school mental health in order to expand funding for various forms of school choice, such as charter schools (Brown et al., 2017).

Increasing the role of the market and private sector in education is entirely consistent with the neoliberal policy of consumer choice and opening up previously restricted industries to profits. However, the cuts to funding are more of a double-edged sword even on neoliberalism's own terms. On one hand, it reduces the size of the government and the burden on the taxpayer (at least at the federal level) by forcing more of the funding of education onto students and their families. This dovetails nicely with neoliberal ideas of making the beneficiary pay for services and avoiding the cross-subsidization of higher education. On the other hand, cuts to job training programs, such as career and technical education and work-federal study programs, harm profits (and are particularly useful to the less-educated workers, the white component of which voted so heavily for Trump) by reducing an important subsidy for training the workforce (Wong, 2017). As is the case in healthcare, while the direction of the Trump administration's education reform is clear, the details are evolving. Certainly the markets are optimistic about Ms. Devos's capacity to neoliberalize education. After Trump's election and the announcement of her confirmation as Secretary (in a tie-breaking vote decided by Vice-President Mike Pence), shares in for-profit educational corporations like K12, Career Education Corp, DeVry, and Capella surged. As one analyst wrote to his clients, "While somewhat of a controversial choice, we believe this appointment will be positive for the private sector (for-profit) education sector, specifically in the K-12 segment where Ms. Devos has been a strong proponent of school reform, particularly charter schools" (Kilgore, 2017).

Politics

> The further a society drifts from the truth, the more it will hate those who speak it. (George Orwell)

In Chapter 6 we argued that the pillars on which meaningful democracy rests have been steadily eroded under neoliberalism. The growing role of finance in and outside of electoral politics has made a mockery of romantic notions of one-person-one-vote. Lofty goals of the common good have been replaced with support of business. The role of the media in providing reliable information on which democratic decisions rely, while always far from perfect and subject to material bias, has been compromised by the rise of alternative news and the shambles that passes for fact on-line. As a candidate, Trump's invitations to his supporters to attack the media at campaign rallies and his desire to lock up his political opponents did not auger well for his commitments to democracy.

One of his first moves as President was to cast doubt on the election's results. Despite winning the actual election (courtesy of the electoral college system), his defeat to Clinton in the popular vote was sufficiently unpalatable that Trump called for a commission on voter fraud to investigate what he speculated were between three and five million illegal ballots cast in favor of his opponent (Gumbal, 2017). The fraud commission was disbanded in 2018 and the issue turned over to Homeland Security. The lack of evidence of voter fraud has not deterred Kris Kobach, the Vice Chair of the commission, and a long-time purveyor of electoral conspiracies, who has blamed "a determined effort by the left" to hamstring the investigation for its failure (Lopez, 2018). It is certainly true that states refused to participate with the commission and, along with many civil rights organizations, accused the commission of violating the democratic right to privacy.

The idea of voter fraud has been a longstanding trope in US politics. Politicians disgruntled with voting trends have frequently speculated that votes for their opponents were not cast by actual living citizens. This specter has had impressive legs considering that all serious studies have concluded that voter fraud is "episodic and rare" (Minnite, 2010, p. 57). The staying power of voter fraud despite the dearth of actual evidence can possibly be explained by the impacts of the preferred solution to the imagined problem. The usually prescribed cure for voter fraud is increased requirements for voters to demonstrate their identity and eligibility. One common example of this is voter ID laws, which require voters to show government-approved forms of ID. This has been an easy sell as a common-sense solution to combat perceived voter fraud, but its distributional consequences on who will vote should be obvious. Marginalized populations, like the poor or disadvantaged minorities, are far less likely to have official ID. A GAO study on voter ID requirements in Kansas and Tennessee found that it decreased overall voter turnout relative to other states and that it particularly suppressed voting by the African American population (General Accounting Office, 2014, p. 52). Unsurprisingly, these measures have been popular in Republican administrations because the kinds of voters who are suppressed tend to favor the Democrats (Gumbal, 2017).

So, Trump was hardly blazing a new trail when he called for a commission on voter fraud. However, this makes it no less damaging. One impact of the voter fraud myth is that it erodes the trust in one of the fundamental institutions of a democratic election—that votes are honestly and correctly tallied. This legitimizes questions about the validity and veracity of electoral outcomes. Its second impact is profoundly undemocratic because the solutions to voter fraud actively disenfranchise the already most marginalized members of the community. Of course, for Trump, as has been the case for many Republicans, that is precisely the point.

The second noteworthy impact of the Trump administration on democracy has been its animosity towards the media, or at least what he has vilified as the "mainstream" media. These attacks are framed in a worryingly aggressive language reminiscent of the diatribes of dictatorial demagogues. Obvious facts that contradict or criticize the President, even about something as trivial and easy to verify as the number of people at his inauguration, are branded "fake news" and those who report it are "the enemy of the people" (Bierman, 2017). Meanwhile the spurious ramblings of a President either deliberately misrepresenting facts or willfully ignorant of them, are defended as accurate. When fact becomes opinion and opinion becomes fact, the very basis for democratic decision making is undermined. In the words of sociologist Patrick Moynihan, a Democratic politician who also served in the Nixon administration, "Everyone is entitled to his own opinion, but not to his own facts" (Bever, 2017). This disparaging of the mainstream media is more than merely about tone and a penchant for hyperbole. After making his "enemy of the people" charge, Trump banned the *New York Times*, CNN and the *Los Angeles Times* from press briefings, inviting only "Trump-friendly outlets" (Bierman, 2017). The punishment of news outlets that criticize an administration and favoritism for those who toe the party line is a long-cherished tactic of anti-democratic governments. It marks the difference between those who view information provision in a society and the resulting informed electorate as a fundamental component of democracy and those who view information provision as partisan manipulation of the beliefs of the population.

This undemocratic turn has not gone unnoticed even by fellow Republicans. In a remarkable speech, Arizona Senator Jeff Flake compared President Trump's relationship with information to Stalin's "authoritarian impulse" and argued that it represented a "challenge to free people and free societies, everywhere" (Abramson, 2018). Politicians from other nations have also been very critical. Former Conservative British Prime Minister David Cameron accused President Trump of "corrupting society" for his attacks on specific news outlets: "President Trump: 'fake news' is not broadcasters criticizing you, it's Russian bots and trolls targeting your democracy" (Wild, 2017).

Conclusion

President Trump has ended business as usual in Washington. He has violated previously respected rules of conduct. His animosity towards the mainstream media and anyone critical of him runs counter to the more civilized and restrained language of previous administrations. On policy matters, on the other hand, things look very much like business as usual, especially with respect to previous Republican administrations. Hacker and Pierson (2010) demonstrated that Republicans tend to take a more comprehensive approach to increasing inequality than Democrats and President Trump looks to continue that trend. The tax cuts ushered in by Trump were similar to those of Presidents Reagan and George W. Bush. His zeal for deregulation was similar to the trends of all the Presidents since 1980 no matter their party affiliation. It was President Clinton's replacement of the New Deal's Aid to Families with Dependent Children with the Temporary Assistance for Needy Families and the Personal Responsibility and Work Opportunity Act that increased poverty particularly among African Americans. The only real change has been the move away, at least in rhetoric and perhaps in policy, from globalization. In terms of a dramatic restructuring of neoliberalism, a few trade restrictions are being asked to do some very heavy lifting. If neoliberalism is responsible for much of what makes America so far from great, it is extremely unlikely that, by strengthening neoliberalism in so many areas, President Trump is going to succeed in "Making American Great Again." And so, in the Trump Presidency we see the neoliberal past as prologue. If its current presentation is, for once, refreshingly transparent, in substance it represents an ever-greater threat to democracy, the environment, and broadly shared prosperity.

References

Abramson, A. (2018). "This Is Reprehensible." Read Jeff Flake's Speech Comparing Trump's Attacks on the Media to Josef Stalin, January 17. *Time*. Retrieved April 30, 2018, from http://time.com/5106069/jeff-flake-donald-trump-press-attacks/.

Aschoff, N. (2017). The Glory Days Are Over, October 2. *Jacobin*. Retrieved January 11, 2018, from jacobinmag.com/2017/03/the-glory-days-are-over.

Baker Hostetler LLP. (2018). *EPA's Fiscal Year 2017 Statistics Reflect Accelerating Decline in Federal Environmental Enforcement*, February 12. Retrieved from

Baker & Hostetler: www.bakerlaw.com/alerts/epas-fiscal-year-2017-statistics-reflect-accelerating-decline-in-federal-environmental-enforcement.

Bever, L. (2017). This GOP Senator Just Attributed a Well-Known Liberal Quote to Ronald Reagan, March 15. *The Washington Post*. Retrieved December 11, 2018, from www.washingtonpost.com/news/the-fix/wp/2017/03/15/this-gop-senator-just-attributed-a-well-known-liberal-quote-to-ronald-reagan/?noredirect=on&utm_term=.e97b146839c5.

Bierman, N. (2017). After Trump Calls Media an Enemy of the People, White House Bars Many News Outlets from Briefing, February 24. *LA Times*. Retrieved April 30, 2018, from www.latimes.com/politics/washington/la-na-essential-washington-updates-after-trump-calls-fake-news-enemy-of-1487963297-htmlstory.html.

Bor, J. (2017). Diverging Life Expectancies and Voting Patterns in the 2016 US Presidential Election. *American Journal of Public Health*, 107(10), 1560–1562.

Bremmer, I. (2017). How 5 of the World's Biggest Trade Deals Have Fared in the Trump Era, November 17. *Time*. Retrieved January 25, 2018, from http://time.com/5027654/donald-trump-trade-america-first/.

Brown, E., Strauss, V., & Douglas-Gabriel, D. (2017). Trump's First Full Education Budget: Deep Cuts to Public School Programs in Pursuit of School Choice, May 17. *The Washington Post*. Retrieved January 26, 2018, from www.washingtonpost.com/local/education/trumps-first-full-education-budget-deep-cuts-to-public-school-programs-in-pursuit-of-school-choice/2017/05/17/2a25a2cc-3a41-11e7-8854-21f359183e8c_story.html?utm_term=.d23810181074.

Carnes, N., & Lupu, N. (2017). It's Time to Bust the Myth: Most Trump Voters Were Not Working Class, June 5. *The Washington Post*.

Collins, G. (2017). No Profit in Betsy DeVos, October 28. *New York Times*.

Committee for a Responsible Federal Budget. (2017). *How Much Will Trump's Tax Plan Cost?* Washington, DC: Committee for a Responsible Federal Budget. Retrieved January 18, 2018, from www.crfb.org/blogs/how-much-will-trumps-tax-plan-cost.

Congressional Budget Office. (2017). *American Healthcare Act.* Washington, DC: Congressional Budget Office.

Crawford-Roberts, A., Roxas, N., Kawachi, I., Berger, S., & Gee, E. (2017). *Coverage Losses Under the Senate Healthcare Bill Could Result in 18,100 to 27,700 Additional Deaths in 2026.* Washington, DC: Center for American Progress.

Dillon, L., Sellers, C., Underhill, V., Shapiro, N., Liss-Ohayon, J., Sullivan, M., and the "EPA Under Siege" Writing Group. (2018). The Environmental Protection Agency in the Early Trump Administration: Prelude to Regulatory Capture. *American Journal of Public Health*, 108(S2), S89–S94.

Donnan, S. (2018). Donald Trump's War n Trade Deficit Backfires, October 1. *Financial Times*. Retrieved January 26, 2018, from www.ft.com/content/33138fda-a20f-11e7-b797-b61809486fe2.

Editorial Board. (2017). A Historic Tax Heist, December 2. *New York Times*. Retrieved January 18, 2018, from www.nytimes.com/2017/12/02/opinion/editorials/a-historic-tax-heist.html.

Environmental Protection Agency. (2018). *Reducing Regulatory Burdens: EPA Withdraws "Once In Always In" Policy for Major Sources under Clean Air Act*, January

25. Retrieved November 28, 2018, from Environmental Protection Agency: www.epa.gov/newsreleases/reducing-regulatory-burdens-epa-withdraws-once-always-policy-major-sources-under-clean.

General Accounting Office. (2014). *Issues Related to State Voter Identification Laws*. Washington, DC: General Accounting Office.

Gillespie, P. (2017). *Trump's Top Trade Issues: Where They Stand*, November 20. Retrieved January 25, 2018, from CNN: http://money.cnn.com/2017/11/20/news/economy/trump-trade/index.html?ref=gazelle.popsugar.com.

Greenstein, R. (2017). *Commentary: With Tax Cuts for the Top, GOP Leaders Now Aim Budget Cuts at the Bottom*, December 21. Retrieved January 18, 2018, from Center for Budget and Policy Priorities: www.cbpp.org/research/federal-tax/commentary-with-tax-cuts-for-the-top-gop-leaders-now-aim-budget-cuts-at-the.

Griggs, T., & Yourish, K. (2018). The Behaviour that Put Scott Pruitt at the Center of Federal Inquiries, April 24. *The New York Times*. Retrieved November 28, 2018, from www.nytimes.com/interactive/2018/04/24/us/scott-pruitt-ethics-federal-inquiries-diagram.html.

Gumbal, A. (2017). America's Shameful History of Voter Suppression, September 13. *The Guardian*. Retrieved November 28, 2018, from www.theguardian.com/us-news/2017/sep/13/america-history-voter-suppression-donald-trump-election-fraud.

Hacker, J., & Pierson, P. (2010). *Winner-Take-All Politics*. New York: Simon & Schuster.

Henry, D. (2017). Trump Signs Bill Undoing Obama Coal Mining Rule, February 16. *The Hill*. Retrieved April 27, 2018, from http://thehill.com/policy/energy-environment/319938-trump-signs-bill-undoing-obama-coal-mining-rule.

Hong, S. (2017). What Gender Gap: Polls Show White Women Preferred Trump to Clinton. *The New Republic*. Retrieved November 28, 2018, from https://newrepublic.com/minutes/138601/gender-gap-exit-polls-show-white-women-voters-actually-preferred-trump-clinton.

Joint Committee on Taxation. (2017). *Macroeconomic Analysis of the Conference Agreement for H.R. 1, the "Tax Cuts and Jobs Act"*. Washington, DC: Joint Committee on Taxation.

Kaplan, S. (2017). EPA Delays Ban on Uses of Hazardous Chemicals, December 19. *The New York Times*. Retrieved April 27, 2018, from www.nytimes.com/2017/12/19/health/epa-toxic-chemicals.html.

Kilgore, T. (2017). K12's Stock Rallies as DeVos Confirmed as Secretary of Education. Retrieved February 12, 2017, from www.foxbusiness.com/markets/k12s-stock-rallies-after-devos-confirmed-as-secretary-of-education.

Klein, N. (2017). Now Let's Fight Back against the Politics of Fear, June 10. Retrieved January 18, 2018, from The Guardian: www.theguardian.com/books/2017/jun/10/naomi-klein-now-fight-back-against-politics-fear-shock-doctrine-trump.

Lopez, G. (2018). *Trump Has Disbanded His Vote Fraud Commission, Blaming State Resistance*, January 3. Retrieved November 28, 2018, from Vox: www.vox.com/policy-and-politics.

Mann, E. (2017). *President Trump's Education Budget*, June 20. Retrieved January 26, 2018, from Brookings: www.brookings.edu/blog/unpacked/2017/06/20/president-trumps-education-budget/.

McCarthy, T. (2017). *Trump's Cabinet Picks: Here Are All of the Appointments So Far*, January 3. Retrieved January 18, 2018, from The Guardian: www.theguardian.com/us-news/2016/dec/09/donald-trump-administration-cabinet-picks-so-far.

McNicholas, C., Mokhiber, Z., & Chaikof, A. (2017). Two Billion Dollars in Stolen Wages Were Recovered for Workers in 2015 and 2016—and That's Just a Drop in the Bucket, December 13. Economic Policy Institute, Retrieved November 29, 2018, from www.epi.org/publication/two-billion-dollars-in-stolen-wages-were-recovered-for-workers-in-2015-and-2016-and-thats-just-a-drop-in-the-bucket/.

Minnite, L. (2010). *The Myth of Voter Fraud.* Ithaca: Cornell Unviersity Press.

Monnat, S. (2016). *Deaths of Despair and Support for Trump in the 2016 Presidential Elections.* The Pennsylvania State University, Department of Agricultural Economics, Sociology and Education Research Brief Research Brief 12/04/16. Retrieved November 28, 2018, from https://smmonnat.expressions.syr.edu/wp-content/.../ElectionBrief_DeathsofDespair.pdf.

Negin, E. (2017). *Trump Vows to Kill 50 Years of Federal Health and Safety Protections*, December 17. Retrieved January 26, 2018, from Union of Concerned Scientists: https://blog.ucsusa.org/elliott-negin/trump-vows-to-kill-50-years-of-federal-health-and-safety-protections.

Olalde, M. (2018). *Obama Official: Trump Cuts Will Leave Coal Clean-Up Agency Unable to Function*, March 15. Retrieved November 28, 2019, from Climate Home News: www.climatechangenews.com/2018/03/15/obama-official-trump-cuts-will-leave-coal-clean-agency-unable-function/.

Peters, M. A. (2018). The End of Neoliberal Globalisation and the Rise of Authoritarian Populism. *Educational Philosophy and Theory*, 50(4), 323–325.

Popken, B. (2016). *Trump's Cabinet Picks Have a Combined Wealth of $14.5B. How Did They All Make Their Money?*, December 7. Retrieved January 18, 2018, from NBC News: www.nbcnews.com/business/economy/trump-s-cabinet-picks-have-combined-wealth-11b-how-did-n692681.

Popovich, N., Albeck-Ripka, L., & Pierre-Louis, K. (2018). 67 Environmental Rules on the Way Out Under Trump, January 31. *The New York Times*. Retrieved April 27, 2018, from www.nytimes.com/interactive/2017/10/05/climate/trump-environment-rules-reversed.html.

President of the United States. (2015). *National Security Strategy 2015.* Retrieved November 28, 2018, from Obama Whitehouse Archives: https://obamawhitehouse.archives.gov/sites/.../2015_national_security_strategy_2.pdf.

President of the United States. (2017). *National Security Strategy 2017.* Retrieved November 28, 2018, from The Whitehouse: www.whitehouse.gov/wp-content/.../2017/12/NSS-Final-12–18–2017–0905.pdf.

Quiggin, J. (2012). *Zombie Economics How Dead Ideas Still Walk among Us.* Princeton: Princeton University Press.

Rothwell, J., & Diego-Rosell, P. (2016). *Explaining Nationalist Political Views: The Case of Donald Trump.* SSRN. Retrieved January 16, 2018, from https://ssrn.com/abstract=2822059 or http://dx.doi.org/10.2139/ssrn.2822059.

Rushe, D. (2018). As State of the Union Nears, Is America Great Again for the Working Class?, January 25. *The Guardian*. Retrieved January 26, 2018, from www.theguardian.com/us-news/2018/jan/25/trump-state-of-union-workers-rights-working-class-record.

Sachs, J. (2017). The GOP Tax Cut Is Daylight Robbery, November 14. Retrieved January 18, 2018, from Boston Globe: www.bostonglobe.com/opinion/2017/11/13/the-gop-tax-cut-daylight-robbery/0FF1Y8MFy7rH8eyEzWA7iM/story.html.

Samuels, R. (2016). *Trump, Conservatives and the Sanders Alternative*, March 2. Retrieved January 16, 2018, from Huffington Post: www.huffingtonpost.com/bob-samuels/psychoanalyzing-trump-con_b_9348856.html.

Schaffner, B., MacWilliams, M., & Nteta, T. (2017). *Explaining White Polarization in the 2016 Vote for President: The Sobering Role of Racism and Sexism.* Herzliya: IDC.

Semuels, A. (2017). The Myth That "Business" Hated Obama's Clean Power Plan, October 10. *The Atlantic*. Retrieved April 26, 2018, from www.theatlantic.com/business/archive/2017/10/business-clean-power-plan/542529/.

Stein, J. (2017). GOP Eyes Post-Tax-Cut Changes to Welfare, Medicare and Social Security, December 1. *Chicago Tribune*. Retrieved January 25, 2018, from www.chicagotribune.com/news/nationworld/ct-gop-welfare-medicare-social-security-cuts-20171201-story.html.

Summers, L. (2017). The Business Roundtable's Outlandish Tax Cut Claims, October 23. Retrieved January 18, 2018, from The Washington Post: www.washingtonpost.com/news/wonk/wp/2017/10/23/lawrence-summers-the-business-roundtables-outlandish-tax-cut-claims/?utm_term=.a0571c93de0b.

Tax Policy Center. (2017a). *Conference Agreement: The Tax Cuts and Jobs Act; Baseline: Current Law; Distribution of Federal Tax Change by Expanded Cash Income Percentile, 2027.* Washington, DC: Urban Institute and Brookings Institution. Retrieved January 1, 2018, from www.taxpolicycenter.org/model-estimates/conference-agreement-tax-cuts-and-jobs-act-dec-2017/t17–0316-conference-agreement.

Tax Policy Center. (2017b). *Tax Policy Center, T17–0312 – Conference Agreement: The Tax Cuts and Jobs Act; Baseline: Current Law; Distribution of Federal Tax Change by Expanded Cash Income Percentile, 2018.* Washington, DC: Urban Institute and Brookings Institution. Retrieved January 18, 2018, from www.taxpolicycenter.org/model-estimates/conference-agreement-tax-cuts-and-jobs-act-dec-2017/t17–0312-conference-agreement.

Tietge, U., Diaz, S., Yang, Z., & Mock, P. (2017). *From Laboratory to Road International: A Comparison of Official and Real-World Fuel Consumption and CO2 Values for Passenger Cars in Europe, the United States, China, and Japan.* Berlin: International Council on Clean Transportation.

Union of Concerned Scientists. (2016). *Who's Fighting the Clean Power Plan and EPA Action on Climate Change?* Retrieved November 28, 2018, from Union of Concerned Scientists: www.ucsusa.org/global-warming/fight-misinformation/whos-fighting-clean-power-plan-and-epa-action-climate#.WuJLVZch3IU.

US Department of the Interior, Bureau of Land Management. (2018). *Instructional Memorandum—Updating Oil and Gas Leasing Reform—Land Use Planning and Lease Parcel Reviews*, January 31. Retrieved November 28, 2018, from Bureau of Land Management: www.blm.gov/policy/im-2018–034

Walsh, D., Mattingly, P., Killough, A., Fox, L., & Liptak, K. (2017). *White House, GOP Celebrate Passing Sweeping Tax Bill*, December 20. Retrieved January 18, 2018, from CNN: www.cnn.com/2017/12/20/politics/house-senate-trump-tax-bill/index.html.

West, C. (2016). Goodbye, American Neoliberalism. A New Era Is Here, November 17. *The Guardian*. Retrieved January 10, 2018, from https://www.theguardian.com/commentisfree/2016/nov/17/american-neoliberalism-cornel-west-2016-election.

Wild, F. (2017). *Cameron Decries Trump's Attacks on the Media*, December 13. Retrieved November 28, 2018, from Bloomberg: www.bloomberg.com/news/articles/2017–12–13/ex-u-k-prime-minister-cameron-decries-trump-attacks-on-media.

Wong, A. (2017). Trump Education Budget Takes Aim at the Working Class, May 23. *The Atlantic*. Retrieved January 26, 2018, from www.theatlantic.com/education/archive/2017/05/trumps-education-budget-takes-aim-at-the-working-class/527718/.

8

Conclusion

Crisis of any kind requires a response. Within the small world of climate-change politics, the options have been boiled down to a shorthand of "mitigation" (reducing the scale of the crisis) and "adaptation" (accommodating ourselves to a new situation). While adaptation is usually framed as defensive spending to protect ourselves from the changing environment, such as building higher sea walls to protect against rising ocean levels, it can also contain a less discussed, more desperate, form of adaptation that is more accurately described as "suffering." In climate terms this would include climate refugees, forced to flee their homes for less damaged locations. Here, the actions of a particular group in response to crisis serve primarily to displace it—to ensure that the costs are borne by other, less powerful people. Neoliberalism was a response to an economic crisis. The crisis was brought on by the economic stagnation of the 1970s created by a fall in profitability. As we have stressed, it was not the only possible response, so we are not in any way suggesting that neoliberalism was a functionally necessary way of dealing with the economic problems of the 1970s. Rather, it was the result of a very successful effort to remake the rules surrounding the economy in favor of business.

Neoliberalism did mitigate the decline in profitability and end the economic stagnation of the 1970s, primarily through lowering costs and expanding spaces for profitable private investment. However, unlike the mitigation–adaptation choice in climate change, where more mitigation results in less need for adaptation, the neoliberal mitigation of the 1970s economic crisis has forced the groups that were on the losing side of the struggle to adapt to a new economic reality. For example, workers have adapted by changing their expectations about their jobs, an adaptation that for many involves a considerable amount of suffering. It is this element that we have sought to highlight in this book, not only in terms of the welfare of working-class people right now but also in terms of the loss of capacities that neoliberalism attempts to effect. Suffering is not always

219

something that is acutely felt. While it can be harsh and immediate, suffering more often builds over time, becomes (barely) tolerable to those who endure it, manifests as a slow degradation of life and its promise. It can be delivered—as in war or other violence, swiftly and without warning. In the case of neoliberalism, the suffering borne by working people has come upon them by small changes (or simply "drift" (see Hacker & Pierson, 2010)) in seemingly distant and esoteric policies, by repeated concessions in the workplace and the near-annihilation of working-class political organizations, by slowly increasing strains on individuals, communities, and families.

To present the working class as "suffering" might strike some as telling at best half of the story. It might be understood as tantamount to presenting the working class as passive victims, as a collection of objects with no agency of their own, taking a beating and then staggering back to take another. Such critics might choose instead to tell stories of working-class resilience, and of enormously deep capacities to adapt, to survive, to mutually support, and these things are true. Resilience, however, is a characteristic required of something or somebody under assault. It is a capacity honed in a fight for continued existence, not one developed in the search for full and flourishing human lives characterized by Nussbaum's "dignity." Resilience, to paraphrase a streetpost flyer that appeared in New Orleans after Hurricane Katrina,[1] is a word used as a precursor to the inflicting of yet another injury. We need to move beyond resilience— beyond simply keeping our heads above water as it rises. Rather, we need to stop the flooding.

In the case of neoliberalism's winnowing away of working-class lives, the source of that flooding is the same one identified by Marx when he spoke of a society riven by a conflict between the two great powers of industrial capitalism. The source of this suffering is a class of people intent on ensuring the expansion of its own power and privilege—not incidentally as part of a generalized social development, and not while dragging the rest of us along on its coattails, but at the horrific cost of our capacity to be fully human agents engaged in the collective construction of our world. They set the rules for its construction, and we are to live the best we can within them. The best we can, for millions in the United States, as we have shown here, is very poorly indeed relative to what is possible. As we hope to have demonstrated, suffering now comes through work—the exact human capacity through which we are capable of our greatest expression and development. Instead, the world of waged work, as the sole means through which millions and millions claw out some access to a dwindling share of social wealth, is a source of humiliation, indignity, insecurity, ill-health, injury, and anxiety. With the very successful undermining of working-class political organizations like unions, it becomes less likely that incomes and conditions under which people work will be protected from the logic of the capitalist labor market. In the workplace, this means workers with less ability to support themselves and their families, less capacity to defend themselves against dangerous work, increases in hours, speed-ups, or layoffs, let alone the capacity to speak to their bosses as an equal social force, cooperating in the creation of things that make for a good quality of life.

Suffering under neoliberalism extends into more typical understandings of the word—the ways our bodies are assaulted and left unmended by a political-economic system that, unless forced to do otherwise, disregards its effects on human health and well-being. Sickness and health, understood commonly to be the product either of "lifestyle choices" or of some cosmic genetic lottery, are much more the products of socially determined distributions of power, income, and wealth. For business, bodies are reconstructed as nothing but carriers of labor power—some necessary, some superfluous. As that vision becomes more and more widely accepted within neoliberalism, even within the working class, debilitating injury, multi-generational sickness, addiction, and early death become unremarkable aspects of life—part of a throwaway culture that is an integral aspect of our current political economic environment. The recent resurgence of black lung among coal miners is just one, so far non-instructive, case in point.

Nor are workers and the unwaged who bear the burden of social reproduction (housework, raising children, keeping communities alive and families intact, tending the ill and the caring for the elderly, etc. ...) the only elements of life caught up in this throwaway society. It is no longer hyperbole to talk about huge swaths of life being treated as disposable by our economic system. Our attention is most urgently drawn to this crisis as a result of climate change, which presents us with a non-negligible risk of making our planet uninhabitable to many existing forms of life. Much like the boosterish language of "resilience," which makes us all feel great about our enduring capacity to bear suffering while our abusers craft bigger and bigger bats, policy elites talk about climate change as a problem for all of us, together, here on "spaceship earth," and which we all must do our part to address. This elides the fact that the American public in the 1960s and 1970s fought long, and occasionally successful, battles against business to force governments into protecting air, water, soil, and wildlife. However, since the early 1980s, business has gained the upper hand in this fight, ensuring that no condition of life, and no living thing in particular, becomes an obstacle to the process of profit-making. Indeed, the better option in their eyes is to turn all of nature into an accumulation front. In this regard climate change must be understood not as the crisis, but as one, admittedly crucial, manifestation of a more systemic problem. These symptoms proliferate, as "planetary boundaries" (Rockström et al., 2009) are exceeded on a number of fronts, and as we produce a massive decline in biodiversity. Again, this is an unrecognized form of suffering, except in the most egregious examples like climate refugees. However, as smoke fills the Western sky, locking people indoors for the summer, as New Yorkers and Floridians keep one eye on the formation of Atlantic storms and hurricanes, as the Dakota are forced to confront dogs and tear gas to defend their water and their rice harvests from the incursion of pipelines, the fact that our flourishing as humans is deeply dependent on land, water, air, and life becomes too clear to ignore. None of this fits within the idea of the "Anthropocene," which sweeps us all equally into complicity for the strata of plastics, radioactive material, and high carbon emissions which now mark our presence geologically. Nor does it fit with the concept of the "plutocene," which targets the 700 million or so "high consumption" individuals on the planet. This is to mistake a problem of power for a problem of poor choices and individual irresponsibility. Only Jason Moore's concept of "capitalocene"—an era whose stratigraphic signature is written through the process of accumulation—captures with any accuracy the geological distillation of power in our time. It is the business class that has created the political economic environment within which our decisions about how to get around, how to generate electricity, how we shelter ourselves, how much care we will take to preserve and care for other life forms as we meet human needs are made. These structures have produced a durable mark on the planet. Neoliberalism marks a period in which our capacities for addressing emergent problems like toxicity, skyrocketing carbon concentrations, and biodiversity collapse, have been crushed or diverted by the resurgent power of business, whose interests do not coincide with the maintenance or construction of a society that respects and protects diverse life and its conditions. Firms do not care how much plastic is in your drinking water. To the contrary, plastic microfilaments pouring out of your tap only opens a new opportunity for profit.

Beyond this, and as troubling as the other, more directly material disintegrations that we have pointed to, is the degradation of working-class political power. While not as obvious a source of immediate suffering as sickness and death, or the miseries suffered at work (or—even worse—lack of work), or even the destruction of ecosystems, the demise of political power and capability is a lasting curse. Not only are we constrained in the moment, having suffered from a "thinning" of what democracy means and with a fat wedge driven between voting and power, but the hopes of finding a way forward that does not involve the immiseration of most of the human population in service of the fourth and fifth homes of the super-rich become diminished. We have entered a sickening downward spiral, in which neoliberalism assaults the bases of broad participation in politics, leaving the political realm as an exclusive space of elite (in the genuine sense of the word rather than the right-wing populist misrepresentation) conflict and cooperation. Some are disenfranchised in the "usual" sense: deprived of the vote through voter ID laws, citizenship status, or as a result of incarceration. Others are deprived of the material wherewithal for politics, as they become priced out of equal participation by the power of corporations and the wealthy to spend without limit on elections and on lobbying. All are denied any credible and independent source of information about the sources and effects of political choices—be they in the realm of foreign policy, economic policy, tax policy, or environmental policy. Will Donald Trump's tax cuts help the poor? Who can say, for sure? Various authoritative voices make different claims, with no apparent basis for evaluation between them apart from hairstyle and pre-existing beliefs. Is climate change a problem, and are we causing it? Who really knows for sure? Lack of perfect clarity on the specific consequences is magnified into "uncertainty in the science," so that at last count, while 70 percent of Americans think global warming is happening, only 49 percent of them were very or extremely sure about that. Only a small majority think that climate change is anthropogenic, despite the 90 percent scientific consensus on this point (Leiserowitz et al., 2018). On what basis, then, are we supposed to take collective political action? If we live in a shared world, we need some shared understanding of its realities, if we are to collectively determine our course. Lacking that, business elites are free to capitalize on uncertainty and to chart our course as it suits them. Finally, education, the great leveller of liberal reformers going back to Adam Smith and J. S. Mill, has become a mechanism of locking in the advantages of wealth, rather than working for their erosion. Like so many other areas of neoliberal life, the basic structures of education from K-12 through post-secondary are remade in the image of the market, with competition, "choice," labor-market readiness, and a dwindling, if not vanished, commitment to universality acting as the guiding principles and constraints. Such a system will not produce democrats by inclination, nor will it, other than in the exception and despite its intentions, provide people with the capacities necessary for democratic citizenship.

Both because of and despite all of this, neoliberal life generates momentary flares of resistance. The teachers' strikes in West Virginia, and then spilling out into the Southeastern US, were one such moment, in which those on the front lines of both producing and living neoliberal life refused to do either any longer on deteriorating terms. The flurry of the Occupy movements which swept across the country from the epicentre in Zuccotti Park, cheek to jowl with Wall Street, named the 1 percent and began, if primarily through slogan, to build solidarity across the 99 percent. Occupy also showed that some people had an intense desire to find a new way of doing politics and of building economies. The Women's March on Washington, in January 2017, was a remarkable event, with hundreds of thousands of people packing the streets of Washington, DC, to protest the misogyny of the newly inaugurated President. Mirror demonstrations were held across the US, and the event addressed issues beyond the traditional comfort zone of liberal feminism: not just reproductive rights, not just equal pay for equal work, but decrying the problems of police brutality and anti-immigration. Black Lives Matter, spurred by black men being shot down and asphyxiated by police, showed that blacks in the US remain in a racial state, despite generations of reforms first hard-won and then reneged upon. The very fact that people in larger and larger numbers are willing to use the word "capitalism" as a reference point for their suffering is relatively new, and a promising development. There was the shocking, for those of us who lived through the politics of the neoliberal ascendance, moment of the Sanders campaign, in which a candidate embraced the previously toxic label of "socialist" and energized huge numbers of mostly young people, while making a highly credible run for the Democratic presidential nomination. Membership in the Democratic Socialists of America is skyrocketing, and candidates running under that banner are winning nominations. Left-wing academics previously on the fringe are being coaxed to write cover stories for the *New York Times Sunday Review*, explaining to its readers why socialism is "suddenly" so appealing to so many (Robin, 2018). One such academic, Corey Robin, is right, we think, that the primary grievance of socialists isn't "that capitalism makes us poor. It's that it makes us unfree." In the neoliberal moment, however, it's doing both. In addition to just plain making many people poorer, and condemning them and their children to remain in that condition barring a miracle, it impoverishes most of us by assaulting the pillars upon which human development rests—things as basic as clean air and drinking water, and as non-negotiable as our health. Capitalism places most of us in authoritarian systems at work, and its neoliberal form increasingly deprives us of political power even in our "democratic" institutions.

Through all of this, Left social forces have yet to produce something with a slower burn—a movement with durability. We didn't see it happen after the cataclysm of the 2008 financial crisis, and we haven't seen one rise in response to President Trump, either. When the Women's March on Washington took place, the *New York Times* reported that "the march is the start of what organizers hope could be a sustained campaign of protest in a polarized America." Celebrity speakers and veteran activists made the call for participants to "not go away"—that is, to use the March as a launching pad for their own organizing efforts. While there are sporadic flare-ups of protest and counter-protest in the streets, frequently between working-class elements of the far-Right and anti-fascists (for example, the tragic moment of Charlottesville, which resulted in the killing of Heather Heyer, or the repeated clashes in Portland,

Oregon), we would have to stretch wildly to translate that into a sign of sustained protest—particularly one aimed from below at the group we have identified here as those responsible for working-class suffering. What we have shown, we hope, in the preceding chapter, is that that for all of the wild spectacle of the Trump administration, for all the scandalized outrage it produces within a more refined element of the ruling class, and for all the claims of its populism, the key fronts of the neoliberal assault on the working class remain on the offensive. Upward redistribution through the tax system, the removal of the already weak protections for our air, water, soil, climate, and non-human life, the undermining of working-class institutions and organizing capacities, the attack on human health that derives from deepening inequality and for-profit care, the privileging above all other rights that of private property, these carry on as usual, moving the legacy of the past forty years forward while the media obsess over Russian bots and pundits decry the erosion of "political norms." The political norm, since around 1980, has been to work to restore profit, power, and wealth to the business class. There is no erosion there. Normally, one expects a book like this to end with a recipe for political change. This is not our goal, and it is generally an academic fool's errand. The requisite social forces will not arrive at our beck and call, and the people who build them are far too busy struggling, raising funds, making calls, developing "shareables," and organizing to pay much attention to such recipes. They are overworked, suffering from burn-out, wrapped up in sectarian fights, under assault from law enforcement, online trolls, and alt-right thugs, and fighting an uphill battle with grim determination. Activists working on environmental, health, race, and gender issues do so in a tense and tenuous relationship with a political force that has a tremendous potential strategic asset: its critical contribution to the production of profit. The labor movement, whose capacity to disrupt the cycle of production and profit is unique among social forces, remains insular and back-footed—a product of its own history of purging its radical elements, of the use of violent repression by capital and the state (Gourevitch, 2015), and of a long, coordinated, and hard-nosed attack through policy. In the absence of a reinvigorated labor movement, working in concert with what sometimes appear to be non-aligned social movements like climate campaigners and Black Lives Matter—whose interests are, in fact, those that should be at the forefront of labor: universal human emancipation and a liveable planet—there is no reason to believe that the bleeding will be stanched. We offer no ray of hope, only an account of the toll taken by neoliberal capitalism on the vast bulk of people in the US, and our blunt assessment of the terrible costs of working-class "adaptation" to the neoliberals' mitigation of the latest round of capitalist crisis.

Note

1 The quote on the sign was attributed to Tracie Washington, of the Louisiana Justice Institute.

References

Gourevitch, A. (2015). Police Work: The Centrality of Labor Repression in American Political History. *Perspectives on Politics*, 13(3), 762–773.

Hacker, J., & Pierson, P. (2010). Winner-Take-All-Politics: Public Policy, Political Organization, and the Precipitous Rise of Top Incomes in the United States. *Politics & Society*, 38(2), 152–204.

Leiserowitz, A., Maiback, E., Roser-Renouf, C., Rosenthal, S., Cutler, M., & Kotcher, J. (2018). *Climate Change in the American Mind*, March. Retrieved March 30, 2018, from Yale Program on Climate Change and Communication: http://climatecommunication.yale.edu/publications/climate-change-american-mind-march-2018/3/.

Robin, C. (2018). The New Socialists, August 25. *New York Times*. Retrieved September 5, 2018, from www.nytimes.com/2018/08/24/opinion/sunday/what-socialism-looks-like-in-2018.html.

Rockström, J., Steffen,,W. Noone, K., et al. (2009). Planetary Boundaries: Exploring the Safe Operating Space for Humanity. *Ecology and Society*, 14(2), 32. Retrieved November 28, 2018, from www.ecologyandsociety.org/vol14/iss2/art32/.

Index

Note: page numbers in *italics* refer to tables or figures. 'n' after a page reference indicates the number of a note on that page.

227